Rules Without Rulers

The Possibilities and Limits of Anarchism

Rules Without Rulers

The Possibilities and Limits of Anarchism

Matthew Wilson

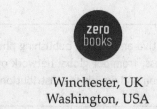

zero
books

Winchester, UK
Washington, USA

First published by Zero Books, 2014
Zero Books is an imprint of John Hunt Publishing Ltd., Laurel House, Station Approach,
Alresford, Hants, SO24 9JH, UK
office1@jhpbooks.net
www.johnhuntpublishing.com
www.zero-books.net

For distributor details and how to order please visit the 'Ordering' section on our website.

Text copyright: Matthew Wilson 2013

ISBN: 978 1 78279 007 5

A CIP catalogue record for this book is available from the British Library.

Design: Lee Nash

Printed and bound by CPI Group (UK) Ltd, Croydon, CR0 4YY

We operate a distinctive and ethical publishing philosophy in all
areas of our business, from our global network of authors to
production and worldwide distribution.

CONTENTS

This book would not exist if it were not for the love and support of my family, and it is dedicated to them for good reason... for Mum, Dad, Paul, Holly, Ernest and Aurora.

Preface.

Although there are many forms of social organisation that exist throughout the world, there is one which everyone, and everything, is undoubtedly affected by. This system, which is often referred to as liberal democracy, but is perhaps more accurately termed polyarchic capitalism, can be defined in numerous ways. For now, let us say just two things about it: first, it isn't working; second, it is nonetheless flourishing. We are immersed in this system, and immersed in the multiple crises that flow from it; these crises are economic, political, social, and environmental. We might also add cultural and moral to the list. Individuals, humans and non-humans alike, suffer in their billions, and the planet itself is increasingly under strain. Actually, the planet will do just fine; but the things that currently live on it might not fare too well, as resources as basic as clean air and fresh water dwindle, and as pollution and waste increase. We know all this. Yet here we are, seemingly incapable of making the necessary changes. In part, this is because we cannot agree on which changes are in fact necessary; can we stop at light-bulbs, or do we need to change capitalism too? And what about the state? What about *us*?

Despite the plurality of visions for another world, there is an increasingly visible trend towards relocalising. Whether they are involved in the Green party, Transition Towns, Earth First!, or countless other more or less radical campaigns, a rapidly growing number of people are coming to believe that the hierarchical and centralised systems we currently live under have had their day, and that, conversely, from food production to politics, it is high time we started to take genuine control over our daily lives. If we didn't already call the system we have *democratic*, it might be a little easier to capture the spirit of this trend; we might then say we are quite simply witnessing a movement towards democracy. But we are told we already have democracy. So what is this movement? Is it a move towards a *real* democracy? If so, what would that mean? Or are we working towards something else? Even if we could agree on where we wanted to get to, could we agree on how to get there?

As we ponder such questions, we look around us to see what is going so self-evidently and catastrophically wrong; but as we search for answers, where then do we turn our gaze? For some, the answer is in plain sight, waiting impatiently to be grasped; anarchism. What better way to deal with a corrupt political system than to somehow depose that system in its entirety? What better way to empower people to take control over their own lives than to build a new politics, a new world, from the bottom-up, with us, each of us, all of us, in control? That is, after all, what anarchism calls for. Yet despite its increasing popularity, and although many of its most basic principles chime with countless other political tendencies, perhaps less radical, but equally impatient for change, anarchism is not what most of us turn to in search for answers. Without knowing it, many people now employ some of its ideas, accept many of its critiques, echo some of its demands; yet we are far from witnessing widespread and wholehearted acceptance of anarchism as a viable alternative. Why not?

Although there are many ways to answer such a question, the following work is ultimately an attempt to address just one reason why anarchism remains a distant dream. That reason? Anarchism. We can blame the corporate media, blame the police, the state, the schools and the history books, none of which do anarchism any real favours; but if anarchism is ever to grow, to inspire, to challenge, it is anarchism itself which needs to be rethought and rearticulated. Although there is much to be said for plenty of anarchist theory and practice, on the whole it is a political movement, a political idea, which is struggling to present itself as a viable alternative. Of perhaps more concern still is how few anarchists appear bothered by this. For too long now, anarchists have avoided asking themselves whether the overwhelming indifference (or worse) towards anarchism may not be at least in part due to the way anarchists themselves have defended their cause. It has been all too easy to blame the people that 'just don't get it'. Although I believe there are far too few critical voices from within the anarchist world, I am not entirely alone in challenging anarchism in this way.

Indeed, numerous critics over the years have made their own particular claims about anarchism's shortcomings, refusing to accept key anarchist views as unquestioned orthodoxy[1]. There is of course no clear cut line between these more critical thinkers and others who have tended to be less so, but I would certainly highlight the work of Gustav Landauer, Errico Malatesta and Michael Taylor. Colin Ward was another such critical friend of anarchism, and I share his concerns with the question of whether or not anarchism is 'respectable'. 'In asking this question', notes Ward, 'I am not concerned about the way we dress, or whether our private lives conform to a statistical norm, or how we earn our living, but with the quality of our anarchist ideas: are our ideas worthy of respect?' (quoted in White 2007, 11). Though I say this with a deep sense of personal regret, not to mention an uneasy feeling of betraying those who have fought and died for anarchism, as well as countless friends involved in anarchist struggles, the answer to Colin Ward's question must, at present, be a resounding *no*.

Anarchism, it has been said, lies like a seed, buried beneath the weight of the state. True enough. But who will tend to it, help it flourish and grow, when what it offers is so vague, so simplistic, so one-sided? People are impatient for change, and even many of those involved in far less radical politics could be easily convinced that more, much more, needs to be done. But to take the leap that anarchism requires, to demand and fight for such a profound change, to run the risk of dismantling capitalism and the state only to find ourselves in an even worse situation, to ask people to do this will require an anarchism that is ready and able to answer the challenging questions that people will quite reasonably ask of it. It is clear that it matters little what horrors our system throws at us, as long as we are left without an alternative. At present, anarchism is not giving people the confidence to believe it can offer that. Fortunately, there is no reason why it cannot do this. At least, no good reason. Through the usual trappings of ideology, not to mention the subtle but powerful blocks to criticism that arise through personal relationships (after all, to criticise a movement is to in some way criticise our friends within it), political cultures have a highly developed immune system; sadly, they keep themselves immune, not from external threats, but from internal critique. Anarchists see this clearly when it comes to capitalism, or communism; when it comes to themselves, the blinkers are there to protect them just the same. It is time we took the blinkers off, stopped, or at least paused, from our critique of the world out there, and looked inwards. People will be convinced by our arguments only when our arguments are convincing.

If my own arguments here are convincing, it is no small part thanks to the help of a great many people who have helped shape my thoughts over the years, who commented on various drafts of this work, and who otherwise supported and encouraged me along the way; naming you all would take too much space, and run the risk of accidentally missing some one out, but you know who you are. So, thank you. That said, Ruth Kinna deserves to be mentioned for sharing her wisdom and good humour, and for sticking with me throughout the writing of this book. Thanks Ruth.

We do not wish to be ruled. And by this very fact, do we not declare that we ourselves wish to rule nobody? (Kropotkin 1970, 98)

Introduction.

In the summer of 2012, I attended a gathering of activists interested in radical social change. The event lasted five days and offered an impressive range of workshops, one of which was a look at the Occupy movement's attempts to organise itself democratically. The workshop started with brief reflections from four speakers (one of whom was myself) before opening up the discussion to everyone there. At some point, the conversation became suddenly heated, as one participant reacted angrily to the news that, in the London Occupy building, a number of social workers, psychiatrists and counsellors had been working with people with serious mental health issues. Occupy, she said, was supposed to be a space where every one felt welcome. No one, she insisted repeatedly, was to be excluded. As such, she was outraged that there would be people such as social workers there. The gaping contradiction in this women's message seemed to mostly go unnoticed. How could it be a space for *everyone*, a space where, categorically, *no one was to be excluded*, if people who happened to work in a particular profession were not allowed to be there?

A few years earlier, and we're in

Stirling, Scotland - 6th July 2005: 2 a.m. [...] From the Horizone eco-village and protest camp [...] a mass exodus is in progress [... O]n the A9 hundreds of people are obstructing the road along a few miles [...] throwing the entire region into a gridlock [....] turn[ing] Perthshire into one big traffic jam. In it, hundreds of secretaries, translators, businessmen and spin doctors are beginning one very long morning [...] In case some one hasn't noticed, anarchism is alive and kicking (Gordon 2008, 1-2).

I'm sure lots of people did indeed notice the anarchist presence in Scotland: one man certainly did. My journey to the G8 summit began two weeks earlier when I left for Scotland from London, on a bike, with sixty other cyclists. The G8 Bikeride travelled up through the country, without motorised support, to join in the protests. Although the ride was never explicitly anarchist, it was organised along anarchist principles, and certainly most of the people who took part would have identified with, for example, the principles of anarchism outlined in Uri Gordon's book from which the above quote is taken. Sometime in the afternoon of the 6th, the ride arrived at a small village called Auchterarder, where large numbers of diverse groups were meeting, with the intention of marching to Gleneagles, where the summit was being held. When we arrived, the main road running through the village and an adjoining park were filled with protesters. As we were about to head off for another ride, to see what was happening nearby, a large man with an unhappy expression stood right in front of me and my bike, preventing me from moving. I didn't know why he was doing what he was doing, but it was clearly intentional. I assumed, given the circumstances, he was a plain-clothes police officer. 'Excuse me' I said. Then, suddenly: 'Bloody anarchists' he yelled, 'we've been sat in traffic jams all morning thanks to you lot. I thought you believed in freedom! What about *my* freedom'? I had been, momentarily, the victim of a one-man blockade. I don't know why he singled me out, and it doesn't really matter; the fact is, he had a point. A few bystanders joined in, supporting the man, and by the end of the day, the feeling of animosity towards (simply) 'anarchists' was plain to see. By blocking roads, not only world leaders, but also a great many protesters had been disrupted by a relatively small number of anarchists. Their tactics had, undeniably, prevented people exercising their *freedom* to protest. Yet freedom, as my one-man blockader correctly suggested, is usually understood as being a fundamental principle of anarchism: so how was the denial of this man's freedom justified?

And some years before that, 18 June 1999, London is the site of an anti-capitalist day of action, and groups of tens, hundreds, sometimes thousands of people are wandering the city, doing their best to evade the police and searching for targets to attack (mostly symbolically, at times physically, but never violently). On the Waterloo Bridge, a thousand or more people find themselves blocked from the north by a line of police, two officers deep. As people are still trying to work out what to do, the sound of horns and shouting sweeps over the bridge from behind the police line, and suddenly another thousand of more people are marching towards the bridge, heading south. The police stand their ground, and so within minutes they are no longer blocking protestors, but being sandwiched between them. Of course, no anti-capitalist action is complete without a large inflatable beach ball, and so when one appeared, the line of police became a net in-between the two blocks of protestors, and a joyous game of volleyball was soon in full swing. Some of the officers took their new role in life with good humour. Many were visibly seething. A few look scared. None of them, it seemed clear, wanted to be there, but their repeated attempts to cut through the crowd were futile. The crowd was mostly good natured, but they were clearly enjoying the fact that the tables had fully turned, and that the police were now being kettled.

Over the last fifteen years or so, the alternative political landscape has shifted dramatically towards a more libertarian, or horizontal, place. At the heart of this shift lies the philosophy of anarchism, a form of politics which takes the notions of freedom and democracy to a radical extreme. Although these new movements and the people who form them are not always explicitly anarchists, they increasingly follow a great many ideas and tactics which stem from the anarchist tradition; as I will explain in greater detail below, it therefore makes sense when trying to understand these movements to explore the anarchist tradition. The anarchist tradition, however, is a diverse and often internally contradictory one, and it is no easy task to tease out the fundamental principles which define it. Nonetheless, I believe we can say here (and I will also defend this position in more depth shortly) that anarchism, or we might more correctly say anarch*ists*, often posit notions of freedom that are absolute in nature. To talk of anarchist coercion, anarchist domination, even anarchist control, is, to many, oxymoronic. So the examples cited above (and I could have mentioned countless more) ought to give the critical mind cause for concern. How genuine is the demand for absolute freedom? What does such a demand even mean? Isn't it the case that, at times, anarchists are ready and willing to negate certain freedoms, to employ censorial or even coercive tactics to fight for what they believe? In part, the following work is an attempt to answer the question posed to me by my temporary blockader; what about *my* freedom? It does so, however, in the form of a wider enquiry into the fundamental principles of anarchism. I begin by asking, then, what conception(s) of freedom do anarchists have? And do other principles at times over-rule the value of liberty, therefore justifying, for example, the denial of my blockader's freedom? If so, what are these principles? So I turn to the question of ethics, to examine which other values might sit alongside, and inform, anarchist visions of freedom. Anarchist approaches to ethics, however, must be understood in relation to another core concept; that of power. Is power understood as necessarily bad, or can it be a positive, creative force? And does it reside simply in certain institutions, such as the state, or within all areas of life? These three concepts then, freedom, ethics, and power, form the basis of the following enquiry. However, exploring these themes has not been a matter of simply detailing what anarchists say they think about such matters; rather, it has been a *critical* engagement, exposing numerous problems and unspoken assumptions within what I call an *anarchist common sense*. Indeed, whilst the concepts of freedom, ethics, and power form the narrative structure of the following work, my discussions of them are propelled by the overarching claim that anarchism is a deeply problematic ideology, which, if it is to be capable of offering a viable vision of an alternative world, is in very real need of a sustained and critical re-assessment.

This view, however, might be dismissed at the out-set, as being simply untrue. Anarchism, it might be argued, is enjoying a considerable surge in interest that has not been seen for well over fifty years; social justice and environmental activists are increasingly embracing anarchist ideas, most notably at the time of writing within the global Occupy movement; and anarchism is receiving attention from academics across the globe. Of course anarchism faces certain challenges, but what ideology doesn't? Surely the high levels of interest generated in recent years suggests that anarchism is in fine health, and any barriers to it becoming more popular still are not the result of anarchism's own failing, but are purely external, emanating from the state, the corporate media, and so on. Anarchism is not considered respectable by the very elites it seeks to get rid of, but that is clearly to be expected; and it evidently *does* meet with the approval of a wide spectrum of people committed to some form of social change. However, I would challenge this view. As both an activist and an academic, I remain unconvinced that anarchism is in a position of strength. Although there has indeed been a great deal of enthusiasm for anarchist ideas within various protest movements, much of this translates into extremely limited tactical shifts. Protests are organised along non-hierarchical lines, more direct action takes the place of marching from *a* to *b*, and so on; this is all well and good, but I believe the legitimate celebration of these achievements now needs to give way to an assessment of how, and in what ways, anarchism can be taken still further. Although anarchism may well be at the heart of much radical political protest, it remains very much marginalised as an alternative political model. In fact, I believe that if sufficient changes do not take place within the movement, it is likely to slide once more into insignificance, to possibly be replaced with a return to a more hierarchical form of leftist politics. Before continuing the discussion of the work itself, then, I want to say a few words on the recent interest in anarchism; in doing so, I hope it will become clear that, for all that has been achieved in its name over the past decade or so, anarchism is still far from being a threat to the established order.

In the Margins, or on the Front-Line?

Despite the myriad human catastrophes endured under 'actually existing socialism', for much of the latter half of the twentieth century, Marxism was still considered, at least in the academic world, as the only viable contender to capitalism; anarchism simply did not appear in the minds, or works, of respectable, leftist academics. At the beginning of the twenty-first century however, this situation has changed dramatically, and anarchism is now reverberating not only through a thoroughly global social movement, but also, increasingly, through the corridors of academic institutions as well. Anarchism has not been so visible for decades. And yet, here in the UK, when discussions about the prospect of a hung parliament and the apparent crisis of democracy dominated the media after the general election in May 2010, not once did I see an anarchist perspective being given column space or air-time. This is just one example, but the point is this: anarchism, for all it has achieved in recent years, remains utterly at odds with most people's understanding of politics; perhaps more importantly, it remains at odds with their under-standing of possibility. Anarchism is simply not seen as being a realistic political philosophy by the vast majority of people. And I am wholly unconcerned here with the *Daily Mail* reading public; what about the people involved in Transition Towns or the Green Party, and even the countless people who have dabbled with

6

radical politics at Climate Camps[2] or G8 summits, for example, but who tend to fall back on more conventional forms of social change sooner or later? For example, there has been a big debate within the Climate Camp movement, which began as an explicitly anarchic network, about the extent to which more conventional political routes should be taken to tackle the issue of climate change, with many arguing that anarchism simply does not have the capacity to respond to such an urgent and global problem[3].

With capitalism teetering on the brink of collapse for several years, a recession as bad as anyone can remember, the global threat of climate change, a looming energy crisis, and, in the UK (and elsewhere), a political system that even mainstream commentators are suggesting is unfit for purpose, with calls for greater democratic accountability on all levels, it has become increasingly possible to imagine that a radically different politics such as anarchism would be embraced by more and more people. Clearly, this hasn't happened, and to find out why, I would suggest anarchists need to take a more critical look at their own ideology, to honestly assess its problems. This might seem like an all too obvious point to make, but woven throughout my critique is an additional claim that anarchists have tended to be far too *un*critical of their own ideology; I discuss some significant reasons as to why this is the case in Chapter 1.

Which Anarchism?

I have so far made a number of broad statements about anarchism, which raises the question; which anarchism, or anarchists, am I talking about? As every anarchist will happily tell you, the anarchist spectrum is a broad one, encompassing many diverse and at times mutually incompatible views of what anarchism is. Anarchism has always been a broad church, with different thinkers in different times and places emphasising certain aspects over others, and, over time, coming to reject particular elements altogether. Can we coherently discuss anarcho-syndicalists of the 1930s in the same breath as anarcha-feminists of the 1980s, for example? As the now infamous dispute between Murray Bookchin (1995) and Bob Black (1997) so clearly demonstrated, a shared ideological *label* does not necessarily entail much else (I discuss this debate briefly in Chapter 6; see also Martin 1998, 39-44 for a useful discussion on the Bookchin and Black debate). Making claims about simply *anarchism*, or *anarchists*, then, with no qualification about which anarchism or anarchists one is discussing, is to obscure these important differences and treat all anarchists as following one coherent and well-defined ideological position; for better or for worse, this is rarely the case. As Leonard Williams puts it: 'sometimes it seems that the only thing that is constant about anarchism is its inconstancy' (Williams 2007, 299).

However, I believe it is both possible and useful to discuss anarchism as a whole. Although at times it is useful to explore a narrowly defined aspect of an ideology (a particular era, or thinker, or theory) it is also useful to stand back and take a broader view. Doing so allows us to see through the many important differences, to uncover some shared problems. This is not to say these differences are ignored, but rather suggests that at times an over-emphasis on diversity may in fact mask and muddle some more fundamental challenges faced by the majority of anarchist thought. It can therefore be worthwhile to put these differences to one side at times, to get down to the nuts and bolts, to discover what I call here *an anarchist common sense*, which, as we shall see, is often far less diverse and unchanging than is often claimed.

Defining the Anarchist Common Sense.

The anthropologist and anarchist David Graeber notes that:

> Anarchism is less about a body of theory than about an attitude, or perhaps a faith: a rejection of certain types of social relation, a confidence that certain others are a much better ones [sic] on which to build a decent or human society, a faith that it would be possible to do so (Graeber 2007, 303).

Whilst academic philosophers may wish to, and be able to, dissect a particular line of thought and demonstrate to what extent it rests on this or that metaphysical understanding of, for example, knowledge, or of human nature, the majority of anarchist thought has not been constructed on such methodical grounds. Indeed, an increasingly common complaint from within anarchism, and an ever present complaint from its detractors, has been this lack of philosophical rigour (McLaughlin 2007). It may be argued, however, that whether or not people are aware of the foundations they rest their philosophy on is beside the point; the foundations are there, and are of no small importance (see Jun, 2010 for an informative discussion of anarchism's philosophical underpinnings). This is no doubt true on one level, but it is worth considering to what extent anarchists' philosophical (or scientific) beliefs come *after* their more basic ethical and political leanings, justifying them retrospectively, rather than being their source. Malatesta makes the point well with regards to Kropotkin, whose '[...] anarchism and communism', he argued, 'were much more the consequence of his sensibility than of reason. In him the heart spoke first and then reason followed to justify and reinforce the impulses of the heart' (Malatesta 1965, 264). Much the same could be said, I would argue, for most anarchists. This is especially relevant when we look to contemporary *activists*, many of whom '[...] overtly disdain abstract or academic theory' (Williams 2007, 298).

So what can be said about this anarchist common sense? Generalisations may at times be useful, but important differences cannot simply be ignored. Firstly, I want to explore the distinction between contemporary and classical anarchism; in doing so, we will see that a number of fundamental anarchist assumptions about freedom, ethics and power, have, in important respects, remained more or less the same over the last century and a half. Saul Newman argues that whilst poststructuralism has

> had a major impact on different areas of scholarship and thought, as well as politics, anarchism tends to have remained largely resistant to these developments and continues to work within an Enlightenment humanist epistemological framework (Newman 2008, 101).

Although there are a few small grains of truth in the claim that certain anarchists have followed a largely Enlightenment inspired philosophical framework, the picture Newman paints is best understood as being mostly false, for two good reasons. Firstly, as we shall see throughout the thesis, early anarchist theorists often demonstrated what could well be seen as a poststructural bent, decades before Foucault and other poststructuralists were even born (see Jun 2012 for a powerful defence of this). Secondly, poststructural thought has had a considerable influence on anarchist theory for many years now, a point which has been widely acknowledged (Purkis & Bowen 1997, 2004; Amster et al 2009; Curran 2006). Indeed, in the last decade, anarchism, it has been argued, has experienced an internal rupture, and a supposedly 'new' anarchism (Graeber 2002), 'revised' (Williams 2007) and 'reloaded' (Gordon 2008) with discourses from feminist, poststructural and post-colonial thought, to name a few, has been born. And it had already been 'reinvented' (Ehrlich et. al. 1979) and 'reinvented, again' (Ehrlich 1996) before that. The distinction between 'capital A Anarchists' and 'small a anarchists' (with 'capital A Anarchists' representing an older, more ideologically strict form of primarily class focused anarchism, and 'small a anarchists' representing a contemporary, ideologically fluid variety, much more in line with poststructuralist theories) presents still further evidence of this philosophical shift (Neal 1997; Graeber 2004; Kuhn 2009, 19). As Leonard Williams suggests:

> In recent decades [...] anarchist thought has moved beyond its central focus on the State or capital to embrace wide-ranging thinking about such matters as the environment, technology, work, and the status of women (Williams 2007, 300).

However, despite such shifts, he goes on to highlight the fact that 'anarchism seems to retain its central character as a viewpoint opposed to the presence of coercion, hierarchy, and authority in human affairs' (ibid.). Importantly, this continuity is not necessarily the result of conscious reflection, and Williams goes on to note that '[o]ne element that remains unquestioned is anarchism's bedrock commitment to opposing authoritarianism in almost any form' (ibid., 311). In other words, despite the many changes that anarchism has undergone, some of its core principles and concerns remain, not only *unchanged*, but also *unquestioned*. The various claims that anarchism has changed so radically in the last half century tell, then, only half the story.

I believe that anarchism is best understood as a set of basic moral demands, which, through a complex network of crisscrossing narratives, are often articulated within certain discursive parameters, including, but not limited to, particular conceptions of human nature, rationality, power, and so on. Rather than resting on these foundations, however, the anarchist project is effectively free-floating, with the primary aim being the achievement of a certain moral rupture from the status quo. This is not to suggest that anything an anarchist might say is mere opportunism, but to highlight the possibility that what really lies at the core of anarchism is not a view of human nature, or of the state, or whatever, but rather a basic libertarian impulse that, when articulated, necessarily becomes intertwined with various other political, ethical, sociological, scientific, and cultural ideas; and, perhaps above all, with often highly contextualised tactical beliefs. Like all ideologies, anarchism is best understood as incorporating a core set of values that exist in a fluctuating relationship with a larger collection of peripheral ideas (Freeden 1996), some of which may be used to retrospectively justify these values.

What unites the vast majority of anarchist thought, old and new, is ultimately a failure to really engage with these issues. Freedom, ethics, power; when we begin to explore these questions, there is no clear, absolute humanist, or anti-humanist, foundation to which we can point. Of course, it is true that some of the earlier anarchists at times applied a profoundly rationalist, scientific approach to their work; my aim is not to deny this, but to stress that there is at least another narrative that can be equally informative. Indeed, throughout anarchist thought there is in fact a strong emphasis on praxis, on anarchy in action, which, however much this may rely implicitly on some metaphysical view or another, is rarely concerned with uncovering what these views might be. As Williams states

> Whether in the form of street demonstrations or an urban bookstore, many of today's anarchists are more focused on getting things done and much less concerned with developing a political philosophy or taking sides in polemical disputes (Williams 2007, 309).

Making a similar point, David Graeber suggests that anarchists are not interested in creating their own High Theory; rather, they see themselves as 'giving a name and voice to a certain kind of insurgent common sense' (Graeber 2009, 213). My feeling is that this *common sense* has not changed dramatically in the last two centuries; it has been added to, stretched, pulled and tugged, and so has inevitably incorporated new concerns, and no doubt abandoned a few, along the way: but its most fundamental elements remain. Crucially, many of those fundamental elements are being incorporated into the theories of the wider radical left; this anarchist common sense and the ideas and tactics it promotes is slowly becoming the common sense of the radical left in general. If anarchism is in fine health, then we can have hope that the movements it inspires will go from strength to strength. If, however, anarchism is haunted by problems, many of which are yet to be fully acknowledged, let alone dealt with, then the future looks considerably less bright. In the following work, I want to get to the heart of the anarchist common sense, revealing and it for what it is, and challenging what is revealed, to see what remains; to uncover the possibilities, and the limits, of anarchism.

Chapter 1

The Case for Anarchy:
Unhelpful Assumptions
& Unchallenged Ideas.

Is this book really necessary? Surely the questions I have so far posed have been asked and answered many times already? Not surprisingly, I think the questions in this book remain in need of answers (and I also think the reasons why such a discussion is necessary are interesting and revealing, and therefore worthy of a chapter of their own). I would argue, in fact, that the majority of anarchist texts, and indeed the majority of anarchists themselves, appear strangely unconcerned with asking whether anarchism really is viable. Indeed, it is not unusual to see the question simply turned on its head. As Randall Amster puts it:

> the question is often posed: How can a society achieve the production, distribution and maintenance of public goods absent a central authority? [...] The problem with such queries is that they are inverted; the real question is how a society premised on coercion and central authority can ever produce, distribute and maintain free individuals (Amster 2009, 296).

However, anarchism is plagued by the charge that it is simply not viable: while other ideologies may be critiqued for their moral failings, anarchism may well find itself applauded for what it argues *for*, but dismissed on the grounds that it is simply impractical (Leach 1996, 186); consider, for example, how the state in liberal theory is frequently referred to as a *necessary evil*, which, we might reasonably infer, suggests that anarchism is seen by at least some liberals as ultimately desirable, but practically unobtainable – or obtainable at too high a cost (Bobbio 2005, 83).

We might imagine, therefore, that anarchists would have devoted a great deal of their time to demonstrating that in fact anarchism is perfectly possible; and, in some ways, they have indeed done so. However, a great deal of this argumentation has taken the form of referring to existing examples of anarchism, rather than defending anarchism theoretically. On the surface, this makes perfect sense: if asked for evidence that a design for a four wheeled carriage could move along the floor powered by a diesel engine, we would save ourselves a great deal of bother by simply pointing to a car. Why waste time embroiling ourselves in theory when the requested proof lies all around us? As Colin Ward famously put it: 'An anarchist society, a society which organises itself without authority, is always in existence, like a seed beneath the snow, buried under the weight of the state' (Ward 1973, 11). The view that anarchism already exists, and has indeed always existed, is extremely important to the anarchist, and has helped shape anarchist thought in a very particular way. However much people may bemoan the lack of philosophical justifications and explanations for anarchist ideas, such critiques are likely to fall on deaf ears: go ahead and make your theoretical critiques, anarchists will respond, anarchism already exists all around us; we do not need to explain or define or defend it, we just need to look for it. Viewed this way, anarchism is not so much a theory at all, but a practice which people have been engaged in throughout our history, and which, in increasingly rare circumstances, people still engage in. As we shall see, this view has been fundamental in shaping the continuing focus of anarchist thought, but it has done so as much by influencing what is *not* said, as what is.

Indeed, as fundamental as it is, the concept of anarchy in action, to use Ward's term, is highly problematic, for a number of reasons. Yet before we explore why, it is worth first taking a look at some examples of these existing anarchies, to get a better sense of what it is anarchists believe we are to look for. In later

Chapters, we shall return to these visions to ask more specific questions, and to see how, when the issues of freedom, ethics and power are critically explored, these examples become much more complex and problematic. In this Chapter, however, a general overview should help establish a useful starting point. We can split these examples of anarchy in action into two main parts: anarchy that exists within non-anarchic systems, that we might call *pockets of anarchy*, and which are to be found in our daily lives, and in deliberately created autonomous spaces; and anarchy that exists in a more absolute sense, as wholesale anarchist societies, such as primitive societies, and the brief but important period of anarchism in Spain.

Pockets of Anarchy.

Colin Ward, one of the most influential and, in my opinion, engaging and honest anarchist writers (or propagandists, as Ward saw himself) wrote a great deal about what he often referred to as *anarchy in action*; experiments in non-hierarchical living that, unlike those of the Spanish anarchists or primitive people, exist *within* the wider environment of the state. They are the famous 'seeds beneath the snow', the pockets of anarchy that may one day grow, along with many others, into fully fledged free societies (Ward 2008), although, as we shall see, Ward questioned the extent to which anarchism could ever be the sole, or even primary form of social life (Ward 1973, 135-136).

The idea that evidence of anarchist practices exist all around us is a common one, and goes back to at least the work of Kropotkin, who advanced various arguments to demonstrate the persistent nature of mutual aid, despite the overbearing presence of the state. In *The Conquest of Bread*, Kropotkin points to numerous examples of what he considers to be evidence for his anarchist philosophy (Kropotkin 1985, 129-142). He cites the European rail and postal networks, the British Lifeboat Institution, and a guild that oversees barge movements on the Dutch canal system to 'prove that men, as soon as their interests do not absolutely clash, act in concert, harmoniously, and perform collective work of a very complex nature' (Kropotkin 1985, 130)[4]. For Kropotkin, such 'spontaneous associations', as he somewhat misleadingly calls them, provide such a convincing argument for anarchism that he confidently and rhetorically puts the onus on defenders of the state to explain how this anarchy could possibly work:

> And the most interesting thing in this organisation is, that there is no European Central Government of Railways! Nothing! [...] Everything is done by contract. So we ask the believers in the State [...] 'how do European railways manage without them'? (Kropotkin 1985, 131-2).

Kropotkin sees in these examples the existence of the anarchist principles of mutual aid and self-government, although he does not suggest the people behind such examples are consciously anarchists. In recent years, the global justice movement, much of which is consciously anarchist, has made similar claims to have demonstrated the viability of these same libertarian principles.

The Global Justice Movement.

The postanarchist Saul Newman argues that:

> one of the ways of demonstrating the capacity of non-state political alternatives is the development of autonomous communities, collectives and organisations that exist beyond the control of the state. The countless experiments in autonomous politics taking place everywhere – squatters' movements, social centres, indigenous collectives, land re-occupation movements, blockades, workers' occupations, alternative media centres, communes, numerous activist networks and so on – are evidence of this possibility (Newman 2010, 116).

Such arguments are commonplace (Morland 2004, 34-7; Heckert 2010, 190-1; de Angelis 2001, 115) and anarchy in action is in fact one of the defining features of contemporary anarchist theory, or, as it is more commonly called, *praxis* (Gordon 2007). Indeed, even within much recent academic work there is often a conscious rejection of theory (or at least being overly theoretical); what matters is what people are actually doing, and what they are doing, we are told, is creating new forms of democracy. Marianne Maeckelbergh, for example, suggests that 'if one wants to know what the alterglobalisation movement is for, one must look at what the alterglobalisation movement *does*' (Maeckelbergh 2009, 4). In doing so, she argues that

> we find that what this movement is doing is radically changing the meaning of democracy and simultaneously constructing a democratic world based on principles of diversity and horizon- tality. [...] Taking an ethnographic approach [...] allows for an exploration of the actual decision-making practices already in place, which make visible the beginnings of an emerging democratic alternative (Maeckelbergh 2009, 4-5).

In other words, Maeckelbergh claims that by looking at the practices of the alterglobalisation movement, its forms of organ- ising, its decision-making structures, its meetings, and so on, we get a glimpse of the 'other world' we hear so much about: we see, then, 'the beginnings of an alternative democratic praxis' (ibid.). Rather than engaging in stale rhetoric and abstract theory, they are *practising* anarchy – anarchy really is 'alive' (Gordon 2008). David Graeber makes a similar point when he argues that activists organise their actions, such as the protests in Seattle, 'according to directly democratic principles and thus provide a living example of how genuine egalitarian decision making might work' (Graeber 2008, 210). In fact, this is a standard position throughout the alterglobalisation movement, which argues not only that another world is possible, but that, thanks to the movement's prefigurative politics, it actually at times lives out that other world, however momentarily.

Absolute Anarchy: Life in Primitive Societies.

Although such examples are rare glimpses of anarchy emerging out of the confines of the state, the state itself is ultimately something of a rarity when the long history of humankind is taken into account (Moseley 2007, 124); the majority of our species' existence has in fact been made up of stateless societies. The state is a relatively new phenomenon, and people certainly existed before the state did: furthermore, it is not only in the past, but also in a few rare places in the present, that people can and do live together in relative peace without state apparatus (Graeber 2007, Chps 5,6,7 & 8). Primitive[5] societies have long been, and continue to be, used by anarchists to demonstrate the viability of a life without the state. Once again, Kropotkin, in his classic text *Mutual Aid* (1902/2008), drew significant conclusions from his (usually indirect) study of primitive life, and argued that, far from being a war of all against all, pre-state societies generally existed in relative peace. There was violence, there were disputes, an d Kropotkin makes no attempt to hide this, but these conflicts were largely kept under control, and daily life was far from being a constant, chaotic battle for survival. Similar arguments are abundant. The Anarchist Teapot[6] (n.d.), for example, in their *Introduction to Anarchy*, note that

> 99 per cent of human existence has been shaped by tribal society, real communities peacefully roaming around eating berries and having a good time without any conception of needing states or government. Their lives were nothing like the constant struggle against hostile nature and other tribes we might imagine.

In fact, many of these 'anarchic cultures have flourished to modern times' but are increasingly coming under threat from the related machinery of 'the state', 'corporations', 'armies', and 'aid workers' (ibid.). It is the state that is the anomaly, not anarchism.

This position has been laid out most starkly by anarcho-primitivists such as John Zerzan (2005) and Derrick Jensen (2006), who believe not only that primitive life shows us that life without the state is possible, but that such forms of life are necessary if we are ever to escape social division and environmental destruction. Anarchists have also drawn on the works of theorists who are not necessarily anarchists but whose work strengthens the basic argument that life without the state is possible; in particular, Pierre Clastres' *Society Against the State* (1987) Marshall Sahlins' *Stone Age Economics* (1974), and James C. Scott's *The Art of Not Being Governed* (2009).

Anarchy in Spain.

Another source of both inspiration and an argument for the feasibility of anarchism is the Spanish Civil War, during which anarchists successfully ran not only large areas of rural Spain, but also, significantly, the industrialised city of Barcelona. Not surprisingly, 'this quintessential moment of anarchism' (Amster et al 2009, 3) features extensively in anarchist writing, and is of course held up as another, and at times, *a more relevant*, example of anarchism's viability. The anarchist period in Spain contains two important elements lacking from examples of primitive societies.

Firstly, those involved were self-consciously *anarchists*. It is often noted that primitive people are at times aware that states exist: in other words, they are aware of other forms of social organisation, yet they consciously remain 'anarchic' (Maddock 1987, 62; Scott 2009). Nonetheless, whilst this is no doubt true, it seems there is an important difference between people explicitly putting into practice the culmination of several decades of anarchist thought, and people who have no such agenda; who have been, in other words, anarchists from birth. Similarly, it is important that the Spanish anarchists were all *raised* within a very different culture, and were in the process of actively creating new forms of social organisation, as opposed to continuing to live out old ones. The anarchist period in Spain demonstrated that people could *become* anarchists, or that societies could become anarchic, regardless of any prior social norms or structures. None of this is intended as a value judgement – neither is better or worse – but these differences are significant. The second difference is one of scale; whilst primitive clans or tribes unite and form alliances with each other in any number of ways, the standard unit of daily life is, by modern terms, tiny. The importance of political equality for anarchism, and the need for face-to-face meetings to ensure this equality is genuine, makes this issue of very real importance, and the scale of anarchism in Spain provides compelling evidence that much larger communities can be run in non-hierarchical ways.

These examples of anarchy in action provide anarchists with an important weapon with which to defend the idea of a stateless society. Whilst many people might believe that *anarchism is a nice idea in theory*, but that *it would never work in practice*, examples of anarchy in action allow anarchists to turn this on its head; anarchism might seem *theoretically* implausible, but it *does* work *in practice*. But do such examples really demonstrate the validity of this claim? And, if they do, what *sort* of anarchy do they provide evidence for? In the following section, I want to critically assess these claims, concluding that whilst there is much to be learnt from these anarchic experiences, their value must be understood to be limited in important ways; in particular, anarchists must acknowledge that *context* is crucial when thinking about alternative social systems; a point which, interestingly, is well recognised, as we shall see, when the idea of blueprints comes under scrutiny, but which is often over-looked when anarchy in action is being discussed. And, as we progress through the work, we will also begin to see that the question of what *forms* of social life these examples demonstrate is crucial; put simply, even *if* anarchism is possible, does a life without the state automatically translate into the sort of world anarchists today wish to see?

Anarchy in Action: A Critical Response.

I readily accept that there is much to be inspired by and to think about in these examples. But can we really learn from them that anarchism, in the twenty-first century, offers a viable alternative to the state? While they may be of tremendous use for anarchists in *thinking about* anarchism, I want to fundamentally challenge the idea that they somehow prove its viability. In fact, these examples raise a number of issues which, when considered honestly, cast an even greater shadow over anarchism's prospects. Although we will return to these examples throughout the work, I want to present a brief analysis of them here.

Pockets of Anarchy.

Kropotkin, as we saw, was so taken with the examples of mutual aid which he saw all around, he confidently asked defenders of the state to explain how it was that the European rail network, for example, could exist without the aid of a national government. Sadly, the answer is a rather simple one: it doesn't. The European rail network, and all the other examples Kropotkin cites, are deeply embedded in numerous ways within the state. Whilst they offer certain interesting and possibly inspiring insights into the ways humans can and do organise, insights that could well be used to advocate an expansion of democratic reforms in the work place, for example, they do not offer any real argument for such reforms on a societal level. It can reasonably be argued that train companies operate within the *safe space provided by the state*; their ability to act together for their mutual benefit is not evidence that the state is unnecessary, but rather evidence that each of the states these companies operate in are doing their job perfectly well, allowing individuals and companies to get on with their daily lives whilst simply ensuring that they are protected from the careless and corrupt, precisely as liberals argue it should. Kropotkin himself says: 'Everything is done by contract'; but who enforces such contracts? That they *could* be enforced without the state is an argument that can well be made, but these examples do nothing to add to such a position, because these contracts *are* in fact safeguarded by the state. What Kropotkin argues, ultimately, is that different groupings of people can come together without an overarching authority *that subsumes them all:* but this does nothing to diminish the liberal argument that states are still ultimately necessary. All of Kropotkin's examples are found with states, and any or all of their positive attributes could reasonably be assumed to be there precisely because of the protection and organisation offered by those states. Again, it could be argued that this isn't the case, but there is no evidence for this; we have not witnessed anarchy in action; at most we have glimpsed its possibilities.

Furthermore, we must take into account the fact that the power of the state does not simply exist in the form of a looming policeman: people learn to police themselves to a great extent, even when the prospects of being caught and punished are extremely low. Interestingly, David Graeber misses this point when he suggests that the fact of activists refraining from physically overpowering a truck driver about to dump toxic waste 'is a remarkable testimony to most activists' dedication to non-violence' (Graeber 2009, 203), but then fully acknowledges it when discussing, not the activists' motives, but those of the truck driver, who is, in similarly refraining from violence, 'likely to be thinking about the possibility of being brought up on charges of negligent homicide' (ibid. 208). Somehow, Graeber assumes the authority of the state is only felt by the truck driver, and not the activists, but makes no attempt to defend such a claim (which is in any case only implicit. What seems clear is that our daily lives are heavily influenced by the knowledge that the state, with the full power of the law behind it, is always present; the fact that some anarchists would prefer that it were not does little to negate the point that people's behaviour is constantly, if often sub-consciously, informed by this reality, and that holds as true for anarchists as anyone else.

What is lacking from these examples is evidence that any of them would work without the various legal and social functions the state is supposed to provide. Once again, the idea of the liberal state is precisely that people *can and should* act together without undue interference from government. Many more examples of these 'seeds beneath the snow' have been given over the years, but they all ultimately suffer the same fate. They do indeed offer anarchists many valuable philosophical and socio-logical insights, and in as much as they do so, it could well be argued that they add considerably to the argument for a life without the state. What they do not do is in any way prove that the state is unnecessary.

The Global Justice Movement.

We can of course apply much the same critique to the examples of anarchy apparently demonstrated by the global justice movement. Within the movement, it is commonly argued that in *temporary autonomous zones* the power of the state is rendered effectively redundant. As an anonymous writer in *Do or Die* puts it: 'Where the barricades begin, the state ends' (anonymous 2003, 22). These claims to have achieved *autonomy* raise questions about how anarchists understand the way power works, and the extent to which anarchists believe people can *escape* certain power relations. Much of the recent work by postanarchists such as Saul Newman argues that anarchists have failed to acknowledge the capacity for other forms of power relations to exist without the state. As Newman suggests:

To insist simply on an autonomous and self-determined space avoids the question of the shape of social and political relations within that space; autonomous spaces can be subject to the worst kinds of authoritarian, repressive and fundamentalist politics. It is clear, then, that autonomy must refer not only to the independence from the state of a particular political and territorial space, but also to the internal micropolitical constitution of that space, to the organisation of social life within it (Newman 2010, 179).

I return to discuss the question of power in Chapter 4, but other considerations arise within these recent examples of anarchist practice. For instance, it is important to note the brief time spans of many of these autonomous zones, most of which are indeed *temporary*: during a two week protest camp, the organisation of daily life is fundamentally different from that of a sustained community. For example, discussions about how the land is to be divided up and used by the people on it are unlikely to ever occur, except as hypothetical campfire chats. Economic questions are for all intents and purposes redundant in such spaces: people bring in money, and resources, from the capitalist world 'outside' and difficult questions around the distribution of goods never arise. Another important factor to consider is the *intentional* element of such projects. Such spaces work effectively in large part because there is a considerable degree of trust and a united sense of purpose, based on shared political, ethical and often cultural views, and of course on many interwoven personal relationships.

Another way to think of this is to see such spaces as creating temporary *communities*. This may be seen as a positive thing, and indeed the idea of community is often considered key to the functioning of an anarchist society (Taylor 1982). However, whilst communities may exist in various forms (we might talk of, for example, an artistic community) for Taylor, for societies to function effectively without the state, the community must be small and *stable* (ibid., 94). If they are to effectively maintain some degree of order, then, they must 'have little turnover in their memberships' (ibid., 91). However, as we shall see in Chapter 5, the idea of consensus-decision making which is almost exclusively used in temporary autonomous zones is premised, according to those who support it, on the ability of individuals to leave one community and enter another with ease (Seeds for Change, 2007; Gordon, 2008: 69; Maeckelbergh, 2009: 226; Graeber 2009, 316). Taylor also stresses the need for members of a community to hold 'beliefs and values in common' (ibid., 26), something which I have suggested is inevitably the case in protest camps, but which is unlikely to be true in larger, or what we might call *un*intentional communities. Such issues raise questions about the need for a strong foundation of shared values within anarchist societies, and the extent to which the need for communities to form and maintain such foundations suggests certain limitations on individuals' ability to move freely from one community to another, or to hold different values These are all questions I return to throughout this work.

Absolute Anarchy: Life in Primitive Societies.

The claim that life in primitive societies can teach us about the possibility of anarchy in the modern world is also problematic: small-scale and traditional communities are, it might be said, not simply quantitatively but also qualitatively different, in important respects. As we saw above, a strong sense of community and of tradition is usually considered fundamental to the orderly functioning of such societies, but this is not something which is currently shared in much of the modern world. Whether we could regain this sense of community, and what it would mean to do so, is, at best, an open question (see Bauman 2001 for some interesting reflections on this subject). However, I want here to focus on another, more specific, problem. Samuel Clark, in his book *Living Without Domination* (2007), presents a more thorough analysis of primitive societies, in particular the Nuer, who he uses to demonstrate 'some human capacities for living together and especially for conflict resolution' and to show that the 'range of human social possibility includes systems of egalitarian social networks, without institutionalised domination, in which violence is limited and conflict can be resolved' (Clark 2007, 119). However, throughout the book, Clark uses the terms 'domination' and '*institutionalised* domination' interchangeably and without comment, but it is far from clear if they are in fact the same thing. Does Clark really present examples of a life without domination, as the title of his book suggests, or simply without *certain forms* of domination? Even if we concede that examples of primitive societies have shown that life without the state is *viable*, we are still left with perhaps a more fundamental question: is it *desirable*? Does it really offer us *freedom*? Or, a better question: what *sort* of freedom does it offer? Life without the state might not be as 'nasty, brutish and short' as Hobbes thought, but can it offer the freedom that we have come to expect after (somewhat ironically, perhaps) several centuries of liberal democracy? Harold Barclay, one of the most prominent anarchist academics to focus on primitive peoples, draws similar conclusions to myself with regards the inevitability of power relations within any form of society (Barclay 2005). As Ernest Gellner argues

> historically, mankind has not always suffered under centralised despotism. ...[Q]uite frequently it was free from such oppression. [However], in the traditional agrarian world [communities] maintain their cohesion, internal discipline and solidarity with the help of much ritual, employed to underscore and enforce social roles and obligations. [...D]iscipline is enforced by a proliferation of minor rules and hence additional possible transgressions, the avoidance

of which puts a heavy and constant burden on each individual [...whose] role is stable and ritually orchestrated. It is both internalised and externalised [...] He knows only too well who he is and what is expected of him: his prospects of redefining his own identity are negligible (Gellner 1994, 6-7).

He concludes: 'Traditional man can sometimes escape the tyranny of kings, but only at the cost of falling under the tyranny of cousins, and of ritual' leading to a life 'which modern man would find intolerably stifling' (Gellner 1994, 7-8). Indeed, only a cursory glance at life in some primitive societies, including many of those held up by anarchists as examples of stateless living, quickly reveals a world that is no stranger to threats, coercion, bullying, violence, punishment, blame; no stranger to, in other words, various forms of domination. Life in stateless societies may have been largely peaceful, and free from coercive *institutions*, but it also limited the life of each individual in ways that, as Gellner argues, we may no longer find acceptable. As Alexander Moseley[7] suggests, 'historically anarchic societies often possessed illiberal cultures that stifled individual creativity', and, therefore, 'the modern anarchist seeks the moral plurality corresponding to modern civilisation without the fastidious conservatism of the primitive' (Moseley 2007, 125). The life of a housewife who spends her day cleaning her husband's shirts and making his dinner, could, after all, be perfectly *peaceful*. The 'capacities and tactics humans have for living together and resolving conflict, without states' that Clark discusses with great admiration (Clark 2007, 110) are also, not surprisingly, used to instil a general conformity of thought and behaviour. As Kropotkin, seemingly approvingly, notes

Primitive folk [...] so much identify their lives with that of the tribe, that each of their acts, however insignificant, is considered as a tribal affair. Their whole behaviour is regulated by an infinite series of unwritten rules of propriety which are the fruit of their common experience as to what is good or bad, that is, beneficial or harmful for their own tribe. Of course, the reasoning upon which their rules of propriety are based sometimes are absurd in the extreme. [...] But, absurd or not, the savage obeys the prescriptions of the common law, however inconvenient they may be. He obeys them even more blindly than the civilised man obeys the prescriptions of the written law. His common law is his religion; it is his very habit of living (Kropotkin 2008, 74).

Later, he summarises the point well when he notes that a 'rebellion against a right decision of the customary law was simply 'inconceivable' because 'law, morality and fact could not be separated from each other in those times' (ibid. 86). Are these the 'tactics and capacities' that Clark, a self-confessed Kropotkinite, has in mind, when he suggests a life without domination is possible? Are we really faced with the choice of domination by, as Gellner puts it, either kings or cousins? Must we decide between institutionalised state regulation, or 'absurd' common law we are compelled to obey? And why are most anarchists so keen to point to primitive societies to defend their politics, yet so slow to ask such obvious questions? Colin Ward is honest enough to acknowledge that this form of social control 'also inhibits many other varieties of non-conforming behaviour as well' (Ward 1973, 128), and he readily conceded he would not like to live in such a society. Earlier in the same work, he explains

[E]arly observers [...] labelled certain societies as anarchistic when a more searching examination might show that they had as effective methods of social control and its enforcement as any authoritarian society, or that certain patterns of behaviour are so rigidly enforced by custom as to make alternatives unthinkable. The anarchist, in making use of anthropological data today, has to ask more sophisticated questions than his predecessors about the role of law in such societies (ibid., 45).

Of course, no one explicitly argues that we either should or could mimic these primitive societies in every respect, but surely then we are faced with the question: if the sorts of cultural tools employed by primitive societies are needed to resolve conflict and maintain stability, are anarchists suggesting we adopt these tools, or that there are moderated forms we can now access which will perform the same function? The former proposal seems highly unappealing, but with regards to the latter, we are left wondering what those forms might be exactly. The closer to primitive life anarchism hopes to be, the less it suggests a life without domination; rather, it merely presents a different form of domination: but the further away we take anarchism in response to this critique, the less useful any comparisons become. At best, the simple claim is made that life is *possible* without the state: but what is possible and what is desirable are two very different things. The question of what sort of freedom anarchism hopes to offer is the basis of Chapter 2.

Anarchy in Spain.

The events that took place throughout Spain in the mid to late 1930s are, without doubt, both inspirational and informative, and they do demonstrate, far more than primitive societies, that anarchism is more than a utopian fantasy. Yet to do justice to the many people that lived and died to defend anarchism, we need to acknowledge that both the context of the civil war, and the beliefs and cultural understanding of those involved, raise questions about the extent to which we can point to this time as some sort of evidence of anarchist success, and, importantly, what sort of freedom was attained. Once again, we need to ask what social processes were employed to make daily life possible, and, having done so, ask whether we would be happy to live under such conditions, or indeed, whether such conditions constitute, despite the lack of an official state, a genuinely libertarian society.

The most obvious factor to take into account is that Spanish anarchism was realised during a time of civil war; a war which cost the lives of half a million people and which ended with a fascist dictatorship in control of the country for the next three and a half decades. I do not want to dwell, however, on the obvious fact that the anarchists ultimately lost. Whilst this is important for some discussions, it is not for mine[8]. What is important is the marked differences of perhaps every aspect of daily life (ethical, political, social, cultural and so on) during an event such as a civil war (Taylor 1982, 37-8). For our purposes here, we might begin by posing some obvious questions. To what extent were differences of opinion amongst anarchists left to one side, were sacrifices made, was self-control exercised, were people united, due to the ever present threat of a fascist victory, in ways that we might not be able to recreate without such a threat? Ultimately, it is perhaps impossible to answer these questions; or, rather, there will be multiple answers. And it may be unrealistic to attempt to disentangle the many and complex emotions that were being experienced; how does one separate, for example, the desire to fight *against* something from the desire to fight *for* something? The Spanish anarchists were indeed fighting against Franco and his troops, but they were also very much fighting to realise their dreams of a libertarian society (which is why they also ended up fighting communists as well as fascists). A question we may want to pose then, without hoping to ever have any generalisable answer, is: can a *common good* unite people in the same way that a *common enemy* so clearly does?[9] Even without answers to such questions, it seems reasonable to conclude that the unusual circumstances that present themselves at such times *must* be taken into account; and that anarchists' reference to the Spanish period as proof of anarchism's viability, without reference to the important contextual issues surrounding this time, are, in this respect, considerably weakened. As one Spanish anarchist put it: 'we ate from the same dish, took part in the same action; we were all in the same situation; when men's lives are at stake there can't be very deep differences' (quoted in Fraser 1981, 430). Such relevant issues must be, but I would argue are generally *not*, taken into account.

There are other things we can learn from this period however. Two important points ought to be considered. The first is that, amongst the Spanish anarchists, *morality* was not, as it has been for many anarchists, a dirty word (a matter, which, again, I return to in Chapter 3). In fact, revolutionary rhetoric was very often endowed with a strong moral sentiment. The Spanish anarchists have at times been compared to medieval millennialists, and whilst this comparison is in many ways unhelpful, as Sam Clark argues (Clark 2007, 121-122) it should also remind us that the anarchists had, as Clark himself acknowledges, an '[a]scetic ideal of purification' (ibid., 121; see also Alexander 2002, 219). Indeed, despite attacks on religious institutions, physically and ideologically, 'puritanism increased as a result of the anarcho-syndicalist revolution' (Fraser 1981, 288). This resulted in many anarchists living according to a strong set of moral values: some of which, such as vegetarianism, would be applauded by many contemporary anarchists, such as Bob Torres (Torres 2007); others, such as a rejection of caffeine and alcohol, I suspect might not be looked upon quite so favourably. (Although there are of course many anarchists who do reject both these things.) Perhaps most disturbingly, in some areas patriarchy, perhaps the most prevalent form of hierarchy throughout human history, remained firmly in place. Inequality between the sexes was often left unaltered; women still occupied traditional roles as cleaners, cooks, child-minders, etc., and were often denied a voice in public meetings. Women were criticised for wearing lipstick, and, whilst free union between men and women was encouraged in some areas, in other anarchist controlled communities, people choosing to live together unmarried were condemned as 'living like animals' (Fraser 1981, 289).

The second point is the unsavoury truth that anarchists were often involved in activities that were a far cry from the libertarian ideals which motivated them. Forced collectivisation and assassinations were, if not common, certainly far from rare. It is, of course, impossible to get the full picture, but there is no doubt that anarchists were involved in coercion in a wide variety of ways. From forcing religious children to be educated along secular principles (ibid., 294-295), to intimidating people to join collectives; from seizing land and machinery, to murdering not only Fascist soldiers, but also members of an Anti-Fascist committee who were accused of cowardice (ibid., 353). Although often keenly aware of their own contradictions, anarchists often felt themselves simply unable to abide absolutely by their libertarian values, and they rapidly created their own forms of authority, including a basic police force (sometimes known as Control Patrols) and law courts (Alexander 2007, 1111-1113). Perhaps not surprisingly, then:

Almost from the beginning of the Civil War, the Spanish anarchists suffered from criticism and even denunciation from the ranks of [some] foreign anarchists who could not forgive the Spaniard's compromise with libertarian principles in the interests of prosecuting the Civil War. The Spanish Anarchists [replied that their critics] had never had to deal with the practical application of their movement's principles (ibid., 1161).

A fact which is conveniently over-looked in most modern accounts of the Spanish anarchists.

What the anarchists achieved in Spain is, I repeat, no doubt inspiring, and I have deliberately focused here on the problems, rather than the many successes; but those problems remain, and to ignore them is to suggest, without argument, that they are irrelevant. It is not my argument here that what happened in Spain *could* not have occurred without these violent and coercive elements, but simply that the historical fact is that it *did* not occur without them. And neither do I claim that the period of Spanish anarchism ought not to be considered successful in its own right. Murray Bookchin, for example, claimed, in a characteristically dismissive manner, that without

> the means for an analysis of their situation [the Spanish anarchists] revealed only a minimal capacity to understand the situation in which they found themselves [...] and no capacity to take 'the next step' to institutionalise a workers' and peasants' form of government (Bookchin 2007, 93)

I offer no such criticism, and, indeed, find such a statement misguided and offensive. My claim is simply that anarchists should do much more to recognise the practical limitations these anarchists encountered when trying to put their libertarian ethos into practice. In other words, any mistakes (if we can call them such) the Spanish anarchists made must be considered as broadly inevitable; the failure to implement a pure anarchy of absolute liberty and equality was not down to any 'minimal capacity to understand the situation', as Bookchin argued, but rather, as I hope to have shown by the end of this work, the unavoidable consequence of organising that complex and troublesome phenomenon, human life. Of course, it might be hoped that any limits to freedom would come about through, and be enforced by, more genuinely democratic processes than often happened in Spain, but I would argue that this is far more likely to be the case if anarchists acknowledge, and thereby anticipate, the problems any libertarian society is likely to face.

Anarchy in Action: Some Lessons.

A number of interesting questions are raised by these examples of anarchy in action. Firstly, there is the distinction between anarchy viewed almost as a philosophical approach, a libertarian tendency, creating and fostering spaces of greater freedom, solidarity and self-governance, *within* a wider political system largely antithetical to these values; and anarchy viewed as a much more comprehensive social system where freedom is absolute, and no coercion or compromise is accepted; and, crucially, where the state no longer exists. In the following chapters, we will return to these competing understandings of what anarchism is, or can be. Regrettably, and worryingly, however, all too often anarchism is presented in what amounts to two radically different ways, with this distinction, crucial though it is, rarely being explicitly acknowledged or discussed. Indeed, it is not always clear how arguments for anarchism as a libertarian *tendency within the state* differ from a standard liberal position; in fact, theorists such as Ward have at times been dismissed as little more than liberal reformists (see Benjamin Franks' discussion on Class War's view about Ward in Franks 2003, 57). Certainly, it is much easier to accept the sort of arguments presented by Kropotkin, and more recently by the likes of Marianne Maeckelbergh, that much greater democratic engagement in all areas of life is possible, *within the state*. Ward was quite unusual in his belief that anarchism may well never be the sole ideology under which a society operates, at times explicitly acknowledging that anarchism was only ever likely to be one strand of the organisational fabric of any society (Ward 2008, 163-4); usually, the underlying assumption appears to be that anarchism in fact needs to, and potentially could, do away with the state entirely. All too frequently, then, these two understandings of anarchy seem to go hand-in-hand, with ideas about one form merging with thoughts about the other, with no real acknowledgement of the fundamental differences between them.

I believe this is one of the biggest pit-falls to be found within anarchist thought, and it can be found almost everywhere we might care to look, from academic texts to agitational pamphlets and flyers. If anarchism is ever to be taken seriously by a significant number of people, this over-sight will need to be addressed.

In Chapter 6 I suggest that the idea of *prefiguration*, that is, anarchy in action within a wider, non-anarchist environment, can play an important role in advancing the anarchist project, especially when it responds openly to the critiques of the following chapters. What I hope to have shown here is that claims that such prefigurative experiments demonstrate the viability of entirely anarchist societies are fundamentally flawed. Whichever way we understand the idea of anarchy in action, we encounter, however, a further paradox when it is placed alongside an equally important idea in the anarchist tool-box; that of blue-prints, or rather, the opposition to them. Although there is much to be said for the resistance to creating blue-prints, I will argue in the following section that this opposition has, like the idea of anarchy in action, helped foster a culture where anarchists all too often fail to ask critical questions about their ideology.

The Anarchist Opposition to Blueprints: Trifling Details, or Necessary Reflections?

I have so far argued that anarchists have, on the whole, failed to critically engage in discussing the viability of anarchy. Above, I suggested that discussions about the existence of stateless societies, and of people working co-operatively without state interference, have been used to defend the basic principles of anarchism. However, anarchists also argue that it is contrary to the anarchist ethos to outline how an anarchist society might work, because to do so is to already limit the freedoms of those who might at some point live in such a place. On the one hand, the claim is made that anarchism already exists, and, on the other, that anarchist forms of social organisation cannot be predefined. But if they already exist, why not at least explain in detail how they work? It might be argued that that is precisely what anarchists do, when they point to anarchy in action, but this only brings us back to the question of precisely how these examples are to be understood. Are they meant as detailed examples that anarchists ought to follow in a strict sense? If so, we are not only faced with the problems I outlined in the discussions above, but also with the question as to what this would constitute if not a blue-print? If that is the case, why then do we so frequently find anarchists opposing blue-prints? From the early theorists onwards, anarchists have taken their libertarian ethos to (one of) its logical conclusions, and argued against the possibility of detailing what an anarchist society would actually be like.

> Diversity is [...] a core anarchist value which leaves little place [...] for detailed blue-prints and designs for a free society (Gordon 2008, 5)

> It is against the nature of anarchism to offer a blue-print for a free society, for free people must decide for themselves how they want to live (Marshall 1993, 625).

> I am really too much of an anarchist to work out a programme for the members of that society; in fact, I do not bother about such trifling details, all I want is freedom, unrestricted liberty for myself and others (Emma Goldman, quoted in Marshall 1993, 398).

Many more such quotes are easily found. Indeed, when reading anarchist literature, they are difficult to avoid. In fact, with a certain irony, the rejection of blue-prints is rolled out with a uniform regularity that can begin to sound like a rather unhealthy mantra. However, this resistance is rooted in a commitment to self-governance, and its concomitant rejection of hierarchical authority, which includes a rejection of any temporal inequality, where those in the present dictate life for those in the future (de Angelis 2001). As Simon Tormey argues, the creation of detailed plans about how the future might look often closes off important space in which to create our own visions of another world (Tormey 2005). And it is true that the rejection of blue-prints does not always and necessarily entail a refusal to discuss the workings of an anarchist community; anarchists tend to be quite comfortable with paradoxes, and this is no exception (see Kinna 2009, 221- 240 for an interesting discussion about the tension between utopian thinking and the rejection of blue-prints). Yet I would argue that, over-all, anti-blueprint rhetoric has had a negative impact on anarchist thought, for three reasons. Firstly, this resistance to blue-prints has itself, with a certain irony, often resulted in closing off the possibilities of imagining a better world. Secondly, the refusal to discuss in more concrete ways the possible workings of an anarchist society has meant that potential problems are not easily anticipated, and are often overlooked entirely. And, finally, the lack of alternative visions, to inform and inspire, has helped maintain the popular view of anarchism as hopelessly unrealistic and naïve. I now discuss these issues in turn.

Firstly, the resistance to creating blue-prints is rooted in a libertarian belief that individuals must be free to define their own utopias, their own visions of alternative worlds. But there is a certain paradox to this position. Although there may be a clear difference between the creation of a manifesto by the vanguard of an authoritarian party, and an individual sharing her hopes and visions around a campfire, the frequent and forceful denouncing of blue-prints has led, I would argue, to a general reluctance to ever present one's own visions, however tentatively, of another world. Rather than opening up space for a *plurality* of visions, as

Tormey suggests is happening within the movement (Tormey 2005), what we see is an extreme reluctance to offer *any* visions; and this should hardly be surprising, because unless we wrap our own visions of a better world within a host of sufficiently humble provisos ... *this is only my view, I don't want to force this on anyone else, and so on...* then the danger is that our vision will itself be denounced as being nothing more than another dreaded blue-print. Indeed, Tormey, seemingly unaware of this paradox, argues, in relation to the Social Forum Process, that

> To the great frustration of all those who would like to see the social forums aid in the construction of a party or movement 'proper', the tone and orientation of such meetings remains resolutely one of negation, of resistance, as opposed to affirmation of an alternative. Resistance opens the way to alternatives; it does not affirm or celebrate one alternative over all others (Tormey 2005, 405).

Yet how can 'resistance open the way to alternatives' if we cannot discuss, or debate, or share our thoughts on what these alternatives might be? Tormey emphasises a *diversity* of visions, yet the strength of his position would appear to *exclude* any vision that is not sufficiently open-ended or vague to meet his approval. Whilst grounded in a valid concern to keep spaces such as the Social Forum, and any forms of politics that stem from them, equal and non-hierarchical, I would suggest that anarchists have often reacted to these concerns in an extreme and ultimately damaging way, denying not only the validity of a vanguard to prescribe how we ought to live, but, in the process, limiting the potential for *anyone* to engage in such thinking. What we are left with is a plurality of silences. As I discuss below, this paradoxical situation can easily be addressed once it is adequately recognised; at present, however, I would suggest this rather simple problem has eluded many anarchists who are, as a result, unduly restricting the radical imagination.

The second problem in need of discussion relates to the fact that, in failing to consider how libertarian communities might actually deal with practical issues, such as the distribution of goods, and the maintenance of social order, anarchists are failing to anticipate and therefore discuss potential problems that may arise if and when an anarchist society comes into being. As we shall see in the following chapters, many important debates, about freedom, ethics, power, and so on, are therefore being ignored or excluded; this happens either because the problems are simply not recognised (because they only arise when more concrete questions about anarchism are asked; something precluded by the rejection of blue-prints) or because, if they are recognised, they are not considered legitimate topics for discussion, because this is again precluded by the rejection of blue-prints. As such, the anarchist has a sort of 'get out of jail free' card; when asked a troubling question about how an anarchist society might resolve a well acknowledged problem, such as how its members might deal with a rapist, for example, they can simply say 'that's not for me to answer'. The result, then, is a lack of engaged, challenging and self-critical debate within anarchism about a number of important issues (Bufe 1994, 1).

And, finally, this lack of clarity and vision makes it extremely difficult to convince people about the merits of anarchism. Michael Albert, who, along with Robin Hahnel, has developed a detailed economic system (Parecon) which is, they argue, compatible with anarchist principles (see Albert 2003; Hahnel 2005) argues that:

> Citizens of developed countries are not going to risk what they have [...] to pursue a goal about which they have no clarity. How often do they have to ask us what we are for before we give them some [...] answers? Offering a political vision that encompasses legislation, implementation, adjudi-

cation, and enforcement, and that shows how each would be effectively accomplished in a non-authoritarian way [...] would not only provide our contemporary activism much-needed long-term hope, it would also inform our immediate responses to today's electoral, law-making, law-enforcing, and court systems, and thus many of our strategic choices. So shouldn't today's anarchist community be generating such political vision? (Albert 2001, 326-7).

Clearly, there is always the danger that ideas offered simply as *options* eventually solidify and turn into unquestioned principles that must be obeyed, but anarchism cannot defend itself absolutely against the ever present authoritarian threat by constantly refusing to provide any ideas about how an anarchist society might function. Furthermore, anarchists need to ask how *inspiring* their demands for a libertarian world are when they are left so deliberately vague. As Trevor Blackwell and Jeremy Seabrook note in their thought-provoking book *The Revolt Against Change*:

Even steel-makers and coal miners have fought to preserve their places of work, once pictured as the most dreadful hell-holes devised by an inhuman system to oppress its captive peoples. [...] Their caution in giving up the familiar for another unknown destination comes from a well-grounded fear that there will be further pain and sacrifice in store (Blackwell & Seabrook 1993, 16).

Of course, even with detailed blue-prints, people will question to what extent any political change will result in its promised benefits, and rightly so; but without *any* real sense of what an anarchist future might look like, is it not reasonable to anticipate an even greater aversion to taking a risk as huge as dismantling the state? This does not mean that anarchists must renounce their principles to win more support, to achieve anarchism at all costs, so to speak; the resistance to this type of politics is of course one of the core elements of the prefigurative ideal. But anarchists must ask themselves whether some more helpful position cannot be found.

In the final chapter I return to the question of blue-prints, and suggest that a balance needs to be struck; anarchists must be wary of creating restrictive plans for societies they themselves may never live in, but they must also seek to expand their vision and create inspiring and useful ideas that can help push anarchist ideas forward. And I will suggest that a greater emphasis on prefigurative politics will help anarchists in finding such a balance, by offering more opportunities for anarchists to engage with difficult moral and political questions, not through abstract theoretical reflection, but as an outcome of living one's everyday life according to anarchist values.

Whilst the rejection of blue-prints is informed by a principled commitment to genuine political equality and freedom, I believe that the anarchist response to this critique itself has a negative and wide-reaching impact on the chances of ever creating such a free society. There is a fundamental difference between offering a solution to a problem as *an option*, and on insisting that everyone must follow that solution. Discussing how an anarchist society *might* deal with problems of anti-social behaviour or disputes about resource allocation, for example, does not mean they *must* deal with them in this way, but it does provide a necessary space for much need critical reflection.

Conclusions.

I started this chapter with the claim that anarchists have failed to address some serious concerns about their ideology, and I suggested that at least two reasons for this were internal to anarchist discourse itself: first, the insistence that anarchism has already been shown to be viable, as is evidenced both by the existence of non-state societies, and by the fact of anarchy in action within existing state structures; and second, the rejection of blue-prints, which stems from anarchism's deeply held commitment to freedom, which negates the rights of a self-selected vanguard to detail how an anarchist society should function. Whilst anarchists can and should learn from anarchist societies, and from the day-to-day practices of people organising their lives without hierarchy, I have argued that there are serious problems when such examples are held up *as proof* that contemporary societies could function without the state; valuable though they are, such examples can only teach us so much about a possible libertarian life. And whilst the rejection of detailed blue-prints should be valued, it too has limitations; this rejection of a vanguardist approach to politics has led, I have argued, to a problematic refusal to engage in discussing a number of difficult questions that anarchism surely must face if it is to be more widely embraced, and if, crucially, it is to work, if ever it gets the chance.

The failure to see the limitations in these approaches has led, therefore, to a number of serious shortcomings in the anarchist project. Questions of freedom, ethics, power, questions any political movement must address, have been left without answers. In the chapters that follow, I want to explore these challenging issues, and to attempt to tease out the underlying anarchist assumptions about them. What *do* anarchists mean by freedom, and how do they hope a free society will actually work? How will issues of crime be resolved, and how will freedom be reconciled with equality? Is there a specifically anarchist approach to ethics, and if there is, what is it? Do anarchists misunderstand the nature of power, and have they therefore underestimated the extent to which it will continue to be a source of problems, even within a libertarian world? Without access to any precise details of what an anarchist society would look like, we must look more thoroughly at these fundamental questions, and see whether anarchists know *themselves* the answers to the basic questions of social organisation. It is, after all, one thing to refuse to outline a blue-print, and another thing entirely to be unable to imagine for oneself what the answers might be.

In Chapter 5, I go on to demonstrate how a failure to consider these issues has resulted in a problematic support for consensus-decision making, a process which, its supporters claim, does in fact respond to problems of freedom, ethics and power, but which, I argue, fundamentally misunderstands them. In the final chapter I return to the matter of anarchy in action, and the question of blue-prints, and make some tentative suggestions as to how they might be re-aligned in response to the issues raised throughout the work.

So we turn now to the question of freedom; are anarchists 'fanatical lovers of liberty', as Bakunin famously declared? Not surprisingly, the answer to this question is complex and, ultimately, incomplete; what will become clear is that freedom is indeed a core anarchist value, but one which is often misunderstood, and which presents very real problems for those who hope to see this value realised in practice.

Chapter 2

Fanatical Lovers of Liberty?
Anarchism and the Limits of Freedom.

Freedom, noted Isaiah Berlin, has been praised by almost 'every moralist in human history' and yet, like 'happiness and goodness, like nature and reality, the meaning of this term is so porous that there is little interpretation that it seems able to resist' (2002, 121). Indeed, if we assume we can gain some understanding of what anarchists mean by freedom by looking at what anarchists believe are some of the living examples of anarchism we saw in the preceding chapter, then we are forced to concede freedom is no less porous for the anarchists than it is for anyone else. The tribes people of the Nuer, for example, might be free from the state, but it is highly questionable whether they have many other sorts of freedom that we might associate with contemporary life.

Freedom: A 'perplexingly polymorphous notion.'

To begin, it might help to think a little about the idea of freedom more generally; to understand it in its wider philosophical and political context. Doing so will, if nothing else, help us keep in mind the fact that anarchism is far from alone in promoting (and struggling with) the basic concept of freedom. Perhaps the simplest but most important thing we might say about freedom is this: freedom is not simple. Not philosophically, and certainly not practically. Indeed, philosophers, political and otherwise, have long considered the idea of freedom, and recognised and discussed the complexity of this powerful word. As Benjamin Gibbs notes

> To investigate freedom is to enter into a labyrinth of concepts
> and principles, and face problems as complicated and

intractable as any in philosophy. We are prone to misconceive and misrepresent this perplexingly polymorphous notion, to abstract from it something thin and stunted which we take to be the real essence of freedom. If such abstractions are applied as principles of social policy, there may be a high price to pay in human suffering. What is brought into being may be *a negation of true freedom* (Gibbs 1976, 10, my emphasis).

In his classic essay *Two Concepts of Liberty*, Isaiah Berlin argues in a similar vein that 'conceptions of freedom directly derive from views of what constitutes a self, a person, a man. Enough manipulation of the definition of man, and freedom can be made to mean whatever the manipulator wishes' (2002, 181). Indeed, freedom has meant a great many things to as many different individuals and ideologies. As anarchists are well aware, freedom is frequently used to defend any number of things they actively fight against; capitalism, liberal democracy, even war, have all been defended on the grounds that they will protect, or extend, freedom. As George Bush II said on the morning of September 11th, 2001, 'freedom itself was attacked this morning by a faceless coward. And freedom will be defended' (Bush, 2001). Bush's closest ally in the fight to spread freedom throughout the world, Tony Blair, argues in a similar fashion: '[A]ll nations that are free value that freedom, will defend it absolutely, but have no wish to trample on the freedom of others' (Blair, 2003).

It is easy enough, especially for radicals, to simply label Bush, Blair and company as hypocrites, or liars; easy, but unsatisfactory. Because whatever the intentions of these particular individuals, the important point is that their ideas of freedom make sense on some level, and they make sense to a great many people. The freedoms offered by liberal democracies, however limited and corrupted they might be considered by some, are, for others, of the highest worth, and the culmination of many centuries of struggle. And, importantly, any limits these democracies place on freedom can be, and often are, justified (at least in the minds of many); more to the point, they are often justified in relation to that very same freedom. As Nikolas Rose points out

> the programmatic and strategic deployment of coercion, whether it be in the name of crime control or the administration of welfare benefits, has been reshaped upon the ground of freedom, so that particular kinds of justification have to be provided for such practices. [... F]or example [...] the argument that the constraint of the few is a condition for the freedom of the many, that limited coercion is necessary to shape or reform pathological individuals [...] or that coercion is needed to eliminate dependency and enforce the autonomy of the will that is the necessary counterpart of freedom (Rose 2004, 10).

Such paradoxes are common, and, as we will see throughout this work, it is a dangerous mistake to assume that they are always the result of disingenuous rhetoric. According to Paul Chambers, for example, for anarchists 'it is a curious suggestion that liberty might be upheld by the denial of liberty' (Chambers 2006, 37); but is it really so curious?[10] That freedoms might be denied to defend other freedoms may well be *paradoxical*, but we might more honestly suggest that such a proposition is *troubling* for anarchists, rather than curious. Indeed, freedom, I would suggest, is fraught with paradox, and the only way to eliminate troubling contradictions is to limit the scope of what we mean by freedom. Which is precisely what many people have attempted to do. As F.A. Hayek put it:

> The most effective way of making people accept the validity of the values they are to serve is to persuade them that they are really the same as those which they [...] have always held [...] And the most efficient technique to this end is to use the

old words but change their meaning [...] The worst sufferer in this respect is, of course, the word liberty. It is a word used as freely in totalitarian states as elsewhere (Hayek 2003, 161-2).

Anarchists may raise a weary eyebrow at such words, coming as they do from such an influential defender of the free market, an economic system that is, for anarchists,[11] antithetical to freedom; but, once again, to do so without reflecting on why it makes sense for a free market liberal to talk in such a way does anarchism no favours. Freedom, it would appear, is inherently problematic and extremely vulnerable to abuse (or, rather, to be simply being *used* in different and often contradictory ways); its content is paradoxical and its meanings are plural. Which brings us back to the question: exactly which forms of freedom *do* anarchists support? What have anarchists themselves said about freedom? If anarchists define themselves as lovers of liberty, and refuse to outline what an anarchist society might look like, how do their visions of freedom differ from those of Hayek, Bush, or Blair?

Anarchist Freedom: An Overview.

Murray Bookchin, one of anarchism's most interesting, prolific, and also problematic theorists, recognised the need for these issues to be at least discussed, if not quite resolved.

Freedom has its forms. [...] At one point or another, a revolutionary people must deal with how it will manage the land and the factories from which it acquires the means of life. It must deal with the manner in which it will arrive at decisions that affect the community as a whole. Thus if revolutionary thought is to be taken seriously, it must speak directly to the problems and forms of social management. It must open to public discussion the problems that are involved in a creative development of liberatory social forms (Bookchin 1974, 143).

Bookchin's enquiries into what such a liberated society might look like, however, increasingly led him away from anarchism, and in the last decade of his life he came to reject the philosophy entirely, describing it as 'the most extreme formulation of liberalism's ideology of unfettered autonomy' (Bookchin 2007, 91). Whilst I would by no means suggest that there can be no coherent anarchist view of freedom, it is perhaps not entirely without reason that, in pressing the question, and refusing to settle for easy answers, Bookchin was left feeling anarchism could not in fact offer any reasonable solutions to the various problems posed by an unswerving commitment to liberty.[12]

Alan Ritter held out higher hopes for anarchism, but nonetheless recognised that too many questions were left unanswered by previous generations of anarchists. He opens his book *Anarchism*, published in 1980, by noting that 'anarchists are commonly regarded as extreme libertarians on the ground that they seek freedom above all else' (Ritter 1980, 9). This view is false, however, because in fact, anarchists rely 'on public censure to control behaviour' (ibid.). How then, Ritter asks, do anarchists justify this control; how, in other words, do they understand *and limit* freedom? 'Although [anarchists] have long deemed this question crucial' he continues, 'no acceptable answer has yet been found' (ibid., 10). Whereas Bookchin's finer points are often sadly lost in a mist of unhelpful vitriol, the opposite problem occurs here; for this is, in fact, a remarkable statement, made with such little fanfare as to be easily overlooked: after more than a century of anarchist thought, Ritter believes the answer to perhaps the single most important question anarchism faces remains unanswered. But was Ritter right? Are anarchists really not extreme libertarians, as they are so often portrayed? In her exploration of contemporary anarchism, Giorel Curran states: 'To anarchists the values of liberty and autonomy are everything, and they staunchly resist all attempts to trample them' (Curran 2006, 20). And, writing many decades earlier, Alexander Berkman argued that:

> Anarchism means that you should be free; that no one should enslave you, boss you, rob you, or impose upon you. It means you should be free to do the things you want to do, and that you should not be compelled to do what you don't want to do (Berkman 1970 [1929], 2).

He goes on to suggest:

> In the fewest words, anarchism teaches that we can live in a society where there is no compulsion of any kind. A life without compulsion naturally means liberty; it means freedom from being forced or coerced, a chance to lead the life that suits you best (ibid., 9, my emphasis).

Anarchist thought is indeed peppered with such categorical statements. L. Susan Brown talks of 'anarchism's concern for individual freedom, *unconstrained by any authority or power*' (Brown 1993, 2, my emphasis), and Uri Gordon suggests that one of three key themes for the contemporary anarchist movement is 'the rejection of all forms of domination' (2008, 6). Yet while Brown rejects *all* authority, and Gordon denounces *all* domination, we can also find hints of subtle distinctions between different *forms* of authority and domination. The title of Sam Clark's book, *Living Without Domination* (Clark 2007) suggests an agreement with Gordon, yet, as I suggested in the previous chapter, his work is ultimately an argument about life, not without domination as such, but *without the state.* In fact, the examples Clark cites suggest multiple and complex relations of power and authority, and any claims that the individuals within these societies are entirely free from domination must be, at best, moderated and tentative. What is unclear in Clark's work, and in the work of many anarchists, is whether such crucial distinctions are over-looked, denied, or considered acceptable. Is all authority and domination really rejected, or only certain forms?

Freedom as Rejection of the State/Authority.

While there is no doubt that domination and authority have been forcefully condemned without qualification, it is equally true that it is their embodiment in the state, its related institutions, and the capitalist economy, which have historically formed, and to some extent continue to form, the basis of anarchist opposition.[13] My point here differs from the postanarchist claim that anarchists have tended to ignore non-state forms of power (Newman 2001; May 1994) (a question I will return to at much greater length in Chapter 4) but it is certainly the case that anarchists' discussions around freedom have often been understood within the parameters of a rejection of particular types of authority or domination; primarily, large-scale, institutional hierarchies. Indeed, it is the rejection of the state that is often taken as being the one element that unifies so many otherwise diverse and contradictory streams of anarchist thought. As Colin Ward puts it, 'for anarchists the state itself is the enemy' (Ward 2004, 2). The term *anarchism* of course means *without rulers* (or some other synonym, such as leaders) and whilst I am cautious about placing too much emphasis on a word alone, especially a word that has a vast and complex history, it is nonetheless evident that it is this rejection of rulers that forms a fundamental bedrock of anarchism. As Ward continues, 'threads of anarchist thought have different emphases. What links them all is their rejection of external authority, whether that of the state, the employer, or the hierarchies of administration and of established institutions like the school and the church' (Ward 2004, 2).

Yet somewhat frustratingly, understanding the fundamental principle of anarchism as being the rejection of centralised authority only shifts the question: we would now need to be clear what was meant by *rejection*, *centralised*, and *authority*.

Rather than analysing these terms in isolation, however, as the analytical philosopher Paul McLaughlin has done (2007), I think it would be more helpful to explore them in relation to other terms and ideas, both directly and indirectly related to the basic concept of freedom. Do anarchists ever talk of acceptable acts of coercion? Are there times when freedom is seen as being legitimately denied? What have *anarchists in action* done when freedoms have conflicted? And does this rejection of authority suggest a support for a negative form of freedom, for example, or is it more compatible with a positive freedom?

Anarchist Freedom: Positive or Negative?

One of the most basic, but nonetheless fundamental, distinctions to be found within discussions of freedom is that between its positive and negative manifestations. As Isaiah Berlin notes, the difference between negative and positive liberty 'is a cardinal issue. These are not two different interpretations of a single concept, but two profoundly divergent and irreconcilable attitudes to the ends of life' (Berlin 2002, 212). On the most basic analysis, negative freedom relates to *freedom from*, whereas positive freedom relates to *freedom to*.[14] On a strictly philosophical reading, I agree with critics of this approach, who have suggested Berlin's distinction is simply wrong: these freedoms are in fact the same thing, referred to in different ways; we are only ever free *from* something in order to be free *to do* something (see Gray 1991, and Gerald C. MacCullum 1967, for some useful explorations of these debates). However, I *would* agree that politically, and practically, the distinction remains a useful way to think through certain issues; hopefully, this point will become clearer as the discussion continues. Taken on this level, we might understand negative freedom as a general stance of non-intervention, where people are best left alone to get on with their lives. Positive freedom, however, is seen as being part of a broader parcel of values, all of which may at times need to be pro-actively defended (see Nursey-Bray 1996, for a useful overview of positive and negative freedoms in relation to anarchist thought).

The quotes we have seen so far would appear to suggest that anarchists adhere to a negative view of freedom, with such freedom being seen as absolute and non-negotiable. Bakunin, for example, famously declared anarchists to be 'fanatical lovers of liberty' (Bakunin 1984, 17). More explicitly, David Graeber and Andrej Grubacic contend that 'anarchism as a whole has tended to advance what liberals like to call 'negative freedoms" (Graeber & Grubacic 2004, 11). Yet we saw earlier how Alan Ritter, while recognising that anarchists are usually *considered* to be defenders of such negative freedom, denied that freedom is in fact the sole value for anarchists, and argued that their libertarian tendencies are tempered by their commitment to other values (Ritter 1980, 39). And, just as we can find plenty of support for negative freedom amongst anarchists, so too there is much to suggest many defend a more positive approach. Herbert Read, for example, suggests that 'we must prefer the values of freedom *and* equality above all other values' (Read 1974, 35, my emphasis), and Nicholas Walter argues that 'freedom and equality are not contradictory, but complementary' (Walter 1979, 43). It is not without reason then that Randall Amster contradicts Graeber by declaring that 'the anarchist is mainly interested in positive liberty' (Amster 1998, 3). It should be made clear that there are no obvious chronological or cultural 'sides' to these disagreements; Amster and Graeber, for example, who argue for differing concepts of freedom, are both contemporary theorists writing about anarchism as it is currently manifest.

So what are we to make of this? Do anarchists simply defend different forms of freedom? This ought not surprise us: it would be somewhat paradoxical, after all, if anarchists were all expected to agree about what sort of freedom they believed to be desirable. Indeed, some may argue that this is precisely the case, and for some anarchists this may well be so. I would argue, however, that on the whole we must draw more critical conclusions. Take Peter Marshall's position. Marshall argues that 'all anarchists share certain common concerns. [...] Above all, they reject all coercive forms of external authority in order to achieve the greatest degree of freedom and equality' (Marshall 1993, 36). Marshall appears to seek to defend an absolute freedom, a negative freedom, and at the same time, to incorporate this freedom with other values (in this case, equality); that is, to also defend a positive form of freedom. Similar statements are commonplace, so we are forced to assume that many anarchists support both positive and negative freedom. But is such a thing possible? Berlin certainly didn't think so, and this approach clearly demands answers to a number of challenging questions. Which values exist alongside freedom, to form this combination of both forms of freedom, a combination which Ritter (1980) calls *communal individuality*? What political and cultural tools are to be used to help mediate between them? What must anarchists do when conflicts between competing freedoms and values occur? How does equality relate to freedom? What about crime (or anti-social behaviour), and security?

Such questions are the standard fare of political philosophy, but where are they to be found within anarchist thought? It is not my intention to suggest that these questions have *never* been asked, but I would suggest honest attempts to answer them are all too rare, and, to the extent such issues have been discussed, any answers arising from such discussions have failed to seep into the broader anarchist conscience; the *anarchist common sense*, in other words, has no ready response. Furthermore, answers such as those presented by Ritter, which I discuss briefly below, are often abstract and presented without reference to any wider context; even a clearly defined defence of, say, positive freedom, which sees equality and freedom as being of equal importance, may give us little idea of how such a position is to be realised *in practice*. At this point, then, I want to explore anarchist approaches to freedom in relation to another key anarchist value, equality, and with reference to an issue that poses problems for any libertarian; that of crime. Doing so, we shall see how the wider anarchist movement understands freedom on a more practical level.

Equal-Liberty.

Discussions about the conflicting demands made by freedom and equality form a significant part of political, moral and economic theory. Robert Nozick's famous discussion of the basketball player Wilt Chamberlain accumulating wealth through the freedom of countless individuals paying to see him play (Nozick 1996, 161-4) is just one example of how complicated this problem is.[15] Indeed, balancing freedoms with other values is a notoriously difficult act to perform, which is one reason why Berlin sees negative and positive freedom as being fundamentally at odds with one another. But perhaps these are merely false dichotomies, which anarchism has seen through? Or perhaps they are real enough within some social structures, but are broken down by the implementation of others, such as anarchism? Is it possible that anarchism is (amongst other things) precisely the resolution of these (supposedly) irresolvable problems? Or, conversely, that other ideologies, such as liberalism, with the aid of capitalism, are responsible for *creating* such problems? Indeed, anarchists often simply deny that this is a genuine problem: freedom and equality are seen as being not only compatible, but in fact mutually re-enforcing. We saw earlier that Nicholas Walter claimed that 'freedom and equality are not contradictory, but complementary' and he goes on to suggest that the 'crucial contribution to political theory made by anarchists is the realisation that freedom and equality are in the end the same thing' (Walter 1979, 43). Iain McKay states simply that 'social equality and individual liberty are inseparable' (McKay 2007, 33), and Saul Newman makes a similar argument: 'Equal-liberty is simply the idea that liberty and equality are inextricably linked, that one cannot be had without the other' (Newman 2010, 20). Understood this way, 'this generous formulation of equal-liberty does not see another's liberty as potentially threatening but, rather, mutually enhancing' (ibid., 21) meaning that 'anarchism provides the fullest development and most radical expression of equal-liberty' (ibid., 24). Newman makes a similar point when discussing the more widely debated question of the relationship between the individual and the community, arguing that the division between personal and collective freedom is not only false, but was recognised as being so by some of the earliest thinkers. For Bakunin and Kropotkin, 'the anarchist idea of freedom embodies and, indeed, maximises ('extended to infinity') the idea of individual liberty or autonomy, refusing to see it in opposition to the liberty of others or to the desire for social equality' (ibid., 144). Such a conception of freedom 'refuses to see an opposition between individual freedom and collective, egalitarian freedom, between the one and the many, any constraint on one involves a constraint on the other' (ibid.). This view, which is 'central to anarchism' (ibid.) fundamentally differentiates it from liberalism and socialism, both of which 'imagine a tension between the individual and society, and between liberty and equality' (ibid., 145). And while liberalism prioritises the individual over the collective, and socialism the collective over the individual, it 'is only anarchism that refuses this opposition' (ibid.).

Rather than seeing conflicts between liberty and equality (or between the individual and the community) as being inevitable, Newman suggests they are the result of a philosophical failing:

Because liberalism is based on the sovereign self-interested individual, it does not have the conceptual language to think in these terms; it sees only a competition of liberties that must be balanced with one another. Unlike anarchism, it cannot imagine liberty as a collective entity, as a social being (ibid., 22-23).

But do all of these problems really come down to differing philosophical positions? Believing in a moral or philosophical equivalence between freedom and equality is simple; providing genuine equality within a community of humans, especially within a community that is currently deeply divided and unequal, is much more difficult. I recognise this is a somewhat question begging statement: what is meant, precisely, by *genuine equality*? Perhaps genuine equality really is dependent on freedom, and conceptions of equality which appear to conflict with freedom (as they do for Nozick, for example) are therefore not real expressions of equality, or freedom, at all. Rather than resolving the issue, however, this merely complicates it further, and leaves us asking yet more questions: what would this genuine equality, and freedom, look like? How would it work in practice? In what ways, precisely, is this anarchist equality different from that sought by other socialists? In what ways, precisely, is this anarchist freedom different from that sought by liberals?

So, just as we have asked what forms of *freedom* anarchists support, we might also enquire what sort of *equality* they believe to be compatible with this freedom. Like freedom, equality can be understood in different ways. Perhaps the most basic distinction is that between responding to, or over-looking, difference; in other words, equality can be understood as treating everyone the same, whereby equality means ignoring their differences, or as treating people differently, whereby equality means respecting their differences (Kymlicka and Norman 2000). The first approach, sometimes referred to as being 'difference-blind', argues that we must look beyond people's individual circumstances and create a level playing field for all. But sometimes, people's differences are *relevant*, and to treat everyone in the *same way* is to, ultimately, deny those differences; in other words, the practical *result* is an *in*equality of treatment. But the second approach, of responding to people's differences, relies on absolute agreement about which differences are relevant, and in how that relevance is to be understood. Without such agreement, there would be a need to enforce the outcome of any decisions which are based on these differences (Nursey-Bray 1996, 106).

In the sorts of temporary autonomous spaces which contemporary anarchists use to defend the viability of anarchism, for example, the provision of food is meant to establish and uphold the ideals of equality; however, this usually means that everyone is given the same amount of food. Clearly, this disadvantages those who are larger, or who have been engaged in more physically demanding activity; whilst people may grumble about this injustice around the camp fire, there are no real attempts within the movement to address these issues. Is the reason for this perhaps an implicit awareness that once such concerns are voiced and addressed, equality would soon become, as it has for liberals, a matter of contention, creating all manner of difficulties? Would people's *differences* lead to *disagreements*? And then would it perhaps become clear that freedom and equality are not so harmoniously aligned? Ultimately, it is just not good enough to morally condemn the conflict between liberty and equality, as Newman and others do, as though it simply exists at the whim of our political leaders, or due to some philosophical error. Those who see a conflict between equality and liberty see it as a problem occurring wherever humans gather: to be sure, it may be greatly exacerbated by certain social arrangements (a capitalist economy being a prime example) but I find it impossible to defend the view that such conflicts and problems are solely the result of these conditions. No doubt they have a huge impact on the extent to which the problem is experienced, and I would defend the view that anarchism is best placed to respond to this conflict in a just manner, but anarchists have failed to argue that no such conflicts would occur at all, or to discuss what they would do when they did. Iain McKay, for example, argues that 'there has been much nonsense written about 'equality' and much of what is commonly believed about it is very strange indeed' (McKay 2007, 31). Certainly, the image McKay himself presents suggests this is the case: anarchists 'have *no* desire to live in a society where everyone gets the same goods, lives in the same kind of house, wears the same uniform, etc.' (ibid., 31), nor do they believe that everyone should be identical. The fact that some people might believe such things 'is a sad reflection on the state of present-day intellectual culture and the corruption of words' (ibid.). It is not clear *who* in fact believes such things, and McKay fails to engage in a more nuanced discussion, trivialising the debate by suggesting that the matter is a simple one once we dismiss the people who believe equality means a life of communist–style clones. More mainstream political theorists concerned with the question of how best to create and sustain an equal society have, however, explored in great detail this problem, and it is clear that equality is, like freedom, far from being a simple matter; as we have seen, equality can be understood as referring to outcomes, or opportunities; it can also refer principally to economic equality, or political equality, or social equality, or a combination of these (for an interesting exploration of the concept of equality by a series of political philosophers see, for instance, Franklin 1997). Furthermore, however equality might be realised in a libertarian society, there is a further problem anarchists must face; namely, the question of how such equality is to be achieved in the first place. How do anarchists hope to *create* equality from such an unequal world; crucially, how do they hope to do this whilst respecting their ideals of freedom?

Even if an agreeable understanding of equality could be

arrived at, there is still the question of how we are to *achieve* an equal society, when the world is currently so unbalanced. We saw earlier that Uri Gordon believed anarchism to be against all forms of domination, yet even he acknowledges that certain groups will need to be forcibly coerced, at least in the *creation of* an anarchist society (Gordon 2008, 68). It is often argued that the ruling class, for example, may be 'forcibly suppressed and coerced into the anarchist society' (Schmidt & van der Walt 2009, 203). This, we are told, is 'not in contradiction with the anti-authoritarian principle. It is force used to remove the existing coercion of the capitalist system and can be seen as an act of legitimate self-defence by the popular classes' (ibid.). Is the claim, then, that freedom and equality will *eventually* be compatible, in an anarchist society? Perhaps. But this only raises more questions. How long will an anarchist society permit people being 'forcibly suppressed'? Until everyone is equal? And how long will that be? And what does this say of the anarchist commitment to a prefigurative politics, where the means and ends of any action are seen to be inseparable? Anarchists must ask themselves how the tasks of redistributing (economic) wealth, and then maintaining an equal distribution, are to be performed in practice: what levels of coercion will be acceptable? How will communities prevent such activities ossifying into institutionalised roles of economic, and then social, control? If *freedom* is the ultimate goal of the anarchist, why is the poor coercing the rich any more acceptable than the rich coercing the poor? Isn't freedom being relegated here, superseded by the need to establish equality? Maybe this is just, but is it *libertarian*? Such questions lead us to ask broader questions about the anarchist position on crime and social control, an issue to which we now turn.

Anarchy and Anti-Social Behaviour.

In the following section, I want to discuss the issue of crime and anti-social behaviour to see how they relate to anarchist demands for absolute freedom, and for an end to all forms of coercion and authority. Such demands have usually led anarchists to reject all forms of law enforcement, such as the police and prison services (Richardson 1987, 274; Wieck 2009, 227). This is perhaps not surprising; the legal system restricts an individual's liberty in a way that is both profound and explicit. Importantly, it presents its coercive authority as necessary and inevitable, and therefore justified; indeed, it even convinces many of those whose liberty it denies of its inherent justice. The rejection of this system then is certainly ethically consistent with the anarchist commitment to freedom, but how would it work in practice? Is this rejection of the law really viable, or is it a morally worthy but ultimately unworkable ideal? Colin Ward was acutely aware of the problem that the anarchist rejection of the law caused:

> Every anarchist propagandist would agree that the aspect of anarchist ideas of social organisation which people find hardest to swallow is the anarchist rejection of the law, the legal system and the agencies of law-enforcement. [...] [People] may ruefully agree with our criticism [of the law ... b]ut they remain sceptical about the idea of a society in which the protection offered by the law is absent (Ward 1973, 126).

Indeed, very often, *anarchy*, in common language, denotes chaos and disorder; and often *violent* chaos and disorder at that (Goodwin 2007, 127). Anarchists often dismiss this negative view of anarchism as the result of equally negative propaganda, as deliberate distortions of what anarchism really means. No doubt they have some justification in taking this view. But there is little doubt too that even without such propaganda, people may reasonably believe that some sort of authority is needed to keep (especially large, modern and plural) societies from disinte-grating into chaos. Importantly, this does not necessarily entail the view that people who see the state as necessary believe that 'man would tear his fellow-man to pieces like wild beasts' (Kropotkin 1985, 129). People may readily concede that the majority of people would not act in such ways. But what about the small minority who might seek to exploit a society without laws? Of course, the majority of people's day-to-day lives are not the result of explicit and direct police enforcement, but we must remember that the state's power operates in multiple ways. Kropotkin argues that we can witness people interacting 'without any intervention of the law', but is this true? As I argued in the previous chapter, the law may not always intervene directly, and explicitly, but can we really assume its background presence has no effect on the way we behave? We do not need to applaud this fact to give it the weight it rightly deserves. Yet Kropotkin's position, echoed by many anarchists, appears to be unjustly dismissive of people's genuine concerns, stereotyping them all as simplistic Hobbesians.

Within the state, then, people's lives are directly and indirectly ordered by the law. From the mundane to the fundamental, a legal system structures and limits the very fabric of society, and so has unavoidable consequences for individual freedom. Whereas anarchism argues that the law is for this very reason unjustifiable, the majority of people see these limitations as acceptable, as an unfortunate paradox, a necessary trade-off, without which we would witness an even greater loss of freedom. Anarchists must defend their claims that freedom will be enhanced without the tools usually believed to be the only ones capable of doing the job, and demonstrate which cultural processes would take the place of our current legal system. So how have anarchists argued for the possibility of (some acceptable level of) social cohesion, without the state, and related legal institutions? Anarchists have advanced arguments to combat claims that life without the state would be 'nasty, brutish and short' by arguing that, whatever view we may have of human nature, the majority of harm (committed *by individuals*)[16] is in fact the result of the way society is *organised*; the majority of crime, it is argued, exists, not *despite* the state, but *because* of it. Massive inequality, of economic wealth, and general life prospects, creates the conditions in which crime will flourish (Pilgrim 1993; Stamm 1995; Kropotkin 1970, 212-18). A more justly organised society would mean that individuals were materially satisfied, so that their need to steal or cheat would be greatly reduced; communities would also be bound with stronger feelings of solidarity, rather than the envy, isolation and anger which flourish in a competitive and unequal world. Whatever anarchists think about human *nature* then (an issue I return to in the following chapter), they place considerable emphasis on the *nurturing* of individuals, not only through childhood, but for one's entire life. Anarchism requires, as Colin Ward argues, a different sort of human *environment*, not a different sort of human *being* (Ward 2008, 154). Well-nourished individuals, morally and gastronomically, are far less likely to commit crimes than the many spiritually and nutritionally malnourished individuals that exist today.

However, anarchists also recognise that not everyone will be motivated by the same communal ideals. To this end, anarchists have usually recognised the need for some form of social control, usually understood as some form of censure or rebuke (Ritter 1980). For example, Alan Ritter suggests that behaviour is 'controlled by penalties, in the form of threatened or actual rebuke' (ibid., 12), yet at no point anywhere in the book does he discuss exactly what form this rebuke might take. Censure is clearly placed by Ritter at a moral distance from coercion, without any concrete suggestions as to what this difference actually means, morally, and in practice. We can only hazard a guess that censure is simply considered as being a relatively mild, verbal (i.e., non-physical) act: yet to the extent that censure is kept at an acceptable level, that is, as long as it remains essentially non-coercive or intrusive, it surely loses any credence as a reliable form of social control. Ritter argues that 'punishment, like authority, far from being at odds with anarchy, is one of its integral features' (Ritter 1980, 76), but if punishment is understood to exist solely as rebuke, which Ritter suggests, then anarchists surely have their work cut out. Kropotkin's examples of censorial taunts (Kropotkin 1980, 69) for example, 'Your mother does not know sewing, your father is blind in one eye' are, let us say, *unlikely* to convince either the criminal to abandon crime or the liberal to abandon the state. Ritter also fails to discuss the extent to which the moral disapproval of a society towards anti-social behaviour may also lead to an oppressive conformity, where alternative lifestyles are also prevented by a community. Once again, it is Colin Ward who most openly and honestly recognises the potential dangers in harnessing the power of communities to encourage appropriate behaviour, because there is often no clear agreement on what is and is not *appropriate*. As such, 'the censorious eyes of neighbours' (Ward 2008, 156) may be used to effectively prohibit not only acts of violence or theft, but could also be used to discourage certain sexual behaviours, for example. Ritter's view relies on a shared understanding of what constitutes good, or appropriate behaviour.

In the following chapter, we return to this question, and ask whether such agreement is possible, or, indeed, desirable. Leaving aside such difficulties for the moment, another problem faces anarchists: such censure is primarily understood as functioning on the level of deterrent, whereby the majority in a community are convinced either of the normative ideals of acting in, broadly speaking, social ways, or, if they are not, of the costs involved in acting in anti-social ways. However, anarchists recognise the potential for what we might call pathological crime; the case of the Mad Axe Man, as Stephen Cullen puts it (Cullen 1993). Serial killers, for example, do not kill for bread, nor are they likely to be prevented from killing by a censorial community that frowns on their homicidal proclivities. What would anarchists do about those people who kill, or rape, not for material gains, but because they are simply disturbed individuals? Anarchists reply with two key arguments: firstly, they argue that these individuals are, again, 'primarily the product of non-anarchist forms of organisation [...] where the civic culture manifests itself in the form of competition, social dislocation, authoritarianism, militarism and sexism' (Cullen 1993, 140). Just as people steal because of the social inequality perpetuated by the state, so they are, at times, more profoundly, emotionally and psychologically corrupted (if that is the right word) by the same system. An anarchist society would foster different values which would not create the sorts of isolated, angry individuals that turn into maniacal killers. Such arguments do not necessarily rely on an essentialist view of a benign human nature, hence my reservation to talk of *corruption*; they can just as easily refer to the possibilities of nurturing people in different ways, one more likely to *create* pathological murderers, the other less so.

The second argument is that these individuals exist today, and the state does little or nothing to protect us from them. As Cullen continues, 'we are just as at risk from them in the most closely policed state as we are in the anarchist utopia' (ibid.). Whilst the fear of prosecution may prevent the casual robber, people with psychological problems profound enough to turn them into murderers are unlikely to be so deterred. Furthermore, the psychologically disturbed nature of their crimes makes it hard for law enforcers to understand, and thus predict, their actions. Even within a state, people can, and do, quite literally get away with murder (and whether or not they 'get away with it', i.e., whether they are eventually punished, makes little difference to their victims). In other words, if anarchic methods of social organisation are likely to fail in such cases, so too are those of the state. Such crimes could well be reduced in a more libertarian society that did not foster violent tendencies, and which did not seek to control its populace by means of oppressive moral conditioning; and to the extent that some such crimes would continue, the anarchist need only point to the obvious fact that they continue now, despite the state and its institutions of law enforcement, and argue that things are unlikely to get any worse.

Can Mutual Aid Protect Us?

How well do these arguments fair? There is good reason to believe that mutual aid and a generally high level of sociability would indeed flourish without the state. As we saw in Chapter 1, solidarity and mutual support are evidenced in all manner of societies that do not have forms of institutionalised control. Even within the state, the majority of people act in ways that foster community cohesion, and it is at least theoretically plausible that, without the law enforcement capabilities the state currently holds, societies could still maintain some degree of social cohesion. This, of course, is the basic argument of mutual aid presented by Kropotkin. Similarly, there is a strong argument to be made that our current economic and political system is profoundly flawed and socially destructive and that there are better ways in which we might organise social life; we can concur, then, that capitalism, and the state, are responsible for a great deal of what we currently unsderstand as crime. However, crime is more than serial killers and people stealing money to feed themselves: people want to know how anarchists would deal with all manner of social problems; domestic violence, for example. And some anarchists concede that such problems are indeed worrying. As one activist notes in an unusual display of honesty and concern:

> One big thing I've always wondered is, what will we do with perpetrators? If we agree that the cops and courts are not our friends; if they do not work to keep us safe; if perpetrators are

not 'out there' but 'in here', what solutions do we magic out of our guts to create safety, justice and healing? (Chen n.d, 7)

It is heartening to see such questions at least being posed, but anarchist discussions that take the question seriously (and there are far too few of them) are either worryingly (but at least honestly) unable to offer any real solutions, or offer entirely unconvincing answers. Invoking the anarchist commitment to freedom, Cullen stresses the point that an anarchist society would be 'undermined by the presence [...] of anarchist prisons' and asks rhetorically: '[Are they] really an option?' (Cullen 1993, 142). As Cullen sees prisons as conflicting with anarchism's commitment to freedom, he concludes that they have no place in an anarchist society. However, he acknowledges that prisons do serve a purpose, and that anarchists would therefore need to find a suitable alternative. Unfortunately, Cullen is unsure what such an alternative might be, and concludes his piece by asking the readers if they have 'Any answers?'(ibid.). Similar discussions display a curiously contradictory acknowledgement of the issue, accepting the lack of any real solution, whilst simply assuming that there must however be one. Class War, for example, state in no uncertain terms that:

The question of what we're actually going to DO when the cops fuck off, has been almost completely ignored by street revolutionaries, but it's one of the most important problems we face. There is no way that people are going to be greatful [sic] to see the back of the filth if they think that muggers, rapists, smack-dealers, wife beaters, and other anti-social bastards are going to have a free hand (Class War, 1986).

So how will anarchists stop the anti-social bastards? The article goes on to conclude: 'There's got to be a better answer than calling the cops or letting it happen. And we need to find it [...]

We need the answers quickly, and we haven't begun to ask the right questions' (ibid.).

It is remarkable that the failure to find an answer, and the recognition that throughout the last hundred odd years of anarchism, such fundamental questions have barely been raised, do little to shake anarchists' faith in a libertarian society: 'there's got to be a better answer', even if we don't know what it is! However, other anarchists are unwilling to concede the problem is unresolved. For example, this position, taken from *The Anarchist Manifesto*: 'actions which are unpopular because they are destructive or selfish will cause the person who committed said actions to be exiled from the society of his or her peers'. A few lines later, the anonymous author goes on to claim that '[a]narchist society does not rely on 'enforcement' or punishment of bad acts' (anarchy.net). But if exile isn't enforcement, or punishment, what is it? Isn't sending people into exile a serious breach of their freedom? And where, exactly, are we to exile them to? To another anarchist community with more hard-hitting taunts: 'Your mother doesn't know sewing, *or* cooking, your father is blind in *both* eyes'? Or are we to hope that at least one state, replete with prisons, continues to exist? Such issues are passed over without comment, and so no answers are given. We are left with a simplistic vision of anarchism, where people are not to be punished but where they can nonetheless somehow be exiled; is it any wonder that people see anarchism as naïve and unrealistic when this is what they are presented with?I will return to assess these problems below; at this point, I want to turn to a more concrete attempt by anarchists to deal with the problem of anti-social behaviour; the concept of 'Tranquillity teams', developed and employed in anarchist spaces such as Climate Camps.

Temporary, and Tranquil, Autonomous Zones.

We find another attempt to respond to the problem of anti-social behaviour within the contemporary anarchist movement: the temporary autonomous zones (TAZs), which I discussed in the previous chapter, often include the role of 'tranquillity teams'. TAZs are far from lacking in organisational structures, but such structures operate according to principles of horizontal decision-making, and are therefore viewed as compatible with anarchist principles. Individuals in a TAZ take on rotating roles, media, transport, food, and so on, to facilitate the day-to-day running of the space. One such role is that of 'tranquillity'. The job of the tranquillity team, usually made up of four people, is to help mediate incidents of conflict, if and when they arise. Often donning deliberately garish, pink plastic cowboys hats in a symbolic display of their non-aggressive and anti-coercive approach, tranquillity teams wander around the camp, never spontaneously interfering but rather waiting to be approached, and for the most part doing very little. Occasionally, however, a confrontation occurs, and then the tranquillity group will do their best to deal with the situation. Generally, they do a remarkably good job; I have personally witnessed a number of tense situations where the anticipated moment of violence has been skilfully prevented from materialising. Other times, however, the aforementioned tool of *exile* has been brought into use. Although the term itself has not been used, at the majority of TAZs I have attended, at least one individual has been removed from the space, sent out, or 'back', for the permanently *un*autonomous zone to deal with. Although such problems ought to have provoked anarchists to ask more probing questions about their capacity to organise life without authority or coercion, they are in fact all too easily framed in ways that down-play their significance: such incidents are rare, and while communities in *temporary* autonomous zones may be culturally ill-equipped to deal with them when they do arise, many anarchists seem to simply assume that fully fledged anarchist societies would develop genuine alternatives in time. These arguments can be turned on their head however: it could be argued that such incidents are rare precisely because these spaces are short-lived; longer term communities would have to deal with problems that simply never arise in a TAZ. What seems clear is that this raises very real questions about the anarchist capacity to protect at all costs the freedom of the individual. If such spaces are intended to demonstrate the viability of anarchist organisation, as is so often claimed, then what can we infer from the need to effectively exile certain individuals? And the best we can do at this stage is indeed make inferences, because there have been no substantial discussions about this issue within the movement.

Another reason for tranquillity team's ability to remain predominantly placid is their extremely limited role: they are there to mediate between parties only when there is a very clear potential for violent behaviour. While this may include psychological as well as physical violence, it is limited to quite clearly defined acts of aggression. Working according to a relatively tight understanding of violence, these teams are generally able to avoid embroiling themselves in messy conflicts which divide the community. However, what constitutes violence, as activists are well aware, is open to considerable debate (Richards 1993). Shared understandings about what sort of behaviour is acceptable, between people involved in tranquillity work and the rest of the community, allow for a generally friction free experience. But what would happen if a community held multiple definitions about what was and was not acceptable behaviour? *Dealing* with violence, or anti-social behaviour is only half the problem; *defining* it is no less difficult, and is therefore a question we now need to explore.

What is Crime Anyway?

As I hinted at earlier, questions around crime, or anti-social behaviour, are not simply questions of *how* certain actions are to be prohibited, but also about *which* actions. On one level, crime can be dealt with by simply deciding that something is no longer a crime. Anarchists could easily resolve the problem of drug related *criminality*, for example, by 'legalising' drugs. Indeed, one way anarchists deal with the problem of crime is to emphasise the extent to which the concept of crime itself is defined by the state (Ward 2008, 153-162). However, this process can travel in both directions: what about those things which are currently legal, like children working fourteen hour days to make our clothes, or throwing those clothes into a giant hole in the ground as soon as we are bored with them, which anarchists might disagree with? The word *crime* has legal connotations which by definition exclude it from positive anarchist discussions; other terms, such as anti-social behaviour, are likely to be considered equally offensive by many: but surely anarchists do disapprove of certain acts and would hope to see their demise in an anarchist society? As we shall see in the following chapter, anarchists do in fact attempt to deny certain actions which they consider to be unacceptable. Fascists are prevented from holding street stalls by activists, for example. This raises the question of whether anarchists are genuinely opposed to coercion *as such*, or simply certain forms of it. When anarchists themselves are in a position to define what is *un*acceptable behaviour, will they be any less inclined to act in ways to deny the freedom of those wishing to engage in acts they disapprove of?

In the *Anarchist FAQ*, Iain McKay suggests 'an anarchist society is non-coercive, that is, one in which violence or the threat of violence will not be used to 'convince' individuals to do anything' (McKay 2007, 29), but then goes on to state categorically that:

Anarchists do not believe that everyone should be able to 'do whatever they like', because some actions obviously involve the denial of the liberty of others. For example, anarchists do not support the 'freedom' to rape, to exploit, or to coerce others. Neither do we tolerate authority (McKay 2007, 31).

What does it mean to say anarchists *do not support* rape? Does it mean they will prevent it from happening, or simply that they will disapprove of it when it does? If it is to be stopped, how? And what would anarchists do with someone who had been found to have already raped someone? And how is rape to be defined exactly? Is consenting sex between an adult and a fourteen year old considered rape, as the law in the UK currently states? And what would anarchists do with an individual *accused* of rape? And there are countless questions of a similar nature: what about pornography, prostitution, drug use, the ownership of weapons, vivisection; the list goes on. McKay suggests that 'some actions *obviously* involved the denial of liberty to others' (my emphasis) but, as we shall see in the following chapter, there is often nothing obvious about such matters; people may well reasonably disagree about what constitutes a denial of liberty.

The question of crime and anti-social behaviour, then, is a major stumbling block for anarchists; in fact, it could justly be argued to be the primary reason why anarchism has remained such a marginal philosophy. Colin Ward certainly thought so. While anarchists may have faith that their rejection of legal authority will not lead to increases in crime, most people remain wholly unconvinced. As Ward comments, '[m]aybe we are not worried [about this lack of faith...b]ut it is our fellow-citizens that we must convince if we are really concerned with gaining acceptance for the anarchist point of view' (Ward 2008, 126). Even an acknowledgement of the injustice of the capitalist system and the crime it no doubt causes is unlikely to lead most people to accept that abandoning the legal system is a reasonable thing to do. But it is not, as we have seen, simply the failure of anarchists to convince others of the arguments that has led to this situation; it is the failure of anarchists to provide arguments even for themselves. And when proposals *are* given, they throw into doubt a supposedly core principles of anarchism: the commitment to freedom. When Schmidt & van der Walt concede that '[a]n anarchist society must also include a measure of legitimate coercive power exercised against those who committed harmful acts against [...] the social order and the freedom of other individuals' (Schmidt & van der Walt 2009, 70) they do so with no acknowledgement of the fundamental questions this so clearly raises. Yet surely we could replace the word *anarchist* with *liberal* in the above sentence; so what does this tell us about the anarchist project? Is it simply the *state* that differentiates anarchism from liberalism? Is anarchism as comfortable with coercive acts as liberalism is, as long as they are performed by the community, and not the state? Is this then the definition of anarchist freedom? *Freedom from the state*, no more, no less?

Conclusions.

In this chapter I have only been able to offer a very small representation of anarchist thought in relation to the idea of freedom, but I believe that what I have provided is broadly reflective of the anarchist common sense. If I am correct, then freedom appears to be primarily understood as an abstract, moral demand; the *practical implications* of a society based on this demand, however, remain unclear. What *is* clear is that such a society would not be organised around a state: at its most basic, we might accept the definition of anarchism as being a rejection of the state, and anarchist freedom as being freedom *from* the state. Clearly, however, most anarchists would hope to support other values, such as equality, and also to challenge other forms of hierarchical structures. Two things follow directly from this. Firstly, we can perhaps conceptualise anarchism as being a regulated system that at times uses coercion, adopts political systems, and so on, but which does so without the state (Nursey-Bray 1996, 107-111). When the political philosopher Jonathan Wolff, for example, states that 'as the anarchist picture of society becomes increasingly realistic and less utopian, it also becomes increasingly difficult to tell it apart from a liberal, democratic, state' (Wolff 2006, 30), what he fails to even entertain is the prospect that there may be other forms of relatively peaceful, and egalitarian social systems besides the 'liberal, democratic state'. However, anarchists must accept some degree of responsibility for this: when pushed, at least some anarchists are apparently willing to concede that some degree of coercion may at times be acceptable. But what this means in practice is far from clear; more importantly, anarchism often *is* presented, by anarchists, as rejecting all forms of coercion, domination, authority, etc. So Wolff can perhaps be forgiven for assuming that anarchism loses its essence the moment it accepts certain restrictions of freedom. Whether anarchists are comfortable with this and are prepared to begin to discuss more honestly how such a society might function, or whether they maintain their unequivocal demands for absolute liberty and refuse to engage with problems of crime, equality, and so on, is something we will return to in subsequent chapters.

And so, secondly, we have begun to see cracks in the libertarian and prefigurative reality of anarchism (although, as I argue in Chapter 6, this need not be considered as a problem, as long as it is recognised). Coercion is acceptable when it is an 'act of legitimate self-defence' (Scmidt & van der Walt 2009, 203): but by what criteria can we judge what is legitimate, and what is not? Ehrlich et. al. claim that in an 'anarchist society, crime would be defined solely as an act harmful to the liberties of others' (Ehrlich et. al. 1996, 12), but if anarchism permits the use of coercion to defend freedom, or prevent harm, we need to ask what sort of freedom anarchists wish to see defended, and what constitutes *harm*. We have already seen briefly how problems relating to freedom can be solved by simply formulating freedom in a particular way. This narrowing of the definition of freedom occurs in all political philosophies, so it should be of no surprise that anarchists have attempted to follow this line of reasoning. The process of defining freedom in a particular way can often, when viewed from outside whichever discursive environment is responsible, appear disingenuous. We saw earlier how the likes of George Bush can define freedom in such a way as to justify a neo-liberal imperialist agenda. But it can also, when we share sufficient values with whoever is responsible for a new definition, appear perfectly reasonable. When anti-fascists disrupt BNP demonstrations, for example, it is easy to convince ourselves that there is no denial of freedom there. In fact, it may even appear grotesque to suggest that there is. Indeed, we saw above how McKay discussed people's 'freedom' to rape, his use of quotations marks suggesting that it would be misplaced to consider this a genuine freedom. And who could disagree? Malatesta makes a similarly uncritical point, also using quotation marks to highlight the supposed absurdity of referring to the freedom to perform certain acts:

> So freedom for everybody and in everything, with the only limit of the equal freedom of others; which does not mean (it is almost ridiculous to have to point this out) that we recognise, and wish to respect, the 'freedom' to exploit, to oppress, to command, which is oppression and certainly not freedom (Malatesta 1965, 53).

Rape may be a relatively easy act for anarchists to denounce without feeling they had breached their libertarian principles, but modern life is full of perplexing moral dilemmas where disagreement, even between anarchists, is extremely common, and where the line between what is legitimate and what is illegitimate, between what is self-defence and what is enforcement of one's principles, becomes far more muddy. Discussing the events in Paris in 1968, Murray Bookchin argued that:

> Having created authentic forms of freedom in which everyone could freely express his viewpoint, the assembly

would have been perfectly justified to have banned all bureau-cratically organised groups from its midst (Bookchin 1974, 254 my emphasis).

It seems to me that such a view either makes perfect sense, or no sense at all, depending, simply, on how we define freedom; for Bookchin there are authentic, and so presumably inauthentic, forms of freedom. But on what basis can we make such a distinction? The idea that freedom takes certain forms, that, for example, it might make no sense to talk of my freedom to shout racist slogans, or my freedom to strike, relies, explicitly or otherwise, on either a metaphysical or ethical understanding of what is either natural and unnatural, or right and wrong, or both. Although, as we shall see in the following chapter, Bookchin did indeed believe that ethics could be objectively grounded in nature, I will argue that anarchists generally do not, and at any rate should not, rely on any overly strong metaphysical ideas. Perhaps anarchists have a view of ethics which does not rely on such foundations, but which allows them to conceptualise freedom in a particular way? If so, any anarchist approach to freedom would rest on the more fundamental question of what an anarchist approach to ethics might be. In the following chapter, I argue that this is partly true, but that to the extent that it is, it too is an untenable position. More commonly, however, I will suggest that rather than having an ethics that informs a particular vision of freedom, anarchists have tended to adopt an ethics *of* freedom, whereby it is freedom itself that is understood to provide a guide to moral behaviour, and not the other way round.

Chapter 3

It's Good to be Free …
But are we Free to be Bad?
Ethics & More Limits of Freedom.

Imagine for a moment you find yourself in a room with two other people. One, a man, is punching and kicking the other, a young girl. In your hand is a stun-gun, which you can use to stop the man without causing any permanent damage. What would you do? What would an anarchist do? It's hard to imagine anyone, anarchist or otherwise, refusing to prevent this man's actions because they felt to do so would be an infringement of his freedom. In fact, for many people it's hard to see this as preventing his freedom at all. At least, not on a moral or political level. Yet surely, on a physical, and on some philosophical level, it is the case that we would be restricting his freedom, preventing him from doing something which he was seemingly intent on persisting with. There can be at least three reasons why we still don't see this as an infringement of freedom, or at least, why we don't feel overly concerned if it was. The first is to in fact accept, in an absolute sense, this was some sort of infringement, but to dismiss this as of no ethical concern because what he was doing justified our actions. Ultimately, we might concede on this line of reasoning that we infringed his freedom, that we coerced him, but we feel comfortable with this, comfortable to the point where, unless pushed to explore fully the theoretical intricacies of our actions, we simply don't register what we did as any sort of infringement. To think of this another way, we might feel that in this instance we restricted someone's freedom, but that, because we did so to defend the freedom of someone else, we are, in principle, still committed to the notion of defending freedom, per se. The second approach is to argue that we did not restrict this man's freedom, because it makes no sense to talk of someone's freedom to do certain things, such as to intentionally cause harm. On this reading, we can only be free to do things which are morally acceptable; we saw hints of this sort of reasoning numerous times in the last chapter. Finally, we might argue that in some way the man's actions were the result of an internal lack of freedom; he was acting against his own will, we might say, and our actions were in accordance with what he would really want. Similar arguments are commonly made when we, for example, restrict the freedom of someone who is mentally ill and a risk to themselves or others. This view entails some form of psychological and/or metaphysical view, about what is natural, or about what we really want contrasted with what we think we want.

This is all rather basic and obvious stuff. But it raises many interesting questions, questions which are by no means easy to answer. And we can complicate it further. Imagine we're now in a shop, a pharmacy, and we see the same man buying some sleeping tablets. These pills are legal, and many people take them for perfectly acceptable reasons. For whatever reason, however, we know that this man wants to use them to drug someone, to take them to a room to assault them. He isn't assaulting anyone in front of us. But we know for certain that that is his plan. So now what do we do now? Furthermore, we also know that these pills are being used by lots of other people for the same reasons, and that those who use them simply to get a good night's sleep could use another pill, which, because it tastes so bitter, is less popular. The existence of this pill means people can, and we suspect will, continue to drug vulnerable people, and if we could prevent the pill being available, we could prevent many such assaults. The company making the pills insists their product is in itself not responsible for such assaults, and refuse to take it off the shelves. And, they receive support from many people who use them as they were intended to be used. So, do we force the people making the pill to stop?

Or, imagine another scenario; Derrick is about to kill. He has a blade in his hands, and his victim is there in front of him. Bob steps in to stop him, and, as an anarchist, justifies this with reference to one of the two arguments made above. But Derrick is also an anarchist, and he denounces Bob as acting contrary to anarchist principles, as restricting his freedom, because he was about to kill a cow, and he believes that that would have been morally acceptable. Bob was defending the freedom of the cow, Derrick is defending his own freedom to kill the cow.

Our views of freedom, it seems clear, always rest on some view of what is morally acceptable, or what is somehow natural. Very few people fully defend any and all acts on the grounds that we must protect freedom above all. Certainly, very few anarchists make such an argument. Furthermore, there is a complex relationship between freedom and any specific context in which we consider it; time and space, the immediacy (or otherwise) of our actions and their consequences, come to bear on our thinking. As we saw with the example of the pill, we tend to feel differently about restricting different actions, even if and when their ultimate outcome is the same. In the following chapter, we will come to see that for many libertarians, be they anarchists or liberals, there is something of a blind-spot when it comes to the arguments made above. Often, the moral or metaphysical content of their views of freedom are hidden, not simply to others, but also to themselves. Their defence of liberty is therefore presented as being independent of any other concerns. But where does this leave us? At the very least, we are left wondering what ethical or metaphysical principles anarchists are committed to; we need to understand those principles, in order to understand the anarchist view of freedom (and, indeed, the anarchist view of anarchism); so before going on to explore this issue, let us first see what anarchists have said on the questions of metaphysics and ethics.

Anarchist Approaches to Ethics: Peter Kropotkin and Murray Bookchin.

Undoubtedly one of anarchism's most famous and influential writers, Kropotkin wrote on a wide variety of topics, including a number of lengthy works on ethics. In works such as *Anarchist Morality* (Kropotkin 1970), he went on to outline some basic principles of an anarchist ethics, as well as providing a basic genealogy of our existing moral order. Advancing the view that there is a biological basis for morality, which goes deeper than mere *human* nature, Kropotkin argued that in our quest to understand morality we 'will never explain it so long as [we] believe it a privilege of human nature, as long as [we] do not descend to animal, plants and rocks to understand it' (Kropotkin 1970, 81). Indeed, it is a 'very striking fact that animals living in societies are also able to distinguish between good and evil, just as man does' (ibid.) He continues to note that

> The idea of good and evil has thus nothing to do with religion or a mystic conscience. It is a natural need of animal races. And when founders of religions, philosophers, and moralists tell us of divine or metaphysical entities, they are only recasting what each ant, each sparrow practices in its little society. Is this useful to society? Then it is good. Is this hurtful? Then it is bad (ibid., 91).

All morality, then, stems from the potential to tap into an innate sense of solidarity and of sympathy (ibid., 94), and in his classic text *Mutual Aid* (Kropotkin 2008), Kropotkin argued that the result of this, namely, *co-operation*, was as important to evolution as competition. This did not challenge Darwin's basic premise, but rather emphasised one side of the evolutionary argument that had been over-looked, or even denied, by the more prominent Social Darwinists who were avidly, and successfully, spreading the message that it was only *competition* that explained our evolution.[17] Kropotkin detailed case after case of mutual aid, from ants and bees to 'savages and barbarians', and finally to examples of contemporary co-operation, to show that working together was *as* beneficial, and often more so, than competing. In demonstrating this, Kropotkin was able to justify an ethics of mutual care, *and* a politics of anarchy, because his argument implied that the Hobbesian justifications for external authority were unfounded. Hobbes' argument relied on a distorted view of human nature, which saw humanity as inherently selfish; in contrast, life without the state was in fact generally peaceful and conflict-free.

Not surprisingly, Kropotkin's view that questions of morality can be resolved by looking to humanity's natural essence, and that we can therefore conceive of an objective 'science of morality' (Kropotkin 1970, 113) has been criticised by postanarchists such as Saul Newman (Newman 2001, 173); below, I shall question the extent to which Kropotkin did see morality as being so objectively grounded. Either way, the important question here is whether Kropotkin's view on these matters seeped into the wider anarchist common sense. Whilst Kropotkin's idea of mutual aid is clearly a prominent one within anarchist thought, I believe it can be explored in ways which break from objective claims about human nature as such. I want to say more about both human nature and mutual aid below, but before doing so, it will be helpful to briefly examine the legacy of Murray Bookchin, to see whether the idea of an ethics grounded in nature has in fact continued to reverberate within the anarchist common sense.

Murray Bookchin was one of the most well-known, influential, and controversial of anarchist thinkers. Credited (by some, at least) with being one of the first thinkers to bring ecological issues and radical politics together,[18] he was both inspirational for and inspired by a generation of activists who came to see the fight to save the planet from environmental destruction as being fundamentally linked with the fight against capitalism and the state. To explain and analyse this relationship, Bookchin developed the concept of *social ecology*, a philosophy 'based on the conviction that nearly all of our present ecological problems originate in deep-seated social problems' (Bookchin 2007, 19). In other words, '[i]ts primary insight is that the ecological crisis is a social crisis of values, with hierarchy the main culprit' (Curran 2006, 157). To the contemporary mind, this is hardly revelatory, but as Giorel Curran notes, 'social ecology has contributed significantly to the greening of anarchism' (ibid.). What many anarchists now take for granted, in other words, is in no small part thanks to the work of Bookchin, although of course, Bookchin's own debt to Kropotkin is always evident (Albrecht 1994, 109-113). However, for Bookchin at least, social ecology was about much more than a recognition of the problems of hierarchy. In *The Philosophy of Social Ecology* (1995), Bookchin outlined in considerable philosophical detail his work of *dialectical naturalism*, which, he argued

> not only grasps reality as an existentially unfolding continuum, but [...] also forms an objective framework for making ethical judgements. The 'what-should-be' becomes an ethical criterion for judging the truth or validity of an objective 'what-is'. Thus ethics is not merely a matter of personal taste or values; it is factually anchored in the world itself as an objective standard of self-realisation (Bookchin 1995, 24).

Very clearly, then, Bookchin argued that ethics could be objectively grounded; questions of what is ethically right or wrong can be answered with reference to hard facts. Yet, for our purposes, the important question here is whether this view receives wider support within the anarchist community. Thomas S. Martin argues that the 'anarchist project has been shaped by Murray Bookchin for the past several decades, and rightly so; he is this generation's Kropotkin, Godwin and Proudhon all rolled into one' (Martin 1998, 39). While there may be some truth in this, it tells only half, or rather a third, of the story. Bookchin, who published work over the best part of five decades, is well known for his apparent ideological shift later in life (Davis 2010), but an equally large disconnect can be found between works such as *The Philosophy of Social Ecology* (1995) and essays such as *Listen, Marxist!* which was re-produced with other influential papers in the popular *Post-Scarcity Anarchism* (1971). There is not, then, simply an 'earlier' and 'later' Bookchin, but also a third, more philosophically inclined strand of his work. So when Giorel Curran states that *The Ecology of Freedom* constitutes 'his major work' (Curran 2006, 163) *and* that Bookchin's analysis 'continues to inspire many' (ibid., 179) we are given a somewhat misleading impression of his impact. Bookchin's influence, I would argue, is by far the strongest in the areas that he himself generally ignored in his own philosophical writing, and explicitly rejected in his own later work; his writings on the events of May '68, for example, and his attacks on the hierarchical politics of the left, reverberate more strongly than his attempts to articulate a comprehensive moral doctrine. As a moral philosopher, advocating the kind of ideas expressed in *The Ecology of Freedom*, it is questionable whether Bookchin ever made much of an impact, beyond a small but dedicated group of adherents, such as Chaz Bufe (1998) and Janet Biehl (1997). His profoundly rationalist and teleological views of nature are unlikely to be held in high esteem by many contemporary thinkers, and there is little evidence of these ideas being replicated and endorsed within the wider anarchist community; they are not, it seems reasonable to suggest, part of the anarchist common sense. And there remains the important question as to whether Bookchin should even be considered an anarchist. It is certainly interesting, and perhaps no coincidence, that Bookchin grew increasingly unhappy with anarchism, and, in his final years, came to argue that '[t]he libertarian opposition to law [...] has been as silly as the image of a snake swallowing its tail' (2007, 95-96). Did Bookchin's moral philosophy lead inevitably to a rejection of anarchist politics? Whatever the case, not only did he himself come to reject anarchism, but many anarchists have rejected, or more often, ignored, a great deal of his work. In short, I would suggest that when we ask what constitutes a broad anarchist approach to ethics, Bookchin's work does *not* provide the answer.

However, following Kropotkin, Bookchin believed that mutual aid was central to an anarchist ethics, and this *has* been taken up within the wider anarchist movement. We need, therefore, to look at this concept in its own right, to see whether it is capable of responding to the questions uncovered in the last chapter: can mutual aid explain what sort of freedom anarchism is intended to deliver? And does mutual aid depend on an essentialist, and benign, view of human nature? I turn now then to explore the question of human nature, before going on to explore the idea of mutual aid.

Human Nature and Mutual Aid.

I argued in the Introduction that the anarchist common sense does not rest on any especially strong or clearly articulated metaphysical assumptions. It is common, however, to encounter the claim that anarchists do rely on an overly positive conception of human nature. This is an especially prevalent view amongst non-anarchists (see, for example, Wolff 1996, 30; Goodwin 2007, 128) but it is also a view shared by a number of contemporary anarchist theorists, such as Saul Newman (2001; 2010) and Todd May (1994). However, as David Morland argues in *Demanding the Impossible?* (1997) this view offers, at best, only a partial account. In fact, anarchists have often been keen to emphasise the negative side of human nature (Hartley 1995); indeed, this is one reason why anarchists believe that authority ought never to be vested in a small group of people, because they are almost certain to abuse their position. Whilst I agree that anarchists do not generally hold a benign view of human nature, it seems clear that they *do* often use a more contextualised understanding of human nature to defend their claims. Without claiming that there is an inherent, unchanging dimension of humanity that we may call its essential nature, anarchists argue that historically, humans have been social animals, and that, as such, we have as a species adopted numerous cultural tools to deal with our shared existence. The idea of mutual aid, then, rests primarily on this understanding of humans as predominantly social animals, for whom, in living socially, it often makes sense to work, not in competition, but co-operatively, to achieve a greater amount of food, security, happiness, love, and whatever else any individual might want; and that they are perfectly capable of doing this without some guiding authority. What mattered to a thinker like Kropotkin, and what is of concern to most anarchists, is whether we can see, in human life, the possibility for sustained co-operation: and the answer is, we do indeed see it. Whatever me might believe about our innate *human nature*, or lack of, our social construction is one which forcibly lends itself, historically and to the present day, through our shared narratives, practices and norms, towards living communally, and doing so in a way that reduces conflict and promotes high levels of sociability. This might then be best understood as human *culture*, rather than human *nature* (although Morland contends that we can still call this nature; Morland 1997, 26-7), but it nonetheless continues to play a fundamental role in shaping our lives, even if, in certain times and places, it is, or has the potential to be, removed or distorted by other, stronger cultural processes. We must be wary of reading too much into this, but it seems to me simply wrong to ignore or dismiss it entirely; indeed, the postanarchist Todd May would appear to accept this when he argues that unless we make some assumptions about humanity's capacity to organise itself without the state, we 'cannot even begin to critique the hierarchies and dominations of a given social order' (May 2007, 27). To this extent, mutual aid, understood as a shared cultural inheritance that is deep-seated and often extremely resistant to threats against it, is a useful way of thinking about the world, as long as all the appropriate provisos are well understood.

However, I would suggest that there remains a serious problem with mutual aid, in the idea of a *common good* which we mutually work towards. Kropotkin argued that, once people were freed 'from existing fetters' (Kropotkin 1970, 102) the tendency towards mutual aid would be more pronounced. If we understand existing fetters as the multiple hierarchies of capitalism, the state, patriarchy, and so on, then I am inclined to agree. However, Kropotkin goes on to suggest that people 'will behave and act always in a direction useful to society' (ibid.). But how do we define what is *useful* for society? This, surely, is an ethical question, and one about which there is reasonable disagreement (Gowans 2000). Bookchin attempted to answer it by looking to nature, as did Kropotkin; but nature cannot answer such questions, and I would argue, once again, that most anarchists do not believe it can. Indeed, Kropotkin appears to recognise the point himself, when he states that the behaviour of what he calls '[...] primitive folk' is 'regulated by an infinite series of unwritten rules of propriety which are the fruit of their common experience as to what is good or bad; that is, beneficial or harmful for their own tribe' (Kropotkin 2008, 74). It is not clear to what extent Kropotkin believed there to be an objective and universal foundation for 'the good'; at times, he appears to acknowledge that what is useful for a community is indeed subjective and contextualised. Yet his writing belies a faith that communities would *tend* towards agreement, at least to the extent that major conflicts would be rare. Whatever Kropotkin may have believed, this is no longer an assumption we can afford to make, and anarchists must now advance with the assumption that *moral disagreement* is always possible between and within human communities. Doing so, we can dispense perhaps entirely with the idea of a benign or malevolent human nature; indeed, we may even note that the desire to work collectively with those other members of our community may make people do things which they would, ethically speaking, otherwise prefer not to. The sticking point for anarchists, then, is not whether humans *are* good, but what humans *believe to be* good, and whether there will be sufficient agreement on this question to allow for a reasonable degree of community cohesion. Furthermore, if we think back to the previous chapter, it is also necessary to ask whether the price to be paid for this *community cohesion* is too high in terms of *personal freedom*; as oppressive as the state is, perhaps a community strong enough to do without institutionalised law enforcement would be more oppressive still. So while mutual aid can be understood as an important element of an anarchist ethics, there must be something beyond it which defines the good society for the anarchist. Mutual aid, in other words, can only ever be one part of an anarchist ethics. And, as we shall now see, the same is true for the equally popular idea of prefiguration.

Prefiguration: Which Means, to What Ends?

Prefiguration refers to two related concepts within anarchist thought; one understanding relates to the idea of anarchy in action, which I discussed in Chapter 1. The other refers to an ethical insistence on the compatibility between means and ends; in other words, it opposes the idea that the means may at times justify the ends. The idea stretches back to the earliest anarchist thinkers: perhaps most famously, Bakunin argued that we cannot expect a libertarian society to come into being using authoritarian means. And, regardless of any other changes anarchism may have been through, the idea has continued to inform anarchist theory and practice ever since (Ehrlich et. al. 1979, 3; Franks 2006). I will discuss prefiguration in Chapter 6 at greater length, but I want here to say a few words on the idea that prefiguration constitutes an anarchist approach to ethics. Although the refusal to subordinate means to ends does indeed suggest a particular ethical stance, and one which directly informs the way anarchists act, it does so in a way that is, in an important (and potentially problematic) sense, extremely open-ended. As Nathan Jun notes:

> The prefigurative principle provides a general procedure for action that does not rely upon transcendent moral concepts [...]. Within the broad ethical boundaries established by prefiguration and the general anarchist commitment to freedom and equality, there is enormous room for diversity of opinion (Jun 2010, 60).

In other words, in and of itself, prefiguration says nothing about *which* means or ends are to be desired, beyond the 'general anarchist commitment to freedom and equality'. But if my arguments in the previous chapter are correct, it is precisely this commitment to freedom and equality which is in need of some prior conception of ethics. As Benjamin Franks argues, prefiguration can be just as coherently adopted by right-wing ideologies, which would of course be opposed to many of the ethical principles espoused by anarchism (Franks 2006). So prefiguration, whilst a worthwhile principle in other respects, will not help us address the concerns I have already raised about how freedom might be understood within anarchist thought. What else, then, have anarchists said about ethics?

Anarchist Approaches to Ethics, Continued.

In his essay *Sexuality/identity/politics*, Jamie Heckert writes that '[o]ne of anarchism's strengths is an emphasis on ethics' (Heckert 2004, 133). This is not an unusual claim. For Benjamin Franks, whereas orthodox Marxism 'prioritises economic discourse [...] anarchism by contrast has foregrounded moral analyses' (Franks

2008, 135) And '[e]thics', according to Janet Biehl, 'lies at the very heart of a truly libertarian movement' (Biehl, n.d.). But which ethics? And where is this emphasis, exactly? In fact, if we look through anarchist texts, from academic publications to activist pamphlets, explicit ethical discussions are something of a rarity. Rather than following a humanist approach to ethics, I would argue that anarchism has tended to have a somewhat ambivalent relationship with it. Like liberalism, a philosophy with which anarchism shares a lot more than many anarchists would assume (or care to admit), anarchism is faced with an inherent difficulty whenever the issue of ethics is raised. With ethics come rules, certain understandings of what is good and bad, and all the possible consequences of normative restrictions that this implies. All this creates a logical difficulty for anyone defending a liber-tarian philosophy, as anarchism undoubtedly is. And especially with the term *morality* (which I understand as synonymous with ethics[19]) we also see a great deal of cultural baggage. *Morality* brings to mind Victorian prudes, more concerned with mastur-bation than mass poverty; it represents unjustified interference by an unjustifiable authority, be it God, the State, the Patriarch, the Priest. Understood as such, it appears to be the very opposite of anarchism. Yet any attempt to condemn such interference, or conversely, to argue in favour of some form of freedom, seems to necessarily entail some type of moral claim (Midgeley 1991). In other words, the very reasons given for rejecting morality are ultimately moral reasons, and this of course holds true for the rejection of those other institutions and ideas that anarchists have always fought against; capitalism, the state, hierarchies, and so on. None of these can be convincingly or coherently critiqued without some recourse to value judgements. When Emma Goldman talks about the 'monster of Morality' then, (Goldman 1972, 127) and suggests that it is 'morality which condemns women to the position of a celibate, a prostitute, or a reckless, incessant breeder of hapless children' (ibid., 129) she is herself expressing her own moral outrage at what she considers to be injustices. What Goldman is attacking is clearly not *morality*, as such, but a *certain form of* morality, a particular set of values, and the methods of their application. This is a common mistake, if we can call it that; perhaps it is fairer to call it a libertarian paradox: the (moral) demand for liberty rejects moral interference but is itself a deeply moral position (Franks 2008, 142). But what lies behind this basic ethical demand? What are its foundations, its limits, its contradictions? What does such a demand for absolute liberty really mean? Is it to be truly limitless? Or limited to the extent that the liberty of one does not interfere with the liberty of another? Or limited by some principle of harm?

Once we start asking such questions (and discovering that, invariably, every answer leads to yet more questions), are we not in danger of finding ourselves on a slippery slope, sliding towards the creation of simply one more morality that tells us what we can and cannot do? Remember how, in the last chapter, we saw anarchists prepared to defend coercion as long as it was used against unethical behaviour, such as economic exploitation. This remains a troubling issue for all libertarians, and I would argue that it is precisely this disturbing difficulty that has so frequently and forcefully encouraged anarchists to push the question of ethics under the carpet, as I shall explore in greater detail in the following sections.

Escape from Ethics.

The anonymous author of an Anarchist Manifesto (Anonymous, anarchy.net) writes in no uncertain terms that 'anarchist morality is simple: do what you will'. Indeed, for some anarchists, morality suggests only and precisely the expression of one's own will; it serves only to ensure an unencumbered realisation of one's desires. Interference is immoral, and everything else is moral (Carter 1993, 143). Yet the notion that anarchist morality is simply that we can do what we will is understood by most anarchists as being simply wrong (Carter, ibid.; see also Marshall 1993, 36-42). More commonly, we find the view that we must temper our actions ourselves. We must accept responsibility alongside freedom (McKay 2007, 26-29; Malatesta 1965, 48). This equilibrium, it is true, was thought by some earlier theorists to be possible at least in part because of a natural harmony to be found within humanity, as long as it was not corrupted by the state: as we saw earlier, Kropotkin and Bookchin often implied that nature would provide the moral laws by which social order would be achieved. Because they were grounded in nature itself, abiding by such laws would not be a restriction of freedom, but rather its fullest expression. However, once again, I would challenge the view that this concept of moral law is (necessarily) as embedded in a humanist ontology as it may appear; rather, I would argue that what is meant by a natural order is a more sociological idea that if members of a society simply leave each other alone to get on with their daily lives, communities will find some sort of balance, and life will be perfectly tolerable. In some ways, this could be understood to be an anti-essentialist position; humans are not inherently in need of an over-arching authority. It is interference, by the state, or the church, that causes so much harm, that is particularly problematic, and therefore immoral. Rather than seeing ethics as explicitly guided by natural teleology, or as a project of rational investigation, then, I would argue that anarchists have simply tended to shy away from ethical enquiry. Indeed, rather than being premised on (any particular sort of) ethics, the anarchist conception of freedom is more coherently understood as *an escape from ethics*. As we shall see shortly, this view is philosophically problematic, and, as I suggested earlier, it is not the whole story, but I would argue that this is a key element of the anarchist common sense, and one which we will do well to explore in greater depth.

We are still left wondering, then, what other ethical substance there may be to the anarchist project. I have suggested that anarchists have often been reluctant to answer such a question.[20] Anarchists are not alone in their reluctance to engage with ethics, however. In fact, I would argue that the fear of ethics has marked much of the political landscape of the second half of the twentieth century. The idea of the *moral atrocity* is intended to signify its *im*moral nature; yet there is also the sense that very often, such atrocities are seen as, and condemned as, the product of morality itself (Tester 1997). Like religious crusades in previous centuries, secular morality has been accused of committing many great crimes in the last hundred years. After the horrors of not only Auschwitz, but, perhaps more importantly, the Stalinist gulags, we have come to see how the desire to shape the world according to certain ethical ideals can lead to tremendous harm. This is not surprising in relation to fascism, but even capitalists, and anarchists, would concede that implementing the communist ideology was never *intended* to result in the murder of millions.[21] If fascism provokes people to ask: how could people have let this happen?, communism has made people (and those on the left in particular) ask: How can we be sure we will not make the same mistakes again? Perhaps more than ever before, we are aware that the road to hell is paved with good intentions.[22]

Interestingly, we see here something of a convergence of anarchist, liberal, and poststructural thought. While anarchism appears to deny the right to ever coerce others, liberalism asks that we be tolerant of others' ethical beliefs, and poststructuralism has filled us with epistemic doubt and moral uncertainty.[23] All three promote a considerable reluctance to act on our moral beliefs, for fear that we may discover our own acts to be simply another form of oppression. Indeed, the more tolerant we become, the more we recognise the relative nature of our own understandings of the world, the more we learn to see great moral 'crimes' as being the result of at least noble intentions. As Kate Soper puts it, we are invited to 'view history as littered with

the victims of such well intentioned visions and utopian projects'
(Soper 1993, 20). We must, then, resist the temptation to compel
others to follow our moral code, or to use our morality to justify
our actions. As Joseph Margolis puts it, we must 'Beware of men
of principle' (Margolis 2004, 16)

Again, we can see this situation as a highly paradoxical one:
the desire to prevent, or to not be complicit in, moral atrocities
leads us to reject morality; but we can only conceive of a moral
atrocity by virtue of our own morality. This condemnation hangs
awkwardly around us, and while it remains emotionally
powerful, it can paralyse us politically; as bad as things are, we
are struck by the fear that if we interfere, we may make things
worse. With the collapse of moral certainty previously offered by
religion (or science), the weight of moral responsibility has fallen
fully onto the shoulders of ordinary men and women. As
Zygmunt Bauman puts it:

> Choices between good and evil are still to be made, this time,
> however, in full daylight, and with full knowledge that a
> choice has been made. [...] With choice comes responsibility.
> And if choice is inevitable, responsibility is unavoidable. No
> secure hiding place is left (Bauman 1995, 7).

However, whilst I agree with Bauman's basic premise, I believe
he is wrong to think that there is no place left to hide. In fact,
contemporary society has found a perfect hiding place within
liberalism itself. And, as that hiding place can be found specifically within its libertarian ethos which promotes individual
freedom, it is perhaps not so surprising to discover that
anarchism has similarly taken shelter there. For reasons I will
explain shortly, a closer look at liberalism and its attempt to
'hide' from moral choices will be beneficial, and revealing, for
anarchists. I turn now then to explore the relationship between
anarchism and liberalism.

Liberalism and Anarchism.

It is worth beginning this discussion by highlighting the fact that although liberalism is the dominant political ideology of our times, anarchists have given it all too little attention. For anarchists in the pub, to call some one a liberal is to mean little more than that they are perhaps well-meaning, but ultimately naive supporters of the state (see Graeber 2009, 355 for just one example of this). Some anarchist academics may have a more thorough knowledge of what liberals really believe, but if they do, they have little to say about it in their work. Engaged discussions by anarchists about liberalism are rare, and when liberalism is mentioned, it is usually presented as a homogeneous tradition that has little more to it than a support for individual freedom that is highly compromised by its equally strong support for the state. When we stop and reflect on this, it ought to be seen as more than a little surprising, for two reasons. Firstly, liberalism is the dominant ideology of our times, and so it would seem of almost obvious importance to anyone interested in politics: after all, it surely makes sense to understand the workings of a philosophy that has a near hegemonic status around much of the globe and which, therefore, will be necessary to challenge if anarchism is to ever grow beyond its currently limited existence. The second reason is that liberalism is, despite some undoubtedly profound differences, in many important ways very similar to anarchism,[24] as we shall soon see. While what this means, and what we can learn from it, is, as I have suggested already, given far too little attention, the resemblance itself is at least acknowledged by some. Saul Newman, for example, states that '[a]narchism might be seen as the wild underside of liberalism' (Newman 2010, 2) and in a similar vein, Giorel Curran suggests 'anarchism champions the individualism and autonomy that liberalism also promotes, albeit rendered differently' (Curran 2006, 21). On rare occasions, this affinity is even recognised by activists; Barbara Esptein notes that one activist she

talked to referred to the anarchist elements of the alter-globalisation movement as "liberalism on steroids', that is, they are in
favour of liberal values, human rights, free speech, diversity, and
militantly so' (Epstein 2001, n.p.). This similarity is of considerable importance to anarchists. Although anarchism has been
argued to have existed outside of theory, that is, to have been put
into practice, clearly liberalism has been exposed to the vast
array of cultural, political, moral and environmental realities of
modern life in a way anarchism never has. Despite the obvious
differences between the two ideologies, I believe we can learn a
great deal from the experience of liberalism's prolonged and
wide-spread realisation, and can ask many useful and interesting
questions about the problems it has faced: importantly, we can
ask whether anarchism might not find itself addressing similar
challenges, were it to be realised on a wider scale. Furthermore,
because of liberalism's dominance, it has attracted a great deal of
critical but reflective attention (unlike anarchism, which is
generally either ignored or simplistically dismissed by those not
already convinced of its merits). I hope to show that what many
critics of liberalism have had to say is also remarkably relevant
for anarchists.

Like anarchism, liberalism strongly supports the ideal of
individual freedom; while this is, for anarchists, entirely negated
by liberals' support for the state, liberals themselves are also well
aware of the tension this creates, and so they too are concerned
about state interference with the freedom of the individual (see,
for instance, Bobbio 2005). Rather than simply dismiss this as
disingenuous hypocrisy, contradiction, or naiveté, as I would
argue many anarchists are prone to doing, I would suggest that
we ought to see this position as being genuinely held and worthy
of our consideration.[25] While fully recognising this tension,
liberals consider the state necessary to maintain a reasonable level
of social order, and also to secure its citizens from external threat.
Individual freedom, while undeniably *threatened* by the state, is

also *enhanced* by the protection the very same state offers; liberals would argue, therefore, that, given the reality of social life *without* the state, freedom of the individual is in fact protected better by liberalism than anarchism (Williams 2000). They do not embrace the state for its own sake, but rather as a problematic necessity; indeed, for some it is a spoken of explicitly as a *necessary evil*. Liberals therefore insist that the limits of state power be restricted to the maintenance of a basic social order, and no more. The state, then, is not intended to interfere with our personal lives, or our personal values. In fact, if the (theoretical) liberal state embodies one fundamental value itself, it is tolerance for other values.

Underlying this position of tolerance and individual freedom is a critique of the possibility of a universal/objective ethics. The notion that values may clash becomes less problematic if we can decide between them in an objective manner, as Bookchin believed was possible. Liberalism, however, is based on the view that we must tolerate different conceptions of the good life; that, in other words, we cannot rely on claims to universally accepted moral truths, although, as we shall see, this position is undermined by a belief in a minimal ethics that underpins all other, broader ethical views. While some anarchists appear to defend a view that there is an objective morality, I have argued that this view is not commonly held, and, furthermore, that it should not be held. But if there is no objective basis for deciding between ethical positions, how can we organise social life so that it does not descend into one huge conflict, or so that one ethical view does not destroy or at least repress all the others? The outcome appears to be either chaos or totalitarianism. It would appear there really is no place to hide; communities, or states, must make ethical decisions, and those decisions will have wide-reaching, and possibly unintentionally illiberal, consequences. Liberals, however, believe that there is somewhere to escape this dilemma, in the idea of the ethically neutral, liberal state, to which we now turn.

Neutrality Explained & Critiqued.

The liberal state, as we have seen, attempts to organise *communal* life without interfering with each individual's *private* life. How? To ensure this non-interference, certain liberals have developed the concept of *neutrality*: the state must be neutral between competing conceptions of the good life. It must not favour one morality over another (Klosko, 2000; see also Kymlicka 2002; Rawls 2001). Neutrality does not entail an absolutely value-free position, but any values which are followed are supposed to be reasonable and agreeable to all by all members of a community, creating, as I noted above, a sort of minimal ethics. To maximise the chances of this working, the state should only intervene when absolutely necessary. Disagreements within the private sphere are both inevitable and acceptable, but, because they are kept at the level of the private/individual, and do not seep into institutional decisions about public life, they ought not cause any significant problems. Problems would only arise to the extent that the state tried to interfere with individuals' moral lives. John Rawls, for example, saw that any attempt to bring about a comprehensive moral unity within a given society would lead to unacceptable levels of state interference (Rawls 2001, 425). But, following the argument of neutrality, he also argued that the state was capable of acting as a sort of impartial security guard, which would step in to defend a set of 'basic rights and liberties' (ibid., 442) when they were threatened. For this to happen, Rawls argued, a society would need to achieve what he called an 'overlapping consensus' (ibid., 421-448 and 473-496), so that it could then provide a 'political conception of justice that can articulate and order in a principled way the political ideals and values of a democratic regime' (ibid., 421). This consensus must be 'endorsed by each of the main religious, philosophical and moral doctrines likely to endure in that society from one generation to the next' (ibid., 473). As we shall see below, and in Chapter 5, many contemporary anarchists have also argued that it is only by reaching consensus that a community can avoid resorting to some form of coercion.

In recent years, however, a growing number of critics (some liberals amongst them) have argued convincingly that the idea of neutrality is fundamentally flawed (Young 1990, 96-122; Kymlicka 1995, 108; Mouffe 1993, 141-144, Cooper 2004, 36). Importantly, this critique has arisen not because they consider the idea of neutrality morally questionable *as such*, but because they consider it an impossible ideal to realise. These critics argue that neutrality is simply not practicable, and they suggest that we need to look more closely at the inevitable problem of *value conflicts* (Young 2001; Carens, 2000). The liberal state is justified by its capacity to maintain a reasonable level of social order, but, in order to do so, it must define certain acts as social, and others as anti-social: defining which acts are social and which are not, however, can never be a value free matter. Critics such as Young argue therefore that the concept of the neutral state is ultimately impossible, because its actions are always guided by certain values and can never be truly neutral. Furthermore, the state cannot help but regulate our private as well as our public lives. In controlling a society's basic infrastructure, its cultural and educational resources, its energy and food production, its health and transport services, and so on, the state is placed unavoidably in a position of having to choose between different courses of action in relation to its administration: but because our values are not merely a private affair, and are in fact often linked in complex and multiple ways to the wider world, physically and discursively, the choices the state makes often have a direct impact, however unintentional, on our moral lives. What this means, ultimately, is that it is not simply narrowly defined anti-social acts, such as murder, that are prohibited and/or regulated by the state, but a whole range of acts and even beliefs that are more or less suppressed by its dominant values.

For liberals, then, the state is justified by its capacity to maintain a reasonable level of social order; but, in order to do so, it must first *define* what that order will consist of. Rawls argued that the state could look to a set of basic liberties in order to decide where it had a right to intervene; that is, it could only properly step in to protect basic liberties, and no more. The problem with this approach is that the notion of basic liberties is an extremely contentious one; is it really the case that a community of people holding diverse moral values will be able to agree on what these basic liberties are? Rawls appears to think so. But freedoms, and all sorts of other values, often *conflict* with one another. We cannot refer to some objective notion of freedom, or some list of basic liberties, in order to decide between conflicting interests, because it is often precisely differing conceptions of freedom that are conflicting. As John Gray notes:

> [Rawls] claims that giving priority to liberty does not require making choices among rival freedoms or making contro-versial judgements about the worth of these freedoms. [...Yet] claims about the greatest liberty cannot be value free. [...] Rawls writes as if any reasonable person can know what the greatest liberty is. The truth is that it is indeterminate to the last degree (Gray 2000, 70).

Rawls' ideal of freedom, a freedom that can contain diverse voices without significant conflict, is not value neutral; what Rawls considers as basic liberties may be considered trivial, or even oppressive, by people of a different moral, political or cultural background. However well intentioned, a list of basic liberties can never be anything other than a list of one's own values; it cannot but reflect what we consider to be morally acceptable and important. This myth of the value neutrality of freedom allows what is in fact a strong conception of the good life to be presented as a set of basic liberties, as a thin, liberal, minimal ethic, a safe space that does no more than protect the diversity of values within it. When this problem is explored in relation to liberal thought, the emphasis is very often on what actions *the state* should or should not take. However, it is hopefully clear that this is the case only because the state is the mechanism by which liberals hope to *resolve* conflict; many, though not all, of the *conflicts themselves* exist independent of the state. So what might this tell us about anarchism, and its own claims to defend freedom? In the following section, I want to argue that anarchism suffers from the same basic problem as liberalism; in particular, I suggest the anarchist support for diversity echoes the liberal rhetoric about neutrality.

Value Conflict, without the State.

I have so far suggested that rather than arguing for a particular set of values, anarchists have been reluctant to articulate a clear ethical code; liberals, I suggested, have followed a similar process, and have argued that the state should organise life according to no more than a minimal, neutral conception of freedom. This, however, has been shown to be problematic, because the organisation of daily life can never in fact be value free, and when competing understandings of which freedoms are important, or of what constitutes the good life, come into conflict, one view will often be subordinated to another. What does this mean, then, for the anarchist understanding of freedom? Does the state create and cause such problems, or will such conflicts be a potential problem for a society without the state?

In fact, although currently the state often *is* the cause of many such conflicts, they can and do also exist independent of it, and when such conflicts arise they do not need the state to come down in favour of one side of the dispute:[26] without state interference, the conflict may simply continue (with whatever repercussions that entails), be resolved in favour of one side or the other, or be eventually settled amicably. Very often, in contemporary societies, the result is a mixture between the first two options; one side becomes and remains dominant, and is generally unthreatened and untroubled by its opposition, whilst the other side remains in a condition of (more or less tolerable) oppression. Iris Marion Young has argued that a profound and systematic denial of freedom, what she calls *structural oppression*, can take place when such conflicts of values and freedoms occur. Importantly for my arguments about anarchism, she notes that 'disadvantage and injustice' arise in such situations, 'not because a tyrannical power coerces [people] but because of the everyday practices of a well-intentioned liberal society'. The oppression that results, then, is 'structural, rather than the result of a few people's choices and policies. Its causes are embedded in unquestioned norms, habits and symbols [... I]n short, the normal processes of everyday life' (Young 1990, 41). In other words, any form of social organisation has the potential to create such a system of structural oppression, which equally has the potential to limit people's freedom in important ways. Bhikhu Parekh makes the point well:

Every culture is also a system of regulation. It approves or disapproves of certain forms of behaviour and ways of life, prescribes rules and norms governing human relations and activities, and enforces these by means of reward and punishment. While it facilitates choices as Raz and Kymlicka argue, it also disciplines them as Foucault argues. It both opens up and closes options, both stabilizes and circum-scribes the moral and social world, creates the conditions of choice but also demands conformity. [...] While valuing the indispensable place of culture in human life, we should also be mindful of its regulative and coercive role and the way it institutionalises, exercises and distributes power. Its system of meaning and norms are not and cannot be neutral between conflicting interests and aspirations (Parekh 2000, 156-157).

What ought to be of real concern to anarchists here is the argument that cultures (which is also to say political positions, even anti-political ones, and systems of morality, even libertarian ones) are argued to be *incapable* of neutrality. As John Gray demonstrates, freedoms conflict and must be decided between, explicitly or implicitly, and, as Young and Parekh argue, certain norms become dominant and thus seriously limit the freedoms of people wishing to live in different ways (see Trujillo 2010 for a discussion of this that is particularly pertinent for many anarchists, focusing as it does on attempts to live sustainable lifestyles). So freedoms, and perhaps we should also say the beliefs and actions that are made possible by those freedoms, conflict, and when they do, one will very often have to submit to the other. To be neutral in these situations is simply to give no assistance to either claim, which will generally mean, to let the stronger side win. By *stronger* I do not only mean physically stronger. There are countless other ways one side of a debate will be in a position to over-rule the others' wishes. One of those ways, of particular importance for liberals *and* anarchists, is by virtue of being able to claim 'neutrality' for their position, whilst accusing the other side of being authoritarian; for example, it is reasonably common to hear anarchists denouncing vegans as fascists, because, in protecting the freedom of animals, they are restricting the freedom of humans to eat those animals. However, clearly both sides are simply presenting different views of freedom, and there is no genuinely neutral position. When these conflicts occur, being neutral does *not* (always) give equal space for both parties to co-exist; it can simply allow space for one to suppress or deny or beat or disperse the other without any third-party interference.

Liberals argue that what Rawls called the 'fact of pluralism' meant that only a liberal politics could protect us from the 'oppressive use of state power'; as we shall see, anarchists also argue that diversity is inevitable (and should be positively embraced) but that it is anarchism which offers people the autonomy needed for this diversity to flourish. We have seen, however, that the liberal idea of neutrality does not defend this plurality as effectively as liberals had hoped; rather, it allows a state, and also, importantly, a culture, to present its own interpretations of liberty as being value-free, thus creating the possibility for it to deny certain other liberties and values whilst declaring itself to be neutral, or to be defending diversity, or freedom. The question now becomes: what evidence is there that anarchist conceptions of freedom and diversity are immune to a similar challenge, especially when we remember the critiques of Young and Parekh, who argue that it is not simply state regulation, but also cultures, habits, norms, and everyday practices that are capable of 'deciding' between conflicting freedoms and values? Young refers to the structural oppression caused, not by a tyrannical regime, but by a 'well-intentioned liberal society'; how much better will a well-intentioned anarchist society fare?

Anarchist Freedom: The story so far.

Ultimately, what all this points to is a denial of there being an unproblematic *common good*. Thinking back to our discussion of human nature and mutual aid, the idea of a benign human nature is problematic, not simply because it relies on an essentialist understanding of the world, but because, even if we think of it as human culture, rather than nature, it relies on the claim that there is, or can be, universal agreement on what it means to be benign; a claim which is, I have argued, untenable. Kropotkin's view that 'people will behave and act always in a direction useful to society' is not, I would argue, problematic because of its suggestion of a positive human nature, but because of the failure to recognise that what is considered *useful* for society is open to dispute. More to the point, what is considered unuseful, or anti-social, is often the source of considerable conflict. This is not to say there can be no arguments made for one good over another; it is not an argument for absolute relativism, and I believe anarchists must begin to engage more with the ethical reflections of theorists such as Todd May and Benjamin Franks (see also, for example, Williams 1993; Mackie 1997; Midgley 1991, for some useful discussions about the possibility of establishing an ethics that is neither entirely subjective, *nor* objective, or universal). But it throws into serious doubt our capacity to organise society in a way that everyone is equally agreeable to. Such an argument denies a human essence, in the strong sense, but it does not deny the capacity for mutual aid: it is not, in other words, a Hobbesian argument that pits neighbour against neighbour in a battle for survival. Rather, it suggests that the sort of diversity anarchism so strongly supports will always have the capacity to lead to conflict, not because people are anti-social, as such, but because people's understandings of what constitutes *the social* differ in important ways.

So far, we have seen that anarchism's conception of freedom is broad and (perhaps deliberately) vague. And I have argued that the idea that this anarchist freedom could be maintained by an inherently benevolent human nature, or by humanity's capacity for rational moral enquiry, is by no means a majority view amongst contemporary anarchists, and is, more importantly, ultimately untenable. But if we can no longer argue for some universal moral code, and if we can no longer conceive of an unproblematic 'common good', then what prospects are there for a truly libertarian community to exist? To begin answering this question, we do not have to wait for, or imagine, such a community: indeed, we need only remind ourselves of the anecdotes with which I opened this work to see that such conflicts occur every day, and that anarchists are as vulnerable to them as anyone else. Contemporary anarchism places considerable value on the notion of *diversity*, which, I have suggested, in many ways parallels the liberal notion of neutrality; it is worth looking now then at the way in which diversity is understood by anarchists.

Freedom in Diversity?

Diversity has long been championed by anarchists,[27] but it is increasingly placed at the very heart of contemporary activist discourses (Maeckelbergh, 2009; Gordon 2009). But what does diversity mean for these activists exactly? Is it limitless, or are there boundaries outside of which *diversity* becomes *division*? Despite its regular evocation, diversity is, I will argue below, a term that, like freedom, is frequently used with all too little reflection. According to Marianne Maeckelbergh:

> Diversity is unavoidable, especially in a globalised world, but diversity leads to difference of opinion and sometimes conflict. Democracy has long been about trying to resolve this basic paradox. The alter-globalisation actors, rather than denying or suppressing conflict, and rather than assuming that conflict is necessarily competitive and dangerous, assume that one can have constructive conflict without competition (Maeckelbergh 2009, 100).

Before looking at how diversity is understood here from an anarchist perspective, it is worth briefly exposing an underlying assumption about liberal politics, expressed in the above quote by Maeckelbergh, but which I believe is common amongst anarchists. Maeckelbergh implicitly suggests here that conventional democratic theorists see conflict as 'competitive and dangerous', and thus try to 'deny or suppress' it. Later, she argues that the movement's understanding of diversity is intended to 'challenge the political project of homogenization implicit in liberal democratisation' (ibid., 109). But is the liberal project really one of homogenization? According to John Rawls, a diversity of doctrines, the fact of pluralism, is not a mere historical condition that will soon pass away [...] diversity of views will persist and may increase. A public and workable agreement on a single general and comprehensive conception [of the good life] could only be maintained by the oppressive use of state power (Rawls 2001, 425).

Perhaps Maeckelbergh is right that the *reality* of the liberal state is one which attempts to limit diversity, though not always successfully, but why? Clearly, to the extent that this is true, there is a radical disconnect between liberal theory and practice. Yet what we have seen so far suggests a strong parallel between liberal and anarchist *theory*, with both ideologies arguing that they defend diversity and individual liberty. As we saw, Maeckelbergh argues that contemporary activists '*assume* that one can have constructive conflict without competition' (my emphasis); but is this any more than an assumption? Maeckelbergh certainly offers no reason as to why this might be the case, yet we have also seen that the reason liberalism fails to protect diversity in practice is not simply down to the role of the state: it is a more fundamental problem about the nature of value conflict. So how does the anarchist view differ? Why would diversity within an anarchist society be non-conflictual, when in a liberal society is so often clearly creates very real problems? As with the question of freedom, there appears to be no acknowledgment within anarchist discourse of the problems a stateless society is likely to face; we are simply presented with a vision of what anarchists want, but no real details as to how they expect to get it, or what they might do if and when things do not go entirely to plan.

For example, its ability to embrace a 'diversity of tactics' was, according to many, one of the principle strengths of the alter-globalisation movement (Tormey 2005), with the slogan 'one no, many yeses' being widely used to give voice to this (Kingsnorth 2003). Yet, as Chris Hurl notes:

While the anti-globalization movement is often celebrated for its apparent diversity, it often remains unclear how this diversity manifests itself in practice. The ambiguous boundaries of the movement serve to obscure its specific social relationships (Hurl 2005, 1).

One activist who embodies this tension is José Bové, an activist who became something of a celebrity within the movement for his direct action against McDonald's (Goaman 2004). McDonald's has become a classic target for anti-capitalist campaigners, but much of the rhetoric against it comes from an animal rights perspective. Bové, however, is a dairy farmer. Recognising the conflicts that freedom raises, a writer from the anarchist collective CrimethInc states that:

> We must create a world in which everything that is possible is also desirable. [...] There will be no reason for guilt, no possibility of hypocrisy or conflict between desires [...] a world empty of meat and dairy products (CrimethInc 2000, 104).

What does this say about the anarchist commitment to diversity? And what would happen to this diversity (and José Bové) if this author succeeded in realising their anarchist vision? Interestingly, within the movement, the limits to diversity are often quite apparent, and so the topic of (at times heated) debates:

> The Dissent! network also jumped through hoops to remain inclusive, albeit with mixed results. At almost every gathering there was a discussion of who should be allowed to participate in the Dissent! network. Could Christians, who might be proselytising an authoritarian religion? How about members of organised political parties? What exactly were the limits and nature of the PGA hallmarks, and who did they include and exclude? (Trocchi et. al. 2005, 66).

Yet whilst these reflections may appear to demonstrate an awareness of the problems I have been raising, in fact we often find that many in the movement are able to assure themselves that, having considered these difficult dilemmas, they have opted for the inclusive approach, and thus resolved any issues diversity may pose; in particular, the idea of consensus, discussed in Chapter 5, is believed to resolve these problems (much as, for liberals, the neutral state is supposed to). Welcoming those beyond the line-up of usual suspects, which usually means allowing Christians and Green Party members into the network, and then coming to a consensus about any shared projects, has allowed a continued feeling of a movement committed to diversity. And a strong focus on practical issues allows deeper ideological differences to be buried, at least temporarily. As Maecklebergh notes:

> Discussions about how the [Dissent! network's] ecovillage should be organised were discussions about philosophy of social change and shared ideals, but safely disguised behind practicalities so as to avoid ideological conflicts (Maeckelbergh 2009, 103).

Interestingly, even when we find an acknowledgement that real ideological differences are not being addressed in the consensus process, as with the quote above, there is no engagement with what this might mean when such differences can no longer be ignored. David Graeber declares that anarchism has often 'celebrated [its] commitment [to negative] freedom as evidence of [its] pluralism, ideological tolerance, or creativity' (Graeber 2006, 5). But the obvious and necessary question, how far does this 'ideological tolerance' actually go, rarely seems to be asked. It is certainly not clear how most anarchists would answer this question, or what their response might be once such limits had been reached; there is, in other words, no anarchist common sense we can point to when considering this. Is this because the obvious response is some denial of freedom, in whatever form it might take? Are anarchists simply unwilling to contemplate what this might mean for their dreams of a libertarian community? One response that is occasionally offered when conflicts cannot be resolved is the idea that groups can divide themselves into smaller units (Maeckelbergh 2009, 106-7; Seeds for Change 2007a). I will discuss this response in greater detail in Chapters 4 and 5, but for now I will simply note that I fail to find it convincing. Diversity then, like freedom, remains a vague and problematic concept; its limitations are rarely discussed, and it fails to offer any real clues as to how the anarchist ideal of absolute freedom is to be realised.

Conclusions.

Why then are freedom and diversity so uncritically accepted and left so unchallenged? I believe the answer, in part, lies in the reason they are supported in the first place. We saw earlier how Zygmunt Bauman claimed that, with the moral certainty of god or science no longer tenable, people would be forced to accept the moral nature of their choices, and to take responsibility for the consequences of such choices. However, we have also seen that liberals, through the concept of neutrality, have attempted to take the ethics out of our (or at least the state's) decisions; while morality still exists in the private realm, we are stripped of any responsibility for it precisely because it has no public conse-quence. Although explicitly motivated by the desire to protect individual freedom from interference by the state and other individuals or groups, I would suggest that the popularity of this idea must at least partly be explained by the protection it gives us from this responsibility. Importantly, this extends well beyond theories of state action: this, I believe, characterizes much of the modern condition. An 'I live my life and you live yours' attitude *appears* to provide precisely the hiding place Bauman believed we no longer had, and it is one which anarchists are as likely as liberals to misuse.

Ethics, then, does explain the anarchist discourse of freedom, but not in the sense of there being a clear moral framework that helps establish the normative parameters of liberty: rather, ethics defines liberty by its absence; freedom is the possibility of a privatised morality that is no longer the concern of society, and thus no longer the concern of anyone hoping to redefine or organise society. Freedom is freedom from moral intrusion, from the moral dictates of others; it is not defined by a certain set of values, but by the idea of a diversity of values. However, this freedom is always potentially limited by the freedom of others. On one level, it is clear that anarchists have always acknowledged this, but the sense in which this limitation was understood was in relation to the individual and her relationship with an otherwise united community with a broadly held agreement about what it meant to act *responsibly*; in other words, issues of *individual crime* have been discussed (although problematically and all too rarely) but issues of broader disagreements between different sections of the same community have mostly been ignored within anarchist thought. This ought to be of very real concern to anarchists, because what the above discussion about values suggests is that it is not simply anti-social acts by certain individuals that will be restricted, but particular ways of life that may be denied. Even without the state, people within communities have *power*, whether they like it or not; and at times, this power may necessarily be used against others, to prevent them living the way they want to live. Anarchist conceptions of both freedom *and* ethics, therefore, need to be understood in relation to power. It is power then which forms the focus of the next chapter.

Chapter 4

The Power of Community,
for Better and for Worse:
The Unavoidable Consequences of Power.

Power is already a central concept within all anarchist theory, but, like freedom and ethics, what anarchists mean when they use the term is often far from clear. In recent years, the charge has been made that, while anarchists may have followed a more sophisticated view of power than that of other socialists, they nonetheless missed some key features of what, it is argued, is a highly complex phenomenon. The postanarchists Saul Newman and Todd May argue that, in particular, Foucault's work on power takes its analysis further than that of the anarchists, seeing power as a diverse and dispersed concept that resides in all aspects of human life, and not simply within the state, or a particular (ruling) class. Others have challenged this view, arguing that in fact anarchists have always understood power as being more than simply the preserve of the state (Antliff 2007). I will review these debates briefly below, but I am not overly concerned with providing an historical analysis of anarchist thought. What concerns me is, first, what the dominant view of power is amongst anarchists today; what, in other words, the anarchist common sense says about power; and, second, what the implications of an appropriately complex and nuanced understanding of power might be for the anarchist commitment to freedom.

The Postanarchist View of Anarchism, and the Poststructural View of Power.

In the last decade or so,[28] a number of theorists commonly referred to as postanarchists have written extensively and critically on the subject of anarchism and power. Although a (rapidly increasing) group of writers have contributed to this postanarchist discourse (such as Sureyyya Evren 2008 and Jason Adams 2003) it is most notably the work of Todd May and Saul Newman which has attracted a great deal of both critical and favourable attention (see, for example, Franks, 2007). Newman and May's critique[29] rests on two basic claims: firstly, that power has traditionally been understood in too simplistic a manner, and that poststructural theorists such as Michel Foucault provide a better analysis. Secondly, they argue that anarchists have understood power in this first, simplistic way, and that anarchists ought therefore to incorporate the insights offered by poststructuralism. The postanarchists' basic argument then is that the analyses of power offered by theorists such as Foucault provide us with a better insight into the world and all its complexity; and it is an analysis that anarchists have not themselves made. To begin, I want to briefly explain this poststructural view of power, before asking whether it does differ so greatly from conceptions offered by anarchists.

Although the poststructural view of power has been widely discussed by numerous thinkers, it is Michel Foucault who is widely regarded as the key theorist in this respect. Through his work as an historian, Foucault aimed to uncover hidden assumptions about the role of institutions and the ideological beliefs that informed them. Foucault came to see that power was deeply ingrained in all social practices, constantly produced and reproduced at every level of society. Like the anarchists, Foucault's analysis of power takes it beyond economics, but he takes it further still, beyond the state, and urges us to look at 'other arenas of power, such as the prison, the family, psychiatric discourse, which have their own strategies and logic' (Newman 2001, 76). Power, then, does not simply exist in certain narrowly defined spheres, such as the state; rather, '[i]t is dispersed, decentred [...] diffused throughout society' (ibid., 78). Such an

analysis sees power in much the same way as we might understand energy, a fundamental part of every element of life, lying
behind every human process. And, like energy, power's effects
may be small, large, productive or destructive, and, importantly,
they are often invisible, or at least hard to pin down. As Todd
May puts it:

> Actions are inseparable from power; that is, from constraints
> upon other actions. And power, in its creative as well as its
> repressive aspects, channels and determines actions in ways
> often outside the grasp of the actors engaging in them. Thus,
> new practices with new constraints arise from the power
> arrangements that infuse social practices. Sometimes those
> new practices and constraints elude anyone's knowledge
> (May 1994, 88).

So the state is not the *source* of power, but rather made up of
various networks of power, which go beyond the state. 'It is
clear' Newman argues, then, 'that Foucault's conception of
power is fundamentally different from that of the anarchists', for
whereas 'anarchists see power as centralised within the state and
radiating downwards to the rest of society, Foucault sees power
as thoroughly dispersed throughout the social fabric' (Newman
2001, 79). Now, it is doubtless true that often, power, for
anarchists, is presented as being morally bad, and existing exclusively within certain institutions such as the state; it therefore
can and should be eliminated, by destroying the state, or the
ruling class. So although the classical anarchists are praised by
the postanarchists for their analysis of power when it comes to
the state, they have not gone far enough in their critique. Unlike
other socialists, anarchists are rightly critical of state power, but
they have fallen at the second hurdle, so to speak, and have
failed to extend this critique beyond the state or other similar
institutions. Such an understanding of power has allowed

anarchists to see society as somehow separate from power, as a power-free space in which the libertarian can flourish; without power, there can be no domination. Anarchism, then, 'creates an essential, moral opposition between society and the state, between humanity and power' (Newman 2001, 47). It is certainly not hard to find evidence of anarchist understandings of power that conform to the critique laid out by postanarchists. According to Dave Morland, 'power is central to anarchist theory, and anarchists, whether old or new, are united in their belief that it should, wherever possible, be uprooted and eliminated' (Morland 2004, 23). And David Thoreau Wieck writes that '[a]narchists [...] propose to reorganise our common life without the crippling destructive principles of power' (Thoreau Wieck 1970, 91).

For the postanarchists, this understanding of power does not exist in isolation: we need to understand it in relation to a broader network of philosophical assumptions within which these ideas about power lie. As Newman claims,

> according to anarchism, human subjectivity emerges in a world of 'natural laws' which are essentially rational and ethical, while the state belongs to the 'artificial' world of power. Thus man and power belong to separate and opposed worlds. Anarchism therefore has a logical point of departure, uncontaminated by power, from which power can be condemned as unnatural, irrational and immoral (Newman 2001, 5).

According to this critique, anarchism's understanding of power is deeply flawed: it sees power as morally bad, and as being confined to certain elements of society, in institutions, such as the state and the church, or in certain classes such as the capitalist or ruling class; and it embeds this view of power within other humanist assumptions, about human nature, rationality, progress, and so on. The result is that anarchists form the overarching view that 'the state [is] essentially evil and society [is] essentially good' (Newman 2001, 28). Despite their critique, Newman, May and other postanarchists maintain a strong affinity with anarchism, and they argue that anarchism has historically come closer to uncovering the complex issues of power than other political ideologies such as Marxism. Through their critique of Marxism, anarchists, according to Newman 'have allowed power to be studied in its own right' (Newman 2001, 37). While acknowledging this achievement, Newman insists the anarchists have simply not gone far enough, and asks whether anarchists have 'not merely replaced the economy with the state as the essential evil in society, from which other evils are derived?' (ibid., 47).

As well as Foucault seeing the place of power as being fundamentally different from that of the anarchists, he makes another distinction, which I believe has been a cause for considerable confusion: this is the idea that power is not repressive, but rather productive. What is meant by this is not that power cannot restrict individuals and be used against them, but rather that individuals do not have an unchanging, natural essence that is free from power itself but which can be repressed by the power of others, especially the state. There is not, in other words, a humanity that exists independent of power, which power then comes along and represses; humanity itself is the product of existing power relations, and this will always be the case. I believe that the emphasis that Newman and May place on this, however, is at times unhelpful to their own argument. Newman, for example, suggests that 'power is not repressive, rather it is productive, and that to see power entirely in terms of repression is to fundamentally misunderstand it' (ibid., 81). But what precisely is being said here? Firstly, he argues that 'power is *not repressive*' (my emphasis) but then that 'to see power *entirely* in terms of repression' (my emphasis) is misplaced. But there is a fundamental difference between arguing power is *not* repressive, and that it is not *only* repressive. Which is it? The confusion, I believe, lies in the use of the word *repression*. For poststructuralists, repression is understood as working against an essential human nature; because they deny such a nature, they deny that power can be repressive. However, for most people, and, I would suggest, at times for Newman and other poststructural thinkers, repression can also simply refer to some form of coercion, or domination. To talk of humans being repressed does not necessarily entail the view that they have an essential humanity that lies beneath the surface. Because Newman's argument rests on the (flawed) assumption that anarchism believes in an essential space free from power, he therefore sees anarchist understandings of repression as being linked to this. But it seems to me that we can do away with an essential human nature and still coherently talk of repression, because, whether the result of nature or social conditioning, or anything else, people still have needs and desires which can be limited by the power of others, and it is this basic fact with which, I would suggest, anarchists are primarily concerned when they talk of the negative, or repressive, aspect of power.

Similarly, poststructuralists (anarchist or otherwise) do see very real imbalances of power, so that the state can indeed be understood as a powerful institution which unjustly dominates the majority of humanity (May 2007, 21). However, in order to correct the traditional emphasis on the state, they tend to over-stress the diffused nature of power. Conversely, I would argue anarchists have tended to do the opposite: while I will go on to argue that anarchists do in fact understand that power infuses all life, they have been primarily concerned with attacking those physical and ideological spaces where power is so blatantly and aggressively displayed. As a result, they tend to emphasise the negative capacities of power (and its existence within institutions such as the state). Indeed, even Newman at times talks of power in this sense: 'Perhaps the whole idea of revolution should be abandoned for a form of resistance to power which is, like power itself, nebulous and dispersed' (ibid., 79). But how can we (and indeed why should we) talk of a resistance to power at all? Surely Newman means a resistance to certain forms of power? A resistance which must, by his account, produce and utilise its very own forms of power. Elsewhere, he notes that 'there is still [...] the raw, brutal inevitability of power and authority' (Newman 2001, 1), and concedes that 'postanarchism shares with anarchism its anti-authoritarian goal of a society without power' (Newman 2010, 69). Once again, I believe such confusion stems quite simply from the multiple meanings of certain terms, in this instance, the word *power*Commonly, power is precisely centralised and repressive/negative: if power is seen by anarchists as being primarily bad, and as deriving primarily from the state, the obvious charge is that they have missed the possibility of power being at times a positive force, and of it existing in other areas of life. However, we might also say that for anarchists, and again, it would seem at times for Newman too, the word 'power' is used to denote the evils of the state, but that they are perfectly aware that there is something else that exists, that is, or can be, positive, and that does, or can, exist outside of the state. Within the context of anarchist writing, propaganda, and activism, the challenge is to attack the state, and the destructive and unequal power relations it embodies. Power, then, like all words, is merely a symbol, and for anarchists it (often) symbolises that which is both bad and inherent in the state: the question is, do they recognise that there is something else, which we may or may not choose to call power, which also exists? Have they, in other words, failed to recognise a certain social phenomenon entirely, or have they simply preferred not to symbolise it with the term power?

This postanarchist critique immediately raises a number of questions. Are they right in their assessment of what the classical theorists thought? Why have they for the most part ignored the work of later anarchists? Do contemporary anarchists have a different understanding of power? Perhaps not surprisingly, this postanarchist critique has itself come under attack. The most common argument is that postanarchism simply misrepresents anarchism: one is certainly left wondering why Newman fails to see that the anarchists he chooses to critique simply talk of power at different times in different ways, in precisely the same way he does; curiously, it would be easy to cherry-pick quotes from Newman's work to show that he, like the classical anarchists, sees power as morally negative. Of course, it would be pointless to do so, but then I would equally suggest that, based on cherry-picked and distorted readings as it is, Newman's work is also largely without merit. Furthermore, the postanarchist identification of a group of classical theorists who are lumped into one metaphysical school is problematic, and their avoidance of later schools of thought which would be less easy to dismiss raises questions about the timeliness and merit of the critique (Franks 2009; Kinna 2007). Another possible critique, which, importantly, appears to be quite rare, is that the post*structural* theory of power which postanarchists embrace is itself wrong: power *should* be seen in a more conventional way[30]. Interestingly, David Graeber, one of the most well-known voices of the new anarchism which supposedly has such close affinities with poststructuralism, is one of an apparently small number of anarchists who has taken umbrage with the Foucauldian turn.

Academics love Michel Foucault's argument that identifies knowledge and power, and insists that brute force is no longer a major factor in social control. They love it because it flatters them: the perfect formula for people who like to think of themselves as political radicals even though all they do is write essays likely to be read by a few dozen other people in an institutional environment. Of course, if any of these academics were to walk into their university library to consult some volume of Foucault without having remembered to bring a valid ID, and decided to enter the stacks anyway, they would soon discover that brute force is really not so far away as they like to imagine; a man with a big stick, trained in exactly how hard to hit people with it, would rapidly appear to eject them. [...] Such a theoretical emphasis opens the way to a theory of the relation of power not with knowledge, but with ignorance and stupidity. Because violence, particularly structural violence, where all the power is on one side, creates ignorance. If you have the power to hit people over the head whenever you want, you don't have to trouble yourself too much figuring out what they think is going on, and therefore, generally speaking, you don't (Graeber 2004, 71-72).

I shall return to this critique below, but for the most part, it would appear that very few anarchists in fact seek to challenge the view of power presented by poststructuralism. So what *do* anarchists have to say about power? In the following section I will suggest that the anarchist common sense understanding of power is indeed more sophisticated than that sketched by the postanarchists: however, I will then go on to argue that the *implications* of this have not been sufficiently considered.

A Response to the Postanarchist Critique: The Anarchist view of Power.

It has been frequently argued that anarchism has changed a great deal in the hundred years since Kropotkin was writing; as we saw in previous chapters, there is apparently a new anarchism, reloaded and fit for the twenty-first century. If the events in Paris in 1968 can be seen as inspiring the poststructural theories that Newman and May hope to synthesise with anarchism, it is clear these events also had a very direct influence on anarchism (and the new left more broadly) at the time, and ever since. (As did other similar movements, such as those of the Dutch Provos, and the German and Italian Autonomen, which have sadly and unjustifiably largely been erased from the popular imagination; see Kempton 2007 and Katsiaficas, 2006, respectively, for a useful history of these movements.) Indeed, Todd May is simply wrong when he suggests that '[o]ne does not normally think of anarchism and recent French philosophical thought as having a natural affinity' (May 2009, 13). On the contrary, the relationship between poststructuralism and anarchism is readily acknowledged by many contemporary anarchists, a point which May and Newman both chose to convenientlyignore. As Giorel Curran notes, there is a strong 'resonance between anarchist and, for example, Foucauldian analyses' (Curran 2006, 30). Not surprisingly then, it is not hard to find evidence of power being understood by anarchists in much the same way as it is by poststructuralists. Uri Gordon puts the point well when he notes that:

> Anarchists are hardly 'against power'. This common misconception is easily shown untrue by anarchist political language, in which 'empowerment' is mentioned as a positive goal. Empowerment is seen as a process where people literally acquire power [...] On the other hand, of course, anarchists want to 'fight the power', or at least 'the powers that be', and resist all systems of domination under which people are systematically subject to power [...] This indicates not a 'rejection of power', but a more nuanced and *differentiated* use of the concept (Gordon 2008, 49 my emphasis).

Here Gordon highlights what I earlier suggested was an important point to consider: namely, that anarchists may use the word power to define that which is repressive and which exists solely within certain institutions, but that this does not mean they do not also understand power in other ways. For many anarchists, power is understood as something that cannot be got rid of, and as something that is not always oppressive; it can be positive or negative, coercive or enabling (Gordon 2008, 48). Marianne Maeckelbergh argues that 'movement actors have highly fluid and context-specific approaches to power' (Maeckelbergh 2009, 101) and, as such, suggests that power is understood in three different ways: 'power as centralised hierarchy, power as decentralised hierarchy and power as decentralised non-hierarchy'(ibid.). The Notes from Nowhere Collective state in no uncertain terms:

> Put simply, power is our ability to do things, to change things. It is the creative force behind all our experience. It is what makes things possible. It's easy to imagine power as something that is outside of us, that is safely guarded and exercised by 'the powerful', a tool wielded by the other, the patriarchs, the capitalists, the oppressors. But power does not just reside in one place. It's not just found in the seat of government, on the screens of the stock exchanges, at the end of the swinging club of the police officer. These are simply places and moments where power has accumulated and become fixed (Notes from Nowhere 2003, 388).

And in his discussion of the Spanish anarchists, Robert Alexander writes clearly that 'their agrarian experiments remain one of the notable aspects of the Spanish anarchists' experience of having, and sharing, power' (Alexander 2002, 217). It is of course debatable whether the Spanish anarchists themselves thought of power this way, but, first published in 1999, Alexander's account at least pre-dates much postanarchist work. And if we look further back into anarchist history, there is evidence that anarchist theories of power were far from simplistic. Even Newman points to what he suggests are contradictions within anarchist thought: Bakunin and Kropotkin both, Newman argues, talk of power in ways that make what he considers to be their *real* view of power 'ambiguous, incomplete, open to question' (Newman 2001, 49), arguing that Bakunin 'perhaps unconsciously exposed the hidden contradiction that lies at the heart of anarchist discourse' (ibid.) when he acknowledged that 'while individuals are naturally moral and sociable, and while society is, therefore, essentially harmonious, individuals also have a dark side, an insatiable desire for power and authority, which jeopardises this harmony' (ibid., 50). Rather than seeing this as a contradiction, however, we could more favourably suggest that Bakunin was offering, as Gordon suggests many anarchists do, a differentiated view of power. The following lines from Bakunin make it abundantly clear that the view of power supposedly unveiled by Foucault was well understood many decades before poststructuralism was even conceived of:

> Social tyranny is often overwhelming and deadly, but it does not exhibit the character of imperative violence, or legalised, formal despotism, which distinguishes State authority. It is not applied like some law which forces the individual to comply [...]. Its effect is gentler, more insinuating and imperceptible, but correspondingly more powerful than that of state authority. It exerts its authority by means of conventions, morals and a multitude of sentiments, prejudices and habits, in the material as well as the mental sphere [...].n(1973, 150).

Such a view certainly sees power as existing outside of the state; but Bakunin continues to note that 'this power may be just as much beneficial as harmful', considering one such benefit to be 'the development of knowledge' (ibid.) Whatever other contrary statements Bakunin may have made, it is clear that he was also capable of seeing power as both positive and negative, as creative and destructive, and as being dispersed throughout society. Writing several decades after Bakunin, Alexander Berkman wrote

in 1929 that all life had become 'a crazy quilt of authority, of
domination and submission, of command and obedience, of
coercion, and subjection, of rulers and ruled, of violence and
force in a thousand and one forms' (Berkman 1973, 8). Of course,
Berkman was more preoccupied with putting his anarchist
principles into practice than writing large tomes of theory, so it
is impossible to know precisely what he meant here, and we
must be wary of reading too much into his words: however, such
an analysis strongly suggests a view of power which sees it as
existing throughout society, and not simply within the state.
Whatever the case is about these earlier theorists' understandings of power, and certainly there will never be a definitive
answer, what I hope is clear by now is that for the majority of
contemporary anarchists, and quite possibly for many of those
writing throughout the last hundred years or more, power is not
understood as simplistically as the postanarchists suggest; the
anarchist common sense about power, I would argue, is not so
dissimilar from that offered by poststructuralist thought.

However, whilst it seems undeniable that anarchists understand power in a more nuanced way than is sometimes
suggested, I believe there is still a significant failure to truly
internalise what this means for a libertarian society. The task of
all anarchists now, I would suggest, must be to move beyond the
deeply flawed postanarchist critique of earlier theorists, and
begin to strengthen and refine the core principles of anarchism in
relation to power (and, indeed, to freedom, ethics, equality and
other concepts which I have suggested are in need of considerable reappraisal). In the following section, I want to explore
two more concrete examples of how power may impact on an
anarchist society; in doing so, I will argue that the anarchist
understandings of freedom and ethics, and of an unproblematic
diversity of interests without conflict or coercion, is ultimately
unrealistic.

The Implications of Power without the State.

I have so far outlined what I believe is a reasonably common understanding of power amongst contemporary anarchists. Although there are undeniably elements of contradiction, and at times a lack of clarity, I suggested that anarchists have long held views about power which are of a similar nature to those views supposedly first articulated by Foucault; at the very least, it is clear that anarchists have been explicitly embracing poststructural discourse for many years. More to the point, this view of power, whoever we might credit with its unveiling, is an analysis I believe we must work with. But what are the implications of this understanding of power? What does this mean for the fanatical lovers of liberty, who hope to create a society of free individuals where no one coerces anyone else? Taking our enquiry to another level, I believe that while anarchists follow this more nuanced view of power, the ramifications for a libertarian society have not been adequately thought through. As I suggested earlier in relation to the classical theorists, anarchists continue to focus their attention on the primary abuses of power perpetuated by the state, and big business. Although this remains an important battle, and one which anarchists must not lose sight of, it is vital that anarchists are more explicit and honest in recognising that, because, as we saw in the last chapter, there are reasonable disagreements about what constitutes the good life, *and* because power can never be overcome, coercion and conflict will remain (at least potential) elements of any society when it comes to resolving such conflicts. In accepting this, and in accepting therefore that the demand for absolute freedom must always be tempered, anarchism must come to terms with the inevitable limits of freedom. To be clear: what follows is a discussion of the *problems* of power; in doing so, I do not deny its positive capacities, but given the over-all focus of this work, my analysis necessarily focuses on the *difficulties* that anarchism faces, and, therefore, on the conflictual potential of power.

Furthermore, there is no denial (certainly not from myself) that power can be and often is *concentrated* in certain areas, *in certain respects*: the editor of a newspaper clearly has more power to influence public opinion than I do. However, what is being claimed here is not that this is not the case, but that this power reverberates throughout society, and is realised, often without consent or knowledge, through the individuals that make up society. The power of the editor is, after all, the power to *influence* other people, to influence what *they* then say, and do; and it is precisely through what they say and do that social norms come to embody those of the newspaper editor. The editor sets the agenda, so to speak, which is then acted upon by countless individuals operating, on various levels and in different ways, throughout society. This is why Graeber is wrong when he says that it is simply the police officer's stick that holds the power. It is also the social respect for the stick (and the police officer using it), the willingness to submit to it, and the various social understandings that come with it; for instance, if I were to be attacked by a random member of the public wielding a stick, other individuals might come to my aid, assuming I am simply being attacked, but if a police officer attacks me, they are likely to assume I am being appropriately dealt with. Equally, I know that if I defend myself against an attack by a member of the public, I am unlikely to be punished for doing so; if I defend myself against an attack by a police officer, even if their actions are entirely inappropriate and unlawful, I am likely to be punished. (Indeed, my own criminal record pays testimony to this.) Of course, it is surely true that our fear of physical violence is very real: we are scared of the stick itself; but this is only half the story.

As I suggested earlier, it is perhaps equally true that poststructural theorists themselves tend to focus on the other half of the story, that which emphasises the less tangible aspects of power. However, I don't believe this suggests a rejection of the relative power of the state, or the stick, for that matter. All it suggests is that philosophers are generally not interested in writing books telling people that policemen have sticks. What Foucault believed was that the less obvious forms of power[31] had escaped people's attention, so it was on this he focused, with good reason.

Indeed, it is the failure to recognise power for what it is that often makes it so problematic. Power can be consciously and deliberately disguised, but it can also work without the knowledge of those who possess it. This is a crucial point for anarchists, and it is here that the arguments of the previous chapter, especially those of Iris Marion Young and Bhikhu Parekh, become so clearly relevant. Power can operate, as Young put it, through 'the normal processes of everyday life' (Young 1990, 41), processes which could lead to extremely oppressive situations for some, *despite* the fact that they take place within 'a well-intentioned liberal society' (ibid.). Importantly, while the stick-wielding policeman is very much a fundamental part of our everyday life, Young is also interested in those articulations of power that are not commonly understood as such, and which do not have the conscious intention of repression or control.

I turn now then to two examples of power that is dispersed, and often hidden, yet which has a considerable impact on those it reaches. Firstly, I explore what Jo Freeman called *the tyranny of structurelessness*, a concept which explores the problems of hidden hierarchies, and one which has been widely discussed in activist circles; I then go on to discuss transport, and in particular the car, to see how the power of the automobile shapes our daily lives.

Jo Freeman and 'The Tyranny of Structurelessness.'

In 1970, the sociologist and feminist activist Jo Freeman wrote a short but widely read article entitled *The Tyranny of Structurelessness*. Although her focus was the feminist movement in America at the time of writing, its wider applicability has long

been recognised by anarchists. In the article, Freeman discusses
the idea of the 'structureless group', a group in which none of its
members hold formal positions of power. Although she never
uses the term hierarchy, clearly the idea of structurelessness
mirrors the anarchist rejection of hierarchies.[32] Freeman's basic
claim is that when formal structures (or hierarchies) within
groups are abandoned, as they were in the feminist
consciousness raising groups in which she participated, these
structures will simply be replaced with *in*formal ones. What was
especially worrying for Freeman was that, because these
informal structures were assumed not to exist, they were effectively beyond critique, and, therefore, invulnerable to
challenges. In a democratic setting where power structures are
formalised, a leader can be voted out of their position, but an
informal leader in a structureless group can potentially be
impossible to remove. As Freeman puts it:

> The idea becomes a smokescreen for the strong or the lucky to
> establish unquestioned hegemony over others. This hegemony
> can easily be established because the idea of 'structure-
> lessness' does not prevent the formation of informal struc-
> tures, but only formal ones (Freeman 1970).

As such, Freeman suggests that this "structurelessness' becomes
a way of masking power' (ibid.). And as she sees the power of
certain individuals to be an inevitable consequence of the structureless group, and because such informality leads to an
increased level of immunity from critique, she suggests that such
power should be formalised.

> If the movement continues deliberately not to select who shall
> exercise power, it does not thereby abolish power. All it does
> is abdicate the right to demand that those who do exercise
> power and influence be responsible for it (ibid.).

However, she goes on to argue that this

> does not mean that we should go to the other extreme and blindly imitate the traditional forms of organisation. But [... s]ome traditional techniques will prove useful, albeit not perfect; some will give us insights into what we should not do [...]. Mostly, we will have to experiment [...] and develop a variety of techniques to use for different situations' (ibid.).

In order that the formalised power structures Freeman advocates are as democratic as possible, she suggests a set of principles which, she argues, can counter the worst effects of hierarchical organisation, going on to conclude that 'we must accept the idea that there is nothing inherently bad about structure itself, only its excessive use' (ibid.). Not surprisingly, Freeman's article generated considerable interest amongst anarchists, who saw her arguments either as a threat to their basic ideological assumptions, or as a welcome note of caution that ought to be listened to carefully. Regrettably, the former response appears to have been more widespread, and I would argue that rather than honestly confront the issues Freeman raises head on, many anarchists have dismissed her critique in an overly dogmatic fashion. Take the following example:

> The problem with this essay is that Freeman was an authoritarian leftist who wrote the essay to attack the anarchistic consciousness-raising groups being organised by feminist women at that time. Freeman was in favour of building mass parties in the Leninist mode and was alarmed at the anarchist ideas taking hold among radical women. [...] The irony, of course, is that contemporary anarchists are using an anti-anarchist essay to criticise problems in their groups and organisations! It is far better to actually talk about group process problems than to wave a decontextualised essay over people's heads (Munson 2010, 4).

I neither know nor care what Freeman's political motivation for writing this pamphlet was: what matters is the argument itself, and it is, in my view, undeniably powerful and worthy of our attention. Some anarchists have, of course, attempted to critique the article in a more helpful manner. Cathy Levine, who wrote an openly anarchistic reply, *The Tyranny of Tyranny* at least acknowledges that Freeman's article was 'written and received in good faith, as an aid to the movement' (Levine 1979, 3). Levine, however, goes on to challenge the basic premise of Freeman's argument, and argues that small, unstructured groups

> [...] multiply the strength of each member. By working collectively in small numbers, the small group utilises the various contributions of each person to their fullest, nurturing and developing individual input, instead of dissipating it in the competitive survival-of-the-fittest/smartest/wittiest spirit of the large organisation (ibid.).

She goes on to suggest that '[c]ontrary to the belief that lack of up-front structures leads to insidious, invisible structures based on elites, the absence of structures in small, mutual trust groups fights elitism on the basic level, the level of personal dynamics' (ibid., 7). Levine does acknowledge that different individuals have different personality traits and different capacities, but she sees the unstructured group as offering the appropriate environment in which such differences can co-exist, rather than compete.

> The small personally involved group learns, first to recognise those stylistic differences, and then to appreciate and work with them; rather than trying to either ignore or annihilate differences in personal style, the small group learns to appreciate and utilise them, thus strengthening the personal power of each individual (ibid.).

Acknowledging that the problems noted by Freeman can, however, exist, Levine believes that they are the result, not of the unstructured group dynamic *per se*, but rather of our social conditioning, which is, at present, deeply embedded in hierarchy. The problem, then 'does not find solution in the formation of structures' (ibid.) but rather in a continuing effort to make unstructured groups work for the benefit of all. So who is right? Freeman argues that unstructured groups inevitably develop a hidden hierarchy, disempowering those individuals kept outside, or below, whereas Levine argues that such groups allow all members to flourish, and that, to the extent this is not always currently the case, this is due to social learning, which could, in a more libertarian context, be overcome. Such attempts at organising without structures or hierarchies have of course continued in the three decades since Levine wrote her reply to Freeman, so how have they fared? Interestingly, Freeman's article is still extremely popular amongst libertarian radicals today, and many of the argument's key themes continue to resonate with those involved in structureless (or horizontal, to use the more contemporary term) groups. Some argue that the anarchist movement has learnt from the critique, and responded with positive theoretical and practical contributions (Dupuis-Déri 2010, 50; Graeber 2009, 233-7). Others have suggested that the critique itself is no longer directly relevant, and that the suggestions Freeman makes to counter the problem are normatively unacceptable and, in terms of the anarchist movement as it currently exists, practically unworkable (Gordon 2009, 62-77). However, I would argue that what the anarchist movement has failed to do is to honestly assess the merits of the argument. What we are given are moral rebuttals that maintain the ethical virtues of horizontal organisation, but no real arguments that convincingly suggest that either Freeman is wrong, or that her concerns have been adequately addressed in the four decades since she wrote the article. Indeed, I would suggest the movement is in some ways haunted by this critique; never being embraced, but never quite going away. We saw in Chapter 2 how Paul Chambers argued that it was 'a curious suggestion that liberty might be upheld by the denial of liberty' (Chambers 2006, 37), and I would suggest we can see a strong parallel here, with anarchists believing it is an equally curious (meaning *incorrect*) suggestion that the greatest equality of power may be maintained by formalised structures of power. In other words, I would argue there is an ideological block to genuinely assessing Freeman's argument. Clearly, some lessons have been learnt since the article was first written, with considerable effort being put into improving the working processes of horizontal groups, by, for example, improving meeting facilitation techniques, a point I return to in the next chapter. But how quickly such improvements will come, what happens in the meantime, and, perhaps most importantly, to what extent we will ever eradicate the problems of hidden hierarchies are not questions that have been appropriately grappled with. It is certainly true that the problems Freeman discusses continue to exist within today's anarchist movement; but if small groups of people dedicated to anarchist principles and who are aware of these concerns and who have attempted, over several decades, to resolve them, are still struggling to find appropriate responses, what does this suggest about the possibility of a thoroughly horizontal society? To put it another way; at what point might we expect the honest anarchist to ask herself whether this is a problem which simply won't go away? Or, if these problems are expected to be dealt with when we have built and had time to experience a more thoroughly horizontal culture, how long will this take, and what are the possible implications before we reach that point? Remember that Marx believed in a stateless world, but saw the state as a useful tool to achieve that ultimate goal; the problem was, as anarchists well understand, that the supposedly transitional period of the state ossified and stuck; but why would the informal hierarchies that even Levine admits are likely to exist in anarchist organising today be any less likely to suffer the same fate? Anarchism, like all political theories, must deal not only with the question of how it will organise society, but with how it seeks to create such a society in the first place, and how it hopes to respond to the difficulties it will no doubt encounter in its attempts to do so.

Although by no means a criticism of Freeman's work, which, it should by now be clear, I think is of vital importance, one of the problems with analysing her article and the responses to it is that they all focus on political movements; but what about problems within wider society, now, and those of a hypothetical future? What are the implications of the analyses of power we have so far seen for our daily lives? Freeman's article demonstrates how individuals can assume a less tangible form of power; ultimately, this power rests on the capacity to influence the thinking of a group of people. I will have more power than you if I have a greater capacity to inspire respect and admiration from those we are both trying to influence, because I am older, funnier, more articulate, better looking, or whatever. I may also be more experienced, or have access to certain information, or equipment, that gives me power over others; something which may be considered as legitimate in certain situations, but which can, over time, ossify into more deep-seated and worrying forms of power (Gordon 2008, 47-77). These capacities to influence are not the only way power can exist in more subtle forms, however. At times, power can have a more dispersed presence, whilst still being invisible to most of those affected by it. Of course, very often these two forms of power will emanate from the same place, and so each will mutually re-enforce the other.

When we think back to the discussion of the previous chapter, where I argued that a plurality of values can lead to conflicting priorities for different members of a community, we might well ask what this maymean for the hopes of a libertarian society.

Different ethical positions will be supported, not only by
different communities, but also by different groups within the
same communities. So while at times communities may agree
about a common good, we must acknowledge that people will
also at times defend their capacity to enjoy *un*common goods.
This will, at times, be unproblematic, but at others, conflicts will
arise. What this means for a libertarian community is that some
lifestyles, understood in the broadest, cultural, political and
moral sense, will necessarily coerce, or be coerced by, other
lifestyles. On a mundane level, if I want to play my music until 6
a.m., my neighbour will struggle to get a good night's sleep.[33]
Hopefully, we could between us come to some mutually conve-
nient arrangement: but when certain values are held by a large
group in any community, the realisation of these values may
have a wide reaching impact, so that it becomes difficult to avoid
the physical reality created by them. Furthermore, such conflicts
will not necessarily arise because of overtly ethical or political
disagreements; some conflicts may arise for what appear[34] to be
amoral or apolitical reasons, as the example of transport, to
which we now turn, demonstrates.

Beyond Horse Power: How the Power of the Car has Shaped Contemporary Lives.

For some, transport may appear to be a somewhat mundane
subject of little political relevance. Of course, many people now
recognise the environmental impact cars have; but beyond this,
transport can hardly be said to excite political theorists in the
same way that gender, or race, or psychiatry, for example, have.
Yet our current transport system is crucial in perpetuating a
number of industries which anarchists have good cause to
denounce: the oil, construction and of course automobile industries, to name but three. The many problems created by these
industries, which can be social as well as environmental,
threaten not only individuals in their local area, but the future of

the human race: the threat of climate change, which is greatly exacerbated by our current transport norms, is just the most obvious of these. Importantly, however, unlike, say, the arms industry, transport is something that we can safely assume anarchists would not want to get rid of entirely. [35] As we shall see, however, power plays an important role in the creation and maintenance of any transport system, so it will continue to pose at least a potential problem for people in an anarchist society. Drawing on the recent work of Aurora Trujillo (2010), I want to show how power, and, in this instance, the power of the automobile, pervades our daily lives in ways which can have far-reaching consequences.

I want to begin though by addressing concerns that some people have about this 'Foucauldian turn'; namely, the fear that such an understanding of power is essentially depoliticising, robbing us of the ability to critique (and indeed condemn) the power of the state, of capitalists, and so on. Understandable as it may be, this fear is ultimately unjustified. Throughout the western world, and increasingly in countries such as India and China, the car is the dominant form of transport: indeed, whilst the following discussion is about transport, it focuses almost exclusively on the car, because the car is at the top of the transport hierarchy, and all other modes of travel are effectively subordinated to it. The car dominates other modes of travel in terms of its levels of use, in terms of economic expenditure (public and private) and, as we shall see, it dominates our cultural and physical landscape, and much else besides. All of this seems perfectly normal. And many would claim it was inevitable. The car offers us the freedom to travel almost anywhere, at any time; it is safe, dry, warm (or cool), comfortable, private, reliable.[36] In short, the growth of the car is often believed to be the result of the qualities of the car itself, and people's natural desire to enjoy those qualities. But the power of the state, and of capitalists, played no small part in what Winfried Wolf

calls 'the resistible rise of the car' (Wolf 1996). Subsidised car
manufacture, and a road building project paid for entirely by the
tax payer, historically, and to this day, are key to the car's success.
The car has been promoted aggressively, not only by its manufac-
turers, but also by governments, as well as, in the early years, a
privileged elite who had access to cars and who therefore
demanded the state provide the necessary infrastructure to meet
their desire to drive. So this initial promotion of the car can be
understood through more traditional understandings of power;
that is, as the result of a centralised and hierarchical power,
operating in a top-down system of coercion and enforcement
(see Wolf 1996, again; and also Paterson 2007).

This state and economic power continues to play an
important role, of course, but over the years, as our increasing
use of the car grew and began to challenge other forms of
transport, the top-down power of the state was, if not quite
replaced, considerably reinforced by a more dispersed network
of power. As the car established its hegemony, life increasingly
came to be designed around the car, physically and culturally. As
more and more cars were made, so an increasing number of
roads needed to be built, and as they rapidly filled up, yet more
quickly followed. As the country became criss-crossed with
tarmac, daily life began to change. People were expected to travel
further for work, and longer journeys were actively encouraged,
by creating out-of-town shopping centres for example. As these
larger shops thrived, local shops began to close at an alarming
rate (Monbiot 2000, 162-208): suddenly, it became a near
necessity to have a car just to do the shopping. Similar processes
took place in relation to all manner of essential services (such as
hospitals), as well as within family and friendship groups.
Parents looked to schools well beyond the local area, in order to
secure a better education for their child, for example.

Although other forms of transport, notably trams and trains
(the horse and carriage was never really a mass means of

transport) helped shape life in similar ways, at least in the bigger cities, their impact was greatly over-shadowed by that of the car. Before the arrival of the car, the majority of people rarely travelled more than a few miles beyond their home, and their communities were underpinned by the stability that this provided; with people walking to work, to the shops, to school, they remained near their homes, and interacted with other members of the communities as they did so. But as the popularity of the car increased, conditions for non-car users became increasingly poor, and often simply dangerous. Public transport was neglected as the car became prioritised by transport planners. In the space of a hundred years, the western world was shaped in no small way by the physical and discursive parameters laid out by the car (see Horton 2006, Illich 1979, Ward 1991, Sloman 2006, and Trujillo 2010 for some interesting discussions about what Andre Gorz (1980) called *The Ideology of the Motor Car*).

The power that operates through and around the car, then, exists within and influences a complex network of physical spaces, behavioural patterns, even ethical norms: for example, what people expect, accept and reject in terms of their transport needs; in institutional regulations, in road traffic laws, the licensing of drivers and vehicles, etc.; and in physical infrastructure, the layout of our roads and cities, and so on. So, when we drive to work, the speed we travel at, the route we take, the way we respond to other roads users (other car drivers, as well as pedestrians and cyclists) the facilities available to us, at our destination and en-route, and much else besides: all these things can be analysed with reference to a complex web of power relations that exist within society.

Perhaps the most important thing to recognise, however, is the extent to which these operations of power are hidden. This happens, not because of any conspiracy to keep them a secret, but because the structures created and consequently reinforced by these networks of power are normalised, and are consequently seen as natural, inevitable even (if indeed we see them at all): 'We take the car for granted as a social good, which renders it nearly invisible as the source of a range of problems' (Lutz & Lutz Fernandez 2010, x-xi). For example, the notion that we have lost our sense of community is an increasingly common complaint, as has the closure of local shops, but how often do people explicitly blame these (and many other problems) on the car, or even acknowledge the part it has unwittingly played? Every year, more than 3,000 people are killed in the UK alone as a result of road traffic accidents: more than 50,000 are seriously injured. Yet compare the public discourse around these deaths to those caused by, say, knife crime. Speed limits of 30 miles per hour or more are the norm even in residential areas, even though travelling at 20 miles per hour has been shown to increase the chances of someone surviving a collision dramatically, as well as greatly reducing the chances of a collision occurring in the first place. However, rather than forcing cars to slow down, pedestrians are increasingly segregated from roads, with, for example, barriers preventing them from crossing them where the authorities deem it unsafe to do so (Davis 1991).

What all this means in practical terms is that other forms of transport, and indeed, certain ways of life, are marginalised or entirely negated by the car's dominance. Fear of the car prevents many people from cycling and the sight of children playing on the streets is increasingly rare (Hillman et al 1990). The street is no longer populated by pedestrians, interacting with one another, but by drivers of dangerous machines. As well as the many immediate effects, on personal health, for example, the broader implications of car culture exacerbate all manner of prevailing ills, social inequality and a decreasing sense of community amongst them.

Whilst the work of Iris Marion Young focuses on the problems of power, diversity and conflict faced by groups which are commonly understood to suffer some form of oppression,

Aurora Trujillo uses Young's framework to show how people holding alternative ethical and political views can be equally marginalised. Like Young, she argues that physical and social barriers exist which can make it extremely difficult for people to live certain ways of life, but that 'this is not only the case for cultural, religious or other groups, such as women, but also for those holding alternative ethical and political values, such as [those trying to live according to certain environmental values]' (Trujillo 2010, 168). This, I believe, is particularly important for anarchists, because it suggests that even when there is no deliberate or conscious attempt to discriminate or oppress, the simple fact of organising daily life can have serious and negative effects on individuals or groups whose lives differ from those of a majority. When diversity and freedom are both supported, as we have seen they are by anarchists, questions need to be asked as to how this will work in practice; clearly, it is not enough to simply defend diversity theoretically. Uri Gordon recognises the point when he acknowledges that

> the rise of diversity to the status of a core anarchist value [...] creates a practical challenge [...] since it raises the possibility of stagnation and renewed hierarchies even in a society where present structures of inequality have been abolished (Gordon 2009, 261).

Anarchists must therefore acknowledge 'the possibility of forms of domination that are hidden from us today and that will only become apparent in the future' (ibid.). Trujillo's work suggests that the car is one such hidden form of domination, which forms significant barriers against people living more localised, sustainable lives. These barriers are the result of a complex network of discourses and actions, many of which are unintentional and often hidden. She suggests that the 'potential disadvantages that [people trying to live sustainably] confront are not intentional. [But] intention is not always a necessary condition in order for injustice to exist' (Trujillo 2010, 72-3). In fact, she finds evidence of

> disadvantages created by the accumulation of otherwise non-harmful actions or situations. These do not only lack a clear or direct intention but are also the result of a series of loosely connected actions or situations. These become problematic only when they are seen in conjunction with one another, uncovering a systematicity that is otherwise difficult to show (ibid.)

And this invisibility has a double effect; not only does it make it difficult for people to recognise and understand it in the first place, but, if and when they do, it creates real barriers to challenging it. Highlighting nicely the paradoxical nature of freedom, these barriers often come in the form of claims of liberty, neutrality, diversity, and so on: for example, those arguing against cars are often denounced for denying the freedom of 'normal' people, for pursuing their *own* particular interests at the expense of others who are simply trying to get on with their own lives. Any attempts to challenge the dominance of the car is denounced as an infringement of people's basic freedoms, a claim repeated incessantly by the road lobby and happily echoed by many in the media. Iris Marion Young puts the point well: 'The standpoint of the privileged, their particular experience and standards, is constructed as normal and neutral'; when others try to expose this, or to demand that their own values are recognised

> [...] their claims are heard as those of biased, selfish special interests that deviate from the impartial general interest. Commitment to an ideal of impartiality thus makes it difficult to expose the partiality of the supposedly general standpoint, and to claim a voice for the oppressed (Young 1990: 115-116).

Importantly, as Trujillo's work makes clear, when Young talks of 'the privileged' this does not necessarily suggest an explicit division between class, or race, for example; rather, just as power must be seen as emanating from all areas of life, so too privilege can exist in a complex network of overlapping relationships; individuals may be privileged simply by virtue of the fact that certain of their understandings of the common good correspond with those of a majority within their community, and whilst they may be privileged in some aspects of their life, they may be oppressed in others.

Individual transport use, then, is heavily influenced by the wider community; at present, an unjust economic and political system has essentially forced the car onto the western world, but having done so, many of us have come to embrace the car, and to argue strongly against any attempts to limit its use. But this use denies others the ability to create the sorts of community *they* want to see: there is, in other words, a conflict, and it is one which is played out on our streets daily. What does this mean for the anarchist commitment to absolute freedom of the individual? Of course, many anarchists today would be strongly in favour of severely curtailing car use, because of the car's environmental and social impact. But people like their cars, and insist on their freedom to drive them, so how would anarchists, opposed to the coercion of the individual, respond to this? More importantly, whatever we, or future communities of anarchists, may think about the car, what is clear is that the organisation of a community will establish itself along certain norms, which will often in turn create certain physical, procedural and cultural parameters that shape our daily lives; and that this can occur in relation to all manner of aspects of daily life. It may be possible for individuals to exist outside of those parameters, but this will not always be the case, and, to the extent that it is, such existence may be accompanied by the very real effects of marginalisation. Living on the normative edges of society is perhaps something which anarchists now take pride in, but what about in a libertarian community, where the individual is supposed to be able to flourish? How will anarchists ensure that not only transport, but all the other elements that make up our daily lives, some fundamental, some trivial, will not result in denying the individual's freedom to live as they choose? Of course, anarchists can provide good moral arguments for restricting car use (or against other actions and beliefs people may wish to follow), but not everyone will accept them: some may argue cars can be greened with new technology, and that they offer a greater liberty than public transport which limits the individual's choice in other ways. It might also be reasonably argued that the break-down of the close-knit community which has been helped significantly by the rise of the car has helped people establish a more genuine autonomy, free from the 'censorious eyes of neighbours', as Colin Ward put it. Ultimately, a choice has got to be made; a choice that may result in people having their freedoms curtailed, and which will result in a certain ordering of daily life. Importantly, decisions which may appear to be technical (i.e., neutral) in nature (such as designing a town's transport system) may result in profound cultural changes that will radically shape the way people live their lives.

Conclusions.

So the reality of power is complex, and the infinite possibilities for its use and abuse (deliberate or otherwise) should be of real concern to anarchists. While the *capacity* of different individuals or groups to defend their own freedoms varies greatly, and so while the state, for instance, must remain a central target of anarchist activity, the somewhat mundane reality is that, whatever the social arrangement a community follows, day-to-day life will be permeated by at least the constant potential for freedoms to be denied. Crucially, power often operates without the awareness of those through whom it works, and for this reason, it is often 'invisible', in the sense that we may not realise where and in which ways it is having an effect. This is especially important for anarchists to realise, if their desire is to maximise the freedom of each individual: not only is the potential for oppression an ever-present threat, but it may be one which is extremely difficult to recognise, as Jo Freeman argued was the case in structureless groups. Anarchists must be humble enough to acknowledge the likelihood that, in many situations, they themselves may struggle to acknowledge the impact *their* choices have on the lives of others.

Saul Newman argues that '[t]he game of politics must now be played within the confines of power' but goes on to suggest that these "confines' are not inexorable and in fact open up unimaginable possibilities for freedom' (Newman 2001, 75). It is not clear, however, how the view of power Newman proposes opens up possibilities for freedom. Certainly, it can be argued that it is better to be aware of a problem than to be unaware of it, and in this sense, anarchists are better off if they come to terms with the complex reality of power[37]; but it does seem that, this aside, the anarchist's demand for absolute freedom must now be considered at best considerably more difficult, if not ultimately untenable. If individuals and communities can continue to exert power on those around them, if different ways of life continue to clash with no way to choose objectively between competing claims, then surely freedom will continue to be limited in an anarchist society. As I suggested earlier, contemporary anarchists are also aware of the problem of power, and they therefore insist that genuine freedom can only be found in genuine self-governance, which effectively means that every decision a community makes must be agreed to by all; they must, in other words, come to a *consensus*. However, being aware of a problem does not necessarily entail fully understanding it, so in the following chapter I will explain the contemporary support for consensus decision making, before going on to argue why it ultimately fails to safeguard individual freedom.

Chapter 5

From Majority Rule to the Tyranny of One: Conflict & Consensus Decision Making.

In the last three chapters, I have challenged the anarchist claim to be able to organise social life in such a way that freedom for the individual would be absolute; a way of organising society, in other words, without recourse to any forms of coercion or domination. However, in recent years, a great many anarchists (especially those involved in the direct action scene) have come to argue that, in order to prevent problems of conflict occurring, or at least to ensure that such conflicts are resolved *without* recourse to institutionalised forms of coercion, communities must come to a *consensus* on the decisions they make.[38] Can consensus perhaps solve the problems I have so far raised, and therefore rescue anarchism's belief in a truly free society? Before going on to explore this question in-depth, it will perhaps help to provide some context to consensus decision-making, in theory and in practice.

The Principles & Processes of Consensus Decision Making.

Since the Battle of Seattle, people have been struggling to name a movement that staunchly resists easy categorisation. Although its opponents (and those who simply aren't that interested) have been happy enough to lump everyone under the problematic term *anti-globalisation movement* (Graeber 2002, 3), those who are involved in or otherwise support the movement have tied themselves into knots, desperate not to do an injustice to the plurality of voices within this diverse human story, but equally keen to have *some* term, to mobilise around, and as a point of analysis and reference; whether it's for an academic article or a slogan on a t-shirt, we need to call this thing *something*. But naming it is only half the problem; *defining* it has proved similarly perplexing. Some call it the new anarchism, but the Zapitistas aren't anarchists; some call it the anti-capitalist, or *alter*-globalisation movement, but that term might include larger NGOs and certain leftist groups that many feel are simply not part of these new discourses of resistance.

One term that, as far as I know, has not been proposed is the *consensus movement*. Yet if one thing unites this movement, and which, conversely, leaves certain other elements out, it is the emphasis on *consensus decision making*, and related ideas of direct democracy, horizontal organisation, and so on. As David Graeber, one of the most prolific and articulate movement commentators, notes:

A constant complaint about the globalisation movement in the progressive press is that, while tactically brilliant, it lacks any central theme or coherent ideology [... But] it is not lacking in ideology. Those new forms of organisation are its ideology. It is about creating and enacting horizontal networks [...] networks based on principles of decentralised, non-hierarchical consensus democracy (Graeber 2002, 70).

Fellow activist and academic Uri Gordon agrees:

One of the most notable features of liberatory struggles today is their saturation with democracy. From the Zapatista consultas in Chiapas to the tactical spokescouncils held amid the tear-gas in Genoa, and throughout the everyday local work of radical grassroots collectives, non-hierarchical and direct-democratic models of organisation and decision-making have become default practice in the global resistance to capitalism and war (Gordon n.d.).

Consensus is not merely a *default* decision making process

however; for many activists, there is simply no acceptable alternative. No matter how long, difficult or tedious a meeting becomes, any attempt to move away from consensus will be viewed by many as an attempt to reintroduce hierarchy and authority through the back door. Consensus, in other words, is considered as being absolutely fundamental within this new movement, and within the school of contemporary anarchism so closely associated with it.

The basic theory of consensus is simple; everyone affected by a decision has a right to participate both in any discussions leading up to the making of that decision, and in the decision making itself (how to define *who* is affected by a decision is a problem I discuss below). When a collective, or community, needs to make a decision, everyone meets to discuss the matter at hand. Depending on the subject, these conversations may be straightforward exchanges of information, or heated debates, or anything in-between. At some point, some one will present a *proposal*. Once the proposal has been presented to the group to discuss, and it is clear everyone understands it, a facilitator will ask if there are any objections (known as blocks, or stand-asides); with everyone participating on an equal footing, ultimately, each individual has the right to block any decision. If there are no objections, the facilitator will again ask if everyone agrees; if they do, then the group has reached consensus. At times, the process is as simple as it appears here; when decisions are controversial, the process may become more convoluted. Often, a contentious proposal will be presented to the group, then discussed, then amended, discussed again, reframed, discussed some more, and so on. Experienced *facilitators*, and the use of numerous *facilitation tools*, can do much to help promote a good decision making process (Seeds for Change 2007a). Conversely, *bad process*, where, to cite a common example, people feel rushed into making a decision, can be seen as devaluing the resulting decision. As we shall see, the *process* involved in making decisions is absolutely integral to the idea of consensus.

The use of consensus decision making has become widespread within large elements of the social justice, peace, and environmental movements, a fact which has provided a great deal of encouragement and inspiration for many contemporary anarchists, because they see it as fitting with anarchist critiques of hierarchy and authority, and with a prefigurative approach to politics. Long-term autonomous spaces, such as lengthy protest camps and social centres, intentional communities, and on-going networks such as Indymedia, are all part of this new discourse of political activism. But it is overwhelmingly the use of consensus in briefer gatherings, the *temporary autonomous zones* we have already encountered, that is the main focus for anarchists, and which is held up as being exemplary of anarchy in action. In the last few years in the UK alone, a significant number of high profile temporary autonomous zones, such as the Hori-Zone eco-village in Scotland, the Camps for Climate Action, and the numerous Occupy! camps, have been organised and run by consensus, providing what many consider to be evidence of the feasibility of this deeply democratic process. The organisational specifics vary from one camp or network to another, but they more or less follow a similar logic, so a rough out-line of how some such spaces are structured should give the unfamiliar reader sufficient understanding of the basic principles, even if the precise details differ.

So a standard process might run something like this: a *network* is usually set up specifically to organise these autonomous zones, and the network's regular (normally bi-monthly) planning meetings are open to all and follow a strongly consensual approach to decision making. Within a larger network, which may consist of around a hundred people, smaller working groups will often be set up to focus on particular aspects of organisation, and these groups may operate with varying degrees of autonomy; but important decisions, including decisions about which decisions are important, will be made in plenary sessions where everyone involved in the network (at least, everyone present at that particular meeting) has a chance not only to speak, but also potentially to block any decision they are unhappy with. When the planning is finally over and these autonomous zones materialise, again, everyone within that space is able to speak and partake in decision making. Systems of *spokescouncils* are set up to help facilitate the day-to-day running of the space (Dupuis-Déri 2010, 52). The gathering will most likely be split up into neighbourhoods (or *barrios* as they are often called) with people freely choosing which neighbourhood to join. Morning meetings are held in each neighbourhood, and a number of spokes*people* (usually two, and ideally never the same people twice) are chosen to go to a following meeting, that of the spokes*council*, made up of each neighbourhood's spokespeople.[39] The spokespeople, or simply *spokes*, are usually not mandated to make decisions, but are simply there to pass information back and forth between the neighbourhoods and the spokescouncil. When decisions are needed, the spokespeople will announce this at the next neighbourhood meeting, or, uncommonly, call an emergency meeting; a decision will then be made by consensus within the neighbourhood, and the spokespeople can then relay this decision back to the spokescouncil. If needed, the process goes back and forth until a decision is reached. Thus, everyone at the camp has the potential to influence all major and many minor decisions, either by positively contributing to the discussion, or by actually blocking a decision. The process is made practically possible by the use of the spokespeople who are, in effect, *true* representatives, as opposed to appointed decision makers who decide for themselves how those who voted for them would want to be represented. Again, spokespeople can *only* consent to a decision in the wider network meeting if everyone in their own neighbourhood has also previously consented; conversely, if some one in their neighbourhood has blocked a decision, they must take that block to the spokescouncil meeting: a consensual decision made by the spokes, therefore, is in effect a decision consented to by *everyone*.

Consensus is also used in other spaces such as social centres, where a smaller affinity group may make decisions as to how the centre is run. People may use the centre and not get involved in the running of it, and may not therefore be involved in the decision making process, but if people are actively involved, then they will automatically gain the right to be involved in decision making. Large networks, such as Indymedia and Radical Routes, and smaller collectives such as Trapese, Rising Tide, and Bicycology, as well as many housing and workers' co-ops also work with consensus, and whilst every group or network may adapt the procedural elements to suit their particular situation, they all apply the same basic principles.

Inspirational, but how Viable?

Inspired, encouraged and excited by this proliferation of consensus in practice, activists have not hesitated in making claims about its effectiveness as a decision making process; they have also been quick to make claims about its applicability in much wider contexts (Dupuis-Déri 2010). Seeds for Change, a small but influential collective which has been promoting and teaching the use of consensus within the movement for many years, claims that consensus is a viable form of politics that can be used, not only in small groups, but 'even whole nations and territories' (Seeds for Change 2007a, 53[40]). Presenting a case study of the G8 Hori-zone eco-village/protest camp, one article implies that the temporary autonomous zone to which the study refers provides a good model of how an anarchist society might actually work:

The ecovillage offered a unique chance to experiment with consensus decision making on a large scale. This was particu-

larly exciting as one of the criticisms always levelled at
consensus is that it might work for 20 people but that it would
be impossible to organise whole communities or even
countries on this basis (59).

In other words, the camp was argued to negate claims that
consensus can only work in small groups, and, conversely,
demonstrated the possibility of consensus being used in much
larger scenarios. Whether explicitly or not, then, the use of
consensus in these autonomous spaces suggests a desire to
organise society at large through similar process, and a belief
that this is possible, which, in turn, suggests, in principle if not
always in name, support for something very much like an
anarchist vision of society. Not surprisingly, then, the increasing
use of consensus is seen as being both a considerable
achievement, and a vindication, of the anarchist movement; and
it is not simply politically inspiring, but also personally
rewarding. Indeed, I concur wholeheartedly with David Graeber
when he says that it 'is difficult to find anyone who has fully
participated in [consensus decision-making] whose sense of
human possibilities has not been profoundly transformed as a
result' (Graeber 2002, 15). The feeling of collectively organising a
gathering of hundreds, maybe thousands of people, of coming to
often difficult decisions after listening to the deeply felt concerns
and arguments of dozens of friends and strangers, the sense of
getting things done without a boss or a leader, all add to a
profound sense of empowerment and possibility.

Nonetheless, I find myself disagreeing with Graeber, and
many in the movement, when he draws the following
conclusion: 'It's one thing to say, 'Another world is possible'. It's
another to experience it, however momentarily' (ibid.). The
common sense view within the movement then is that the use of
consensus amongst activists offers not only a workable model for
a genuinely democratic politics, but also provides evidence of its

success; it is *anarchy in action*. But have we really experienced this *other world*? Have these experiments in consensus been simply smaller examples of what a truly decentralised, horizontal society could look like? Have we in fact witnessed *anarchy in action*? Many seem to think so; but whilst I share much of the excitement and enthusiasm, I would argue there are a number of serious problems that face this radically democratic process. I have already touched on some of these issues in Chapter 1, but here I want to explore them in greater depth, and specifically in relation to the use of consensus. So my primary task in the rest of this chapter is to shed some light on these problems and to encourage some much needed reflection, especially in light of the arguments presented in the previous chapters. These are not, however, simply problems about consensus: as I hope to demonstrate, the lessons we might take from the following discussion have very real implications for the libertarian dreams of anarchism more generally.

Consensus: A Dissenting Voice... A Tyranny of One.

We saw above that any individual involved in a decision making process is able to block a decision.

Although this might understandably be seen as constituting the right to veto, some activists in fact argue that it should not viewed in this way (Gordon, n.d.), and it is important to understand the reasoning behind this. If an individual, or a number of individuals, do block a decision, attempts will be made to accommodate their concerns; the idea is, however, that if the decision is likely to be blocked, more work needs to be done amending the proposal *before it is presented to the group for agreement*. In other words, it is the *process* of refining and altering proposals, of listening to everyone's concerns carefully and genuinely, that makes consensus work; and, as I suggested earlier, it is this process that many see as being the most important element of consensus. The block is there, at least in one sense, not *as a veto*, but as a tool to ensure *the need for a veto* never arises. In other words, it is felt that this process can only exist, or rather, is safeguarded by, the need to ultimately arrive at consensus. More conventional democratic debate which may theoretically incorporate similar normative ideals, such as giving everyone a voice, attempting to address everyone's concerns, and so on, can easily turn into little more than a façade, when everyone involved knows that the final decision in any particular process will fall on a limited number of individuals, who may or may not take their responsibility to adhere to these ideals seriously; *if we have the power to decide, or even if we know we're going to win the vote, why bother trying to resolve the concerns of a minority?* The knowledge that everyone has the capacity to block a decision, therefore, helps ensure that debates and decision-making processes are undertaken with a genuine and deeply felt commitment to values of equality, horizontality, and mutual respect. In other words, they are safeguarded from becoming a tokenistic gesture, as many would argue standard election processes are today (Plumwood 1995, 101).

I agree that there is much to be said in favour of the processes and tools developed by activists, and such techniques must surely be considered a useful element of any democratic politics that anarchists might hope to build. The skills and knowledge developed through the use of consensus are helping transform not only the nature of decision making; they are also fundamentally challenging the way in which politics is understood; in consensus, political decisions are not simply *consented to* by the people, but are *created by* the people. However, the *process* used by practitioners of consensus can be disentangled from the need to in fact *reach consensus*; indeed, I would argue it *needs* to be, because whilst the right to block decisions may well help this process in some respects, the price paid for such insurance may often be too high. Whatever the block brings to the process of decision making, it also clearly does in fact provide the capacity to veto, as some in the movement acknowledge (Graeber 2002, 71). Clearly, the ability for one individual, or a small minority,[41] to block a decision can lead to a situation where some members of a community are forced to accept the opinions of others; precisely the situation consensus is intended to ensure does not happen. As well as being inherently unjust, this process has the clear potential to tend towards a stagnating conservatism, where any new ideas about how a community might function will need the agreement of everyone in order to be implemented. In particular, new members of a community, and indeed children, as they become more active in decision making, may potentially be disenfranchised, as previously agreed to decisions will need a whole new consensus to over-rule them; whilst such consensus is always possible, it is equally possible that absolute agreement may not be reached, meaning that decisions made a generation ago will remain in force, even if the majority of the community has changed their opinions on the matter. So, in effect, consensus has the potential to add political weight to cultural traditions, which may over time make for some decidedly *il*liberal communities. The possibility of blocking decisions also creates scope for unsavoury bargaining and the formation of alliances, with, for example, people agreeing not to block a decision in return for some form of reward.

We might also ask at what stage consensus is deemed to be workable within the wider world; even if communities could be expected to *eventually* agree on all decisions, how long would it be before people who are perfectly happy with the status quo would stop blocking each and every decision that would otherwise chip away at their favoured forms of social organisation, their current privileges, and so on? At what point, in other words, is consensus expected to be a viable form of politics outside of the temporary autonomous zones in which it is currently practised? Crucial though it is, I have yet to see this question discussed within the movement. If we remind ourselves of some of the discussions in Chapter 2, are we, for example, to assume that consensus would only be implemented after the ruling classes had been 'forcibly suppressed and coerced into the anarchist society' (Schmidt & van der Walt 2009, 203)?

Consensus and the Common Good.

Anarchists claim that these recent experiments in consensus offer insights into how more libertarian forms of decision making may work, not only in small groups, but, as we saw earlier, amongst 'potentially tens or *hundreds of thousands* of people' (Seeds for Change 2007b, 5, my emphasis). As such, they point to 'what functioning direct democracy could actually look like' (Graeber 2002, 70). In short, consensus is frequently presented as offering a viable model for organising large, modern societies. However, activists also acknowledge that 'a necessary condition of consensus' is that 'we're all on the same side' and have 'overall shared aims' (Seeds for Change, n.d, 7). Consensus, in other words, will only work in groups that share 'fundamental principles' (Graeber 2002, 71). Indeed, activists have developed the idea of *principled* blocks, which relate to the founding principles of a group. For example: if a group is set up to stop a pipe-line being built, then some one in the group could make a principled block against the group's plans to support another pipe-line ten miles down the road, arguing that the group's core principles are opposed to pipe-lines per se. But a vegan could not raise a principled block against the group supporting a local dairy farm, because veganism is not part of the group's core principles. Groups using consensus, then, must have a shared understanding about their principles and values; this not only helps the group reach consensus, but can in effect justify the group rejecting a block because it is unprincipled. Conversely, groups with plural values, or unclear aims, will be less likely to reach consensus. Indeed, when 'people are not united by a common aim they will struggle to come to the deep understanding and respect necessary for consensus' (Seeds for Change 2007b, 4). But what, exactly, is meant by 'deep understanding'? If deep understanding and respect are necessary for consensus, what happens when they are absent, and consensus cannot be reached? How does this fit with those earlier claims, made by the same collective, that consensus is possible within entire nations? Surely there are many groups that will not be able to respect or understand one another? Isn't this precisely why many people regard the state and other institutions of authority, not with a rosy optimism, but as necessary evils? And how does this relate to the anarchist support for diversity? Doesn't the need for people to be 'united by a common aim' suggest very real limits to this diversity?

Does this support for consensus therefore suggest a failure to acknowledge, or realise, the potential for serious moral disagreements, as I suggested is often the case in Chapter 3? Are these *new* anarchists still committed to an Enlightenment inspired philosophy which sees morality as somehow naturally grounded, or which believes in the capacity for moral reasoning to be conducted on entirely rational grounds? Postanarchists such as Saul Newman and Todd May would certainly argue that this was the case for classical theorists, but what of their contemporaries (about which, curiously, they have almost nothing to say)? Unfortunately, as I argued in Chapter 1, and in the previous section, the emphasis on practice all too often side-lines overt discussions about such matters, and it is far from clear exactly what reasoning is taking place in such contexts; perhaps, as I suggested, there is no underlying philosophical assumptions at all, and such problems are simply being overlooked. Whatever the case, it seems clear that some reasonable agreement on what constitutes a common good, or some shared sense of values, is seen to be necessary for consensus to work; as such, the arguments I presented in Chapter 3 must considerably weaken the view that consensus is in fact a viable form of decision making in large, permanent, and unintentional communities.

So rather than offering a considered response to the critiques I have so far made, consensus appears to be supported *despite* them. And just as the anarchist approach to ethics failed to understand the extent to which power would continue to operate in an anarchist society, so too with consensus we see a similar failure to understand the consequences of a community unable to come to consensus, or how *power* will play out in communities that have internal disagreements about what constitutes the good life. I turn now to discuss this further problem.

Standing Aside; The Unavoidable Consequences of Decisions.

We saw at the end of Chapter 2 that within anarchist theory, freedom, even when viewed positively, is usually understood as an absence of institutional authority; that of the state, the church, the police force. When disagreements arise within a community, it is the state which imposes order; anarchism, however, denies both the moral legitimacy and the practical need for such an imposition; consensus decision making is in many ways the logical outcome of this. But I have argued that communities are unlikely to be able to reach consensus on every matter. One response to this is the use of the block, but I have also argued this too is unsatisfactory from an anarchist perspective, because it has the potential to simply shift authority from the majority to a minority. However, another option offered by practitioners of consensus is that of the *stand-aside*. The stand-aside is a commonly used and necessary element of the consensus process. According to the Seeds for Change collective, 'standing aside = not being involved in implementing a decision *or its consequences*' (Seeds for Change 2007a, 9, my emphasis).

Here we see a clear recognition of the fact that if a decision is not agreed by everyone, then there may well be some degree of coercion needed to enforce it; *unless* people block it, *or* stand aside. Although I have suggested that the block has not received the critical attention it deserves, on rare occasions it is nonetheless recognised that blocking a decision is problematic. The stand-aside, however, is intended to resolve this problem, because it allows a decision to go ahead whilst allowing those unhappy with it to be free from the decision's consequences; rather than resulting in a tyranny of a minority, then, the minority can simply stand-aside from majority decisions it disagrees with. This of course is the hope of the wider anarchist movement, whichever form of decision making is used. As Harold Barclay puts it:

> The fundamental difference between anarchist and democratic doctrine [...] is that the minority in the anarchist situation is not compelled by threat of police action to accept the majority decision. In anarchist theory, even if a decision were reached by a majority vote, it cannot be forced on the minority (Barclay 1997, 155).

Robert Graham argues in a similar vein that within anarchist theory, '[w]hat the majority cannot do is force the minority to obey its decisions' (Graham 2004, 22). Yet as we saw in the last chapter, even if we live without government, without the police, without institutionalised hierarchical authority, we still have to make decisions that will limit or deny entirely the freedom of others to pursue particular goals or values; these may be small, trivial issues, but they may well be fundamental to someone's idea of the good life. Graham, and other anarchists, might believe the majority *should* not force a minority to obey its decision, but would anarchism ensure that it *could* not, even if it didn't want to? In other words, can people really stand-aside, in the sense that they can avoid the consequences of certain decisions?

Anarchists who defend consensus appear at one and the same time to understand and miss this problem. David Graeber suggests that 'any society not based on violence ultimately needs to be based on consensus' (Graeber 2004, 34). If communities cannot reach consensus, forms of coercion[42] will somehow be imposed, even without a state; in other words, coercion, of one sort or another, is *the inevitable consequence of unresolved disagreements*. Surely then we are back to the absolute need for all members of a community to agree with every decision that affects them, something I have suggested in Chapter 3 is extremely unlikely in large, plural societies. Once again, it is useful to briefly consider the liberal response to these questions; doing so, we see further parallels between liberal and anarchist thought. As we saw in Chapter 3, the liberal philosopher John Rawls argued that a 'public and workable agreement on a single general and comprehensive conception [of the good life] could only be maintained by the oppressive use of state power' (Rawls 2001, 425). In recognising the fact of pluralism, and the unhappy consequences of any attempt to unify divergent interests, Rawls therefore sought to limit the actions of the state:

> Since there is no reasonable religious, philosophical or moral doctrine affirmed by all citizens, the conception of justice affirmed in a well-ordered democratic society must be a conception limited to what I shall call 'the domain of the political' and its values (Rawls 2000, 220).

In other words, because agreement cannot always be reached, we must limit the extent to which political decisions extend into people's daily lives. For Rawls, the state deals only with the political sphere, maintaining a broadly neutral social order in which individuals can pursue their own 'good life', without any, or any undue, interference from the state. However, Rawls' domain of the political suffers in much the same way as the concept of neutrality; how, precisely, are we to define a 'domain of the political' which is somehow separated from people's personal lives? For a number of fairly obvious reasons, anarchists have not employed the same imagery and language as Rawls, but I want to argue that in fact, a very similar *logic* is being used to define and defend consensus, and, in particular, the concept of standing-aside. Activists tend to talk about *action*, rather than *politics*: as Graeber puts it, '[d]ebate always focuses on particular courses of action; it's taken for granted that no one will ever convert anyone entirely to their point of view. The motto might be, 'If you're willing to act like an anarchist now, your long-term vision is pretty much your own business" (Graeber 2002, 72), and elsewhere he writes that the 'assumption behind all good consensus process is that one should not even try to convert others to one's overall point of view; the point of consensus process is to allow a group to decide on a common course of action' (Graeber 2004, 84-85). Like Rawls, then, anarchists appear to be suggesting that we can somehow separate the effects of certain decisions, into the 'realm of the political', or to specific actions; those opposed to such decisions need simply to avoid those actions, to stand-aside. Again, these ideas are echoed within wider anarchist thought. As Nicholas Walter argues,

> anarchists disagree little about private life, and there is not much of a problem here [...] All that is needed for the liberation of the individual is the emancipation from old prejudices and the achievement of a certain standard of living. The real problem is the liberation of society (Walter 1979, 55).

What we have here seems to be more or less the Rawlsian view of an overlapping consensus simply articulated in different terms; instead of the political domain, activists talk about action, but the idea is essentially the same: find points of agreement, and work with those, and leave the rest to some private realm: people's long-term visions are pretty much their own business, as Graeber put it.

But while we see here some acknowledgment of the *potential* power of a majority to force its decisions on a minority, even *without the state*, there is clearly a failure to properly consider the fact that this potential is very often realised regardless of the will of the majority: the stand aside, or the division between the public and private, fail to fully understand the distributed *effects* of this power. In other words, the stand-aside ignores the reality that, unless the minority leaves the community entirely, that minority will, with regards to many decisions, be seriously impacted by those decisions. A society that allows hard drug use does not force me to consume those drugs, but if I remain in that society, I have to live with the consequences of that policy. Put another way: how would I *stand-aside* from such a policy? Simply not taking drugs is surely no use, as it would clearly not help me address my concerns about serious drug use in my community. Clearly, any society could potentially encounter an endless number of similar problems, where the effects of a decision are unavoidably felt by those who opposed it.

As with the block, the possibility of standing aside is hugely problematic then, but there is no real sense within the movement that this is the case, and it continues to be promoted as a workable response to the majority of conflicts. However, at rare times anarchists recognise that conflicts will be so great that other options must be considered; namely, the splitting of a group, or the leaving of certain individuals within it. Whilst this may appear to negate my previous claims, I would suggest that even though this does suggest some acknowledgement of the potential for unresolvable conflict, the emphasis is overwhelmingly placed on the appropriateness of the stand-aside in most instances. My claim, then, is not that anarchists have entirely failed to see that standing-aside is not always feasible, but that they have failed to understand just how vulnerable the stand-aside is to the problems just discussed. Furthermore, the proposed solution, which I now turn to, is perhaps more problematic still.

Agreeing to Disagree... At a Reasonable Distance.

Although I have argued that there is a general silence with regards to the difficulties of consensus, occasionally anarchists are forced to recognise that there will be times when consensus cannot be reached; unfortunately, however, the standard response to this possibility is also hugely problematic. In fact, I would suggest that it simply fails outright to address these concerns.

When such dilemmas arise, many anarchists argue, the response is not to resolve them with, for example, another decision making process,[43] or an appeal to other values, but rather that one or more, or possibly all, parties involved simply go their separate ways (Seeds for Change 2007; Gordon 2008, 69; Maeckelbergh 2009, 226; Graeber 2009, 316). In a typical statement, David Graeber suggests that even when a decision is being made which has a 'bearing on the structure of the group, there's no one forcing [anyone] to stay' (ibid.). Or, as Ed Stamm notes, '[e]ach *community* can debate the issue of 'actual harm' for itself, and people can relocate according to their preference' (Stamn 1995, n.p, my emphasis). Marianne Maeckelbergh expands on such arguments, and argues that the possibility of individuals leaving communities, and even entire communities separating, must be considered a necessary element of an anarchist politics:

Above all, a decentralised democratic system needs to have a constituency that is not fixed but fluid. Individuals and groups [...] must have the option to sever links, to leave a group and to 'stand aside', so that one does not get held to a decision when one does not agree with it; otherwise consensus becomes much more difficult to reach, and outcomes become potentially 'oppressive'. For this fluidity of constituency to be possible, what constitutes 'the people' cannot be determined by geography. It would have to be determined by topic or issue and continuously reconstituted decision-by-decision. As challenging as this may sound, it is not impossible (Maeckelbergh 2009, 226).

These are common responses to difficulties arising within *activist groups*, and although this often results in situations that are less than ideal, it does indeed provide a practical response to the breakdown of the consensus process in these limited situations; the problem comes when such *groups*, and the problems they encounter and the tactics and theories they develop to resolve those problems, are held up as examples of how an anarchist *society* may function. The Seeds for Change collective again:

> One example is the Muscogee (Creek) Nation, where in those situations where consensus could not be achieved, people were free to move and set up their own community with the support, not the enmity, of the town they were leaving (Seeds for Change 2007b, 4).

The notion that, when a dispute arises between two or more groups within a community, resolution can be found by such groups reducing their proximity to each other may seem to some to be a remarkably naïve response. And, in fact, it is. Cultures, and the sociability we witness wherever we witness human life, are malleable and capable of ruptures, but only to a point. Cultures cannot simply pack up and leave. Neither can a shared history. Neither can knowledge grounded in a direct relationship with the land, its topography and weather, its flora and fauna. In other words, and contrary to Marianne Maeckelbergh's hopes, what constitutes a community very often will be determined by geography (and cultures grounded in that geography). Whilst nomadic movement might have been a feature of early humankind, it has not been so for the majority of humanity for a very long time. Contemporary mobility, much lauded within western ideologies, capitalism in particular, is still the preserve of a minority; at least, the enjoyable and rewarding form of it. Forced relocation, as a response to extreme conditions such as war or drought, are themselves the cause of considerable suffering. Less dramatically, but perhaps no less painfully, forced movement for reasons of seeking employment, to cite just one example, creates all sorts of personal and social problems. As Michael Walzer notes in a discussion concerning the negative effects of increased social mobility, '[m]oving may be a personal adventure in our standard cultural mythologies, but it is as often a family trauma in real life' (Walzer 1995, 60). Even if a group was willing to leave, it is far from clear that they would have somewhere else to go. At one time, it may have been easy enough for some members of a community to drift a few miles away, clear some trees, and build a new village or town. But nowadays land is scarce, and throughout much of the world there would appear to be little scope for communities to literally start afresh. The other option is for people to move to other existing communities; but what is to say they will be welcomed, that they will be able to cope with a sudden influx of new people, or that those leaving would want to begin a new life in an entirely new community? Even if we assume a group would be willing to move on and leave their houses and history behind, it is far from clear that there would always be somewhere suitable for them to go.

Which brings us to another problem; which group should leave? One writer notes: 'If no resolution is possible, the dissenting individuals can form another grouping or leave without fear of persecution by the rest of the group' (Stamm, 1995). But given the problems outlined above, it seems reasonable to assume that there would be resistance to moving, and therefore that no parties involved in the dispute would be happy to volunteer to be the ones to move on. We can also go on to consider that there are already clearly tensions within the community, such that separation is considered the only solution;

it seems unlikely that such a fragmented community would be able to agree on which party ought to be the one to leave. Stamm's suggestion, that it is the 'dissenters' who leave, not only relies on there being a clear understanding within the *whole* community of who the dissenters are, which seems morally and practically unreasonable, but also appears to punish them for their dissent; hardly an appropriate anarchist response. Yet apparently a rather common one. Michael Schmidt and Lucien van der Walt note unproblematically that

> [g]iven that the anarchist society would be a voluntary associ-
> ation, membership assumed a basic commitment and values
> of that society. Those who disagreed with those values were
> under no obligation to remain within a society with which
> they were at odds (Schmidt and van der Walt 2009, 70).

More worrying, they go on to note that 'equally, that society was under no obligation to maintain such persons' (ibid.). Such rhetoric sounds like that of the contemporary British state, with its border controls and citizen tests, and hints at worse still. One is reminded of the 'if you don't like it, move to Russia' nonsense of McCarthy-era America. It does at least acknowledge the problem of maintaining a libertarian society when members of it hold differing values; but if the response is one that would not look out of place in the right wing press, this raises very serious concerns for the anarchist project.

All things being equal then, the idea that, when disagree-
ments or conflicts arise, the proposed solution that one group simply moves away seems to be a far from satisfactory response. Indeed, as Sam Clark notes, it was circumscription, when 'people who would prefer not to submit to an incipient state are either unable to leave, or think the costs of doing so too high' that played a necessary, though not sufficient, part in the evolution of early states (Clark 2007, 80; see also Taylor 1982, 58). Not only

does this provide some historical evidence, therefore, that people will in fact be unable to move on even when they would like to, it also suggests that an inability to do so can lead to the creation of a powerful, dominant group or ideology, and possibly from this some form of state, that can force its norms on to weaker members of the community, who are forced for whatever reason to remain. True, it may well be the case that moving on *does* occasionally offer a realistic solution in a number of situations, especially for small numbers of individuals, but that this will always, or even often be the case seems extremely implausible.

The following responses, it might be argued, are question begging, in that they assume social conditions that may not exist in an anarchist society. Anarchism, so this argument may continue, will, *because* of the problems I outline, necessitate radically new forms of living, including, but perhaps not limited to, a renewal of nomadic lifestyles *by all* communities. To this I would simply respond that if anarchism *is* only viable by returning to nomadic lifestyles, we might reasonably question to what extent it can in all honesty be considered viable, and indeed *desirable*, at all.

Duty, Responsibility, and Care.

There is another problem with the response that conflicts can be resolved by groups separating themselves from one another. The concept of duty is, I accept, a problematic one; can people be said to have moral duties towards others, except when they are the result of certain actions, for example promises? I do not have space to pursue any in-depth discussions here; nonetheless, I think we can legitimately raise the basic concept of duty as a likely and valid source of objection to the idea of relocation; perhaps most effectively, we can utilise its negation, that is, the idea of abandonment.

One anonymous anarchist writer notes that '[s]ome communities will be dedicated to crime and drug use, and other commu-

nities will be intolerant of such choices and will defend against
them' (anarchy.net). It is of course hard to imagine an entire
community dedicated to crime; in fact, it is not clear how we
would conceptualise *crime* within a community if all its members
were committed to it. But we can leave these objections aside; the
point that the author here is making (I assume) is that some
communities will follow certain moral norms, and others will
follow others, and that, aside from one community defending
itself from another, interaction between the two need not occur.
The obvious objection to this is that many disagreements that are
likely to arise will involve a third party. If this dispute is of the
sort: John doesn't think Sarah should do *x* to *herself*, then we can
agree that Sarah will have a convincing case in saying that John
ought to mind his own business.[44] But if John doesn't agree with
Sarah doing *x* to *someone else*, then we immediately enter a very
different situation and quickly encounter a number of complica-
tions: Does the third party consent? *Can* he/she/they consent? Is
their consent considered genuine, informed, even relevant? How
would a concerned community know that they could protect the
third party any more appropriately? How do we separate and
understand paternalism and guardianship, authority and care?

Many moral disagreements will involve the treatment of a
third party, by which we can understand individuals, groups,
non-human animals and the natural environment, and even
man-made environments and objects. A simple example: a
community becomes divided about the use of children for hard
labour; some parents are using their own children to perform
hard, possibly dangerous tasks. The community is split as to
whether this is acceptable. A solution is offered whereby the
town is divided into two new, autonomous communities; one for
those opposed to such treatment, one for those in favour or
without strong opinions. Leaving aside all the problems of
physical relocation raised above, there remains a significant
objection to this proposed solution; if the disagreement comes in

the first place on behalf of a third party, i.e. the children, simply separating the community is not going to be a satisfactory response, because at least some of the third party in question will continue to suffer from the wrong that is the source of the conflict to begin with; so this is no resolution at all. At best, a situation would arise where two adjacent communities existed in a state of mutual antagonism, which is far from ideal. More likely, there would be an attempt by those opposed to the children's working conditions to force such behaviour to end, in order to defend the children in question. As we saw in Chapter 2, anarchists appear to be in favour of using coercion to stop exploitation, so why would this not be the case in this example? I think it is fair to assume that most anarchists would be of the opinion that to simply abandon an oppressed group in order to prevent conflict within a community is not a satisfactory response, and it seems that the issue of duty remains as a serious obstacle to the idea of resolution through relocation. That said, it is worth posing the question here, though I can do no more than that, as to whether anarchism can or should be seen as embodying an ethics of extreme toleration, in which even those acts we strongly disagree with are allowed, because to attempt to stop them will inevitably lead to a greater harm. I am not convinced by this, and it raises a number of paradoxical questions, such as why anarchism would exist at all, *at least as it defines itself against the state*, hierarchy, and so on. Still, it does appear occasionally that in a partial, and thus highly problematic and often disingenuous way, the idea of 'live and let live' motivates some elements of anarchism.

For practical and dutiful reasons then, the response that, when consensus fails, groups can simply divide themselves up into new, smaller communities is simply not an adequate response. The chances of diverse and permanent communities always reaching consensus must be doubted, and the proposed response to resolving problems when consensus is not reached must be considered untenable, undesirable, and often both. But what

about when consensus *is* reached? Surely that ought to be
something which we at least aim to reach? In fact, there are
reasons for concern even when consensus decision making runs
according to plan.

The Successes of Consensus?

Whatever criticisms I might lay at the door of consensus, it
continues to be applauded by most of those involved in the
contemporary anarchist movement, and anyone who has been
involved in a group or space organised using consensus will
understand why. In the setting where consensus is used, it is at
times an effective tool which, although sometimes difficult (and
remarkably tedious), really does get results. As we saw earlier,
many inspiring examples can be found of consensus in action,
and if and when it is experienced, it creates an undeniably strong
feeling that this is how politics ought to work; *this is what
democracy looks like*. At times I believe these feeling are justified,
but only at times. Anarchists also need to ask whether on some
occasions there is simply the belief that consensus has been
achieved when in fact it has not, or whether, when it has been
reached, it is done so in such a way that raises concerns about its
ultimate value. There are obvious ways that both these scenarios
might occur, and, in fact, practitioners of consensus are usually
keenly aware of them; the manipulation of individuals, the
withholding of certain information, emotional cajoling or even
blackmail, and so on. But there are other, less obvious ways in
which the process can be corrupted.

For John Rawls, the consensus process was backed up by a set
of basic liberties which could not be questioned; consensus, in
other words, needed to be premised on a predefined set of
values. This was a pragmatic response, intended to make the
overarching aim of consensus viable. Whilst anarchists might
reject this idea when presented in such an explicit manner,
preferring to believe that no freedoms will be denied, and no

coercion permitted, we have already seen how certain beliefs and actions are in fact readily denied, and how anarchists accept that shared values are crucial for consensus to work. It seems reasonable to assume that many of the values held now by anarchists, such as a commitment to anti-fascism, would be carried into an anarchist community, thus becoming the guidelines for an anarchist set of basic liberties. Consensus would have to rest on an underlying moral framework which would not be open to challenge, at least not easily. This may be as much as any libertarian can hope for; communities would certainly seem to need *some* degree of shared values, but the idea of consensus must therefore be understood to be to some degree predetermined and limited, and the consequences of this ought to be more honestly acknowledged. As I suggested earlier, there appears to be an under-acknowledged tension between the desire to have a genuinely open, libertarian process, and the recognition that consensus is limited by the need for agreement about certain values. This tension can theoretically be resolved without recourse to coercion, if it is assumed that all members of a community will freely choose sufficiently compatible moral values, and it would seem that this is the unspoken hope of practitioners of consensus. Furthermore, there is the important question (which I have space only to comment briefly on here, though it is one worth pursuing in more detail elsewhere) as to the limits of the discursive methodology employed by practitioners of consensus. The implicit assumption with the consensus model is that we are rational agents who can articulate our needs and desires in ways which will be understandable by other, similarly rational agents. This approach clearly echoes the work of Jürgen Habermas (1993) though not surprisingly his work appears to be little known within the activist community. Habermas' notion of deliberative democracy suggests that, in what he called an 'ideal speech situation', people would be able to reach agreement through rational debate; we might well say

that the facilitation tools used by activists are an attempt to reach
such an ideal speech situation. This position, however, has been
critiqued by feminists and others (see, Mehhan, 1995; Devaux
2000) for assuming, as John Rawls does, that there can be a
neutral and public form of reason which everyone is equally able
and willing to employ when engaging in ethical and political
discourse. As Monique Deveaux states:

> The view that participants in dialogue are likely to be
> persuaded by the same public reason relies in part on a
> distorted view [...] about the main source of political [...]
> disagreement in plural societies (Devaux 2000, 152).

Rather, we must acknowledge that many disagreements stem
from 'group based differences in our ethical and cultural frame-
works' (ibid). Reason, in other words, is not a universal tool
which anyone can use, and even when it is used, it is used differently by different people. Just as Rawls failed to see that his view
of basic liberties was inherently skewed to reflect his own values,
so too is the notion of reason itself. Whilst the use of reason, and
the potential to engage in rational debate, should by no means be
dismissed entirely, we must acknowledge that there are clear
limitations to this approach. The power of values (which may or
may not be articulated rationally), of tradition, of emotion, of
personal and group psychologies, all these things come into play
when people are discussing how their lives are to be organised,
and these place certain limits on the likelihood of achieving
consensus through reasoned debate.

Conclusions.

For contemporary anarchists, consensus is increasingly seen as a
fundamental part of anarchism; in fact, we might go further, and
suggest that it is seen as the very expression of anarchism;
consensus and anarchism are not simply linked, they are the

same thing. As we saw earlier, David Graeber argues in relation to the globalisation movement that these 'new forms of organisation are its ideology' (Graeber 2002, 9). But if my arguments so far are right, or even partially so, contemporary anarchists need to recognise the intrinsic limits of consensus, *and* understand that anarchism is about more than a decision making process. However, I want to end this chapter with some more positive thoughts. Consensus can be an effective tool in certain situations; the workplace for example, or perhaps in neighbourhood associations and other similar, small-scale scenarios. Furthermore, the tools used by practitioners of consensus could play an important role in making other decision making processes as democratic as possible. Of course, the question as to how much consensus *as result* makes consensus *as process* so effective must for now remain an open one; if people know that at the end of a discussion, a vote will be taken, can that discussion ever be as genuinely focused on resolution as it would be if consensus was required? Whatever the answer (and indeed, there is likely to be no *one* answer for all situations) I believe that the tools of the consensus process can be disentangled from the view that absolute consensus is always possible.

Proponents of consensus, and indeed all anarchists, must also begin to ask broader questions about the organisation of social life; questions which, I have argued, do not arise in temporary autonomous zones, and which are all too rarely asked. How long do decisions made by a community last? Are they open to constant review, to be re-negotiated whenever some one changes their mind? What happens if some one arrives from a new community; can she demand old decisions be opened up for debate? And what about children? At what age does their consent become valued? They, after all, will have to live with some decisions longer than those who are making them. And we might also ask, given the increasingly connected world we live in, how we decide which decisions affect which people; burning coal in

Glasgow could be argued to affect indigenous communities in northern Canada, and there are of course many such less extreme examples that a community might be expected to ponder, so how exactly is such connectivity to be understood? Perhaps some global spokescouncil might be considered; the movement certainly prides itself on making consensus decisions about large protests that concern and involve tens of thousands of people all over the world; but again, we need to ask more practically oriented questions about day-to-day life in anarchist communities. At the moment, such discussions are simply not being had.

If consensus is not always possible, then the anarchist commitment to freedom remains as problematic as it appeared to be in previous chapters. Anarchists are left facing the problems of conflict, of values, of power, and they must begin to accept this, and to work towards a libertarian politics that can offer, not absolute freedom, but a much greater freedom, and a much deeper level of social, political and economic equality, than liberalism, or communism, have been able to provide. Although such a project is undoubtedly vast, and my central aim of this work has been to argue for the need to discuss such a politics, rather than define my own view of what it may look like, in the final chapter I want to offer my own tentative thoughts; reflecting on the problems I have so far outlined, and accepting the limits of freedom, I believe a less perfect, but far more viable anarchist politics *can* be imagined.

Chapter 6

Melting the Snow: How Anarchism Prefigures Anarchy.

A goal which is infinitely remote is not a goal at all, it is a deception (Alexander Herzen, quoted in Ward 2008, 164).

So far, it would be fair to say that my analysis of anarchism has been highly critical. Yet none of what I have had to say has been written with the intention of encouraging the reader to abandon anarchism (or to continue dismissing it). In fact, my rather grandiose hope is that, in challenging anarchism so thoroughly, I will not have killed it, but made it stronger. Of course, what *it* is, that is, what sort of anarchism I hope to salvage, remains to be seen, and may not be to everyone's taste. Addressing the concerns I have raised will certainly require tampering with a number of anarchist taboos, and may ultimately be seen as making too many compromises. The reader must judge for herself if my solutions are acceptable. However my tentative responses to these problems are received, what I hope is now less contentious is my claim that anarchism is currently ill-equipped as a political philosophy, suffering as it does from a number of significant problems. Such problems will need to be over-come, or at least considered with greater honesty, if anarchism is to receive significantly wider support than it currently does; and if it is to succeed (if and when it gets the chance) in its efforts to create a fairer world. I hope, in other words, to have at the very least demonstrated that *something* needs to be done.

Before beginning this final chapter, it is worth recapping the main arguments so far. In the first chapter, I suggested that claims that anarchism can and indeed does exist in practice must be critically scrutinised; the much-lauded examples of anarchy in action,

I suggested, did not correspond to the absolute ideals of anarchism as a means of organising modern, plural and large societies. In Chapter 2, I argued that freedom will always need to be moderated in some way, partly because, as I showed in Chapter 3, people holding different ethical values will at times disagree about which freedoms should be promoted or denied. In Chapter 4, I suggested that even without the state, communities will continue to embody networks of power, which will endorse (and, indeed, enforce) certain values over others; anarchists cannot walk away from this reality, no matter what their ethical ideal might be, and no matter what form of social organisation (or lack of) they adopt. The anarchist support for absolute freedom, and the concomitant rejection of all forms of domination, appears to be indefensible. In the previous chapter I turned to the idea of consensus-decision making, to see if this could provide a satisfactory response to the problems identified in the earlier sections of the work. In fact, I argued it could not. Anarchists must come to terms with the limitations that this critique suggests; power can and will be used to defend certain liberties over others, certain values over others, certain ways of life over others. Rather than constituting a dismissal of anarchism, however, I believe that anarchism should be understood, not as a negation of this reality, but as an attempt to respond to it in a certain way.

In this final chapter, I want to outline a number of responses to the challenges anarchism faces. However, I have argued that anarchism encounters *numerous* problems, and although some may be considered as being interdependent, it would be far too simplistic to claim that everything I have argued so far is reducible to one core problem; even if this were the case, I would argue against attempts to pin down the one, true, logical response to it. It is not my contention then that what follows in this chapter is logically dictated by the problems I have presented, and, clearly, not every position I defend here purports to solve every issue previously raised. Rather, this chapter offers a more holistic response to a complex set of problems, and makes no claims to be either entirely sufficient, or absolute. My hope is that it is, simply, helpful. However, with little space left, I can do no more than offer sketches, but this is perhaps the way it should be. I do not intend to trample on anarchist principles to such an extent that I believe a perfect blueprint can or should be constructed; but I do believe that anarchism would benefit from more detailed discussions about how life without the state might look. The time has come for anarchism to recognise that it needs to engage with the difficult questions of how it would organise society in the twenty-first century, and, more importantly, what it hopes to offer people, today. Fortuitously, these two concerns, anarchism's present, and its future, are intimately linked by anarchists' commitment to a prefigurative form of politics. And it is through a prefigurative approach that anarchism can, I believe, make a real difference, here, now, and beyond. However, whilst the value of prefiguration is widely recognised within the anarchist movement, once again we encounter confusion, contradiction, and a general lack of analysis when we scratch beneath the surface of the anarchist common sense. If prefiguration is to be more usefully employed, like so many other anarchist ideas, it first needs to be better understood.

Prefiguration: What, When and How?

So, what is prefiguration exactly? And, more importantly, how does it figure in the anarchist common sense? Perhaps the most important thing to begin by noting is that prefiguration actually refers to two different though closely related ideas. Firstly, prefiguration suggests a consistency between means and ends, a consistency which is viewed as being central to the anarchist tradition (Ehrlich et. al. 1979, 3). For example, unlike Marx, who believed the state could be used in the initial stages of a post-revolutionary society but who also argued that the state would eventually wither away, anarchists stress the importance of only employing political tactics which are commensurate with their ultimate goals. If you want a world without a state, you cannot use the state to achieve this aim. Secondly, prefiguration is understood as the realisation of one's politics in the here and now, as opposed to waiting for the revolution; it is the famous building of the new society in the shell of the old. Although these two understandings are clearly linked, there is also a tension between them. On the one hand, there is a demand for consistency between means and ends, and on the other, for an anarchist politics to be *lived*, here and now. But how can means and ends remain consistent within a wider context deeply antagonistic to anarchist principles?

The traditional answer to this dilemma has been to withdraw from situations where such conflicts might arise: party politics, hierarchical organisations, and so on, and, conversely, to create spaces of autonomy where no such compromises are necessary. Yet whilst entirely understandable and laudable, this response raises questions and problems of its own. Firstly, as I argued in Chapter 1, it helps create and re-enforce the notion that anarchy in action can and does exist in some sort of bubble, independent of the wider world that surrounds it, leading many anarchists to cite such activities as examples of anarchism's viability. In continuing to see such examples of anarchy in action as being simply small-scale and temporary articulations of what we might expect from a genuinely anarchistic society, with little or no acknowledgement of the wider context within which they exist, anarchists fail to see that their current practices do not sufficiently answer the question *how would an anarchist society actually work*? This creates a sort of theoretical vacuum, whereby anarchists consistently fail to see that a fully functioning anarchist society would need to address all manner of problems that simply don't arise in their autonomous spaces. In short, it means anarchists don't ask enough questions of themselves, or provide enough answers. In part because of this, and in part because of the commitment to only using libertarian means, anarchists consciously refrain from creating blue-prints, which are seen as either unnecessary (because we have the answers already, through examples of anarchy in action) or because to do so would be to impose a temporal hierarchy (authoritarian means) by defining the social and political structures of a society which does not yet exist.

Secondly, this leads to a somewhat dogmatic and often arbitrary set of mostly unspoken codes of what is and what is not acceptable anarchist behaviour. The assumption that anarchists can operate autonomous of the state, or of capitalism, is ultimately flawed: an anarchist social centre may be run along libertarian principles, but will always remain a part of a more complex relationship. In other words, they do not, and *cannot*, create a purely libertarian space. This does not automatically negate the worth of such experiments, but it raises a further question as to how this relationship is understood: why are some compromised means (using money, for example) acceptable, and others (becoming a councillor, say, or voting within anarchist groups) not? To think of this another way, we can begin to see that there is in fact no truly *autonomous* zone, temporary or otherwise; anarchy in action currently exists in a complex and multi-faceted relationship with liberalism and capitalism (not to mention religious and other discourses). For the time-being at least, anarchism must come to terms with its interdependence with a world that is often at odds with its own strict ethical principles: doing so may help anarchists recognise that they are already forced to make concessions to some of their more strict principles; this does not mean that anarchists should simply start to compromise more and more, but it does suggest the need for a renewed assessment of what constitutes appropriate anarchist action.

Finally, in a similar vein, prefiguration currently presents anarchists with what I would suggest are unnecessary obstacles, because anarchists themselves have a number of unrealistic expectations about the nature of an anarchist society. But if anarchists hold unrealistic expectations about possible *ends*, as I have argued they do in relation to their basic libertarian ideals, for example, then the *means* they use to reach them are likely to be too stringent. Crucially, this is *not* an argument for compromise or pragmatism. I am not suggesting that anarchists ought to sever the link between means and ends, which would be to ultimately reject prefiguration. Rather, anarchists must accept that the ends they seek must be understood as necessarily partial; anarchism will never provide a perfectly libertarian end, so anarchist means to achieve liberation need not be perfectly libertarian either. To cite an example already discussed in the previous chapter; the idea of consensus is given so much weight within contemporary anarchism because it is understood as the only decision-making procedure that will not result in any form of coercion. Voting, on the other hand, is condemned as inherently authoritarian. However, if my analysis so far is correct, such a critique of voting, in otherwise egalitarian environments, loses some of this strength, because we come to see that there will always be times when some degree of conflict, and coercion, is possible. Simply put: consensus will not always be possible, and if anarchists continue to argue that it is, then they are destined to be chasing an illusionary dream, and, what is worse, liable therefore to ignore or reject more viable alternatives.

I believe that, when appropriately acknowledged, all of these concerns can be viewed positively and turned to anarchism's advantage; we can begin to see experiments with prefiguration as a blurring of the boundaries between anarchism and liberal democracy[45], creating space both for anarchist theory to grow, and for liberal democratic theory to be pulled in an increasingly libertarian direction. Some readers may well argue that this is indeed a compromise, allowing anarchism to be contaminated by liberal democracy; or, we can reverse this, and see liberal democracy as increasingly contaminated by anarchism (Plumwood 1995, 102-3). I believe anarchists ought to embrace the latter option[46]; crucially, anarchists must stop seeing this interaction as a compromise that sullies the good name of anarchism, and begin to see it as an opportunity. As Colin Ward put it, the 'choice between libertarian and authoritarian solutions is not a once-and-for-all cataclysmic struggle, it is a series of running engagements' (Ward 2008, 164). However, in the idea of the temporary autonomous zone, as it is commonly understood, anarchy in action has too often resulted, not in running *engagements*, but in running *away* from situations which are deemed contrary to anarchism's basic principles; the fear of corruption, of working with 'impure means', has resulted in a tendency towards *dis*engagement. Yet anarchism, in its rejection of hierarchical and centralised authority, can be understood as offering a continuing critique of the way in which liberal politics currently manifest[47], alongside very real strategies for reducing such authoritarian forms of social organisation; but it can do so most effectively by practising forms of prefigurative politics which engage with the wider world, in anarchistic ways. Doing so, it seems to me, is the surest way to create, not more and more temporary and autonomous spaces, but the seeds of a new world which may one day become permanent and wide-spread. Furthermore, whilst these examples of anarchy must be understood to provide only partial glimpses of what a fully-fledged anarchist society might look like, these insights are nonetheless extremely important; we simply need to accept that they do not provide anything like a full picture.

Although there are certainly some notable exceptions to the picture I have painted (the work of the Haringey Solidarity Group being just one[48)] I believe that currently anarchists are not making the best use of prefigurative politics, and that a serious engagement with its problems and potential is much needed. In order to open up more spaces in which anarchist politics can have a direct impact, I want now then to explore how prefigurative politics could function more effectively, taking into account not only the concerns presented in this chapter, but also the earlier discussions about freedom, power, and ethics; to do so, I separate prefiguration into what I call *social* and *personal* prefigurative politics. Such a division is primarily a theoretical tool, to help analyse more clearly what are in fact two overlapping and mutually dependent ideas.

Social Prefiguration: Building the New Society.

The creation of libertarian alternatives to those things usually provided by the state, or the capitalist market (housing, places of work, healthcare, education, and so on) is a long established tool within anarchist politics; as such, I do not want to spend too much time discussing the precise details of such projects. However, within the contemporary anarchist movement, such projects are, whilst valued, nonetheless given considerably less priority than those forms of action with which the term *direct action* is usually associated: summit mobilisations, blockades, office occupations, etc.; in other words, protests.[49] It seems worthwhile, therefore, to highlight why social prefiguration is such a useful tool; indeed, *more* useful, I would suggest, than the direct action protests which currently consume the majority of anarchists' energy.

Social prefiguration, as I understand it, is the creation of spaces and processes which fulfil the needs and desires of members of any community, and which do so along anarchist principles of horizontal control and mutual aid, as well as incorporating other values which anarchists might well be expected to endorse, such as sustainability. The results of such prefiguration are what Chris Carlsson calls 'nowtopia' (Carlsson 2008); more commonly, the concept of 'DIY' is used within activist circles (Holtzman et. al. 2007; Trapese Collective 2007). Such initiatives may exist outside of the established order, and may even be illegal, or open to legal dispute; squats and land-based projects where semi-permanent communities are created without planning permission being examples of this. Other projects may have more direct, and even, to some extent, agreeable, relationships with the wider world; for example, housing and workers' co-ops, which rely on mortgages and market exchange respectively, and which are more open and amenable to pro-actively engaging with members of the wider community. Home or community education, of children and adults, alternative health care projects, community allotments, cultural spaces and events, environmental schemes (composting, tree-planting and so on), bike workshops, local economic trading schemes, and countless other projects exist with more or less participation with the wider community and its established institutions, norms and practices. As such, few, if any, of these can be said to be fully prefigurative, in the sense that, to some extent, they are all reliant on, or restricted by, non-anarchistic methods of social organisation. Furthermore, although they create alternatives to profit-making companies and state run services, they do not directly challenge them; although there will clearly be points of tension and possibly conflict, it is possible for both to co-exist. In particular, workers' co-operatives still operate within the market paradigm, which is consistent with Proudhonian mutualism (see Prichard 2010), but which is opposed by the majority of anarchists. As such, it is common within the anarchist movement to see such activities as little more than reformism. Although they are generally accepted, and indeed appreciated on a personal level, they are often dismissed in strategic terms; all well and good, but hardly revolutionary (see McKay 2010). However, whilst social prefiguration is not *sufficient* in and of itself for bringing about radical social change, I believe it is *necessary*, and that it should be given much greater emphasis within the anarchist movement.

Such spaces provide opportunities for experimentation and education that cannot be found elsewhere. This is absolutely vital, because any shift towards a more libertarian world is likely to meet a great many obstacles, but whilst some, such as explicit military intervention, are acknowledged, the psychological and discursive barriers people (anarchists included) are liable to encounter are too often over-looked. This becomes especially true when the critiques raised in previous chapters are recalled; if and when the state disappears, humanity will not simply exist in a peaceful and harmonious community. Nor can we simply make a rational choice one day to act as good anarchists, rather than as efficient, individual consumers. Learning how to work, live, and play in horizontal communities is not something that can be taken from theory to practice at the individual's choosing. Our habits and norms, which currently reflect a competitive and hierarchical world, need to be undone, and consciously replaced with new values. Such projects become, in the words of Chris Carlsson, 'a breeding ground for strategic and tactical thinking and practices that confront the everyday objectification to which capitalism reduces us all' (Carlsson 2008, 4) and therefore 'constitute the beginnings of new kinds of communities' (ibid., 6). Errico Malatesta made a similar argument, and whilst stressing that co-operatives were not revolutionary in and of themselves, he

> recognise[d] the extreme usefulness that co-operatives, by accustoming managers to run their own affairs, the organisation of their work and other activities, can have at the beginning of a revolution as experienced organisations capable of dealing with the distribution of goods and serving as nerve centres for the mass of the population (Malatesta 1965, 115-6).

Proudhon also defended such a position, arguing that the more people began to *live* their politics on a daily basis, especially in the workplace, the closer they would be to creating a better society. As Alex Prichard explains, Proudhon 'advocated a gradualist (r)evolution' which 'could be achieved through the socialisation of title through workers' co-operatives and trade and communal federations' (Prichard 2010, 108). Such processes take time, and as painfully slow as it may seem, if anarchists take their politics seriously, such work must begin here, and now.

However, there is a further criticism of such initiatives, and especially workers' co-ops, which suggests that, based on market principles and embedded within a wider capitalist context, they are forced to make too many compromises. As Iain McKay argues, 'Eco-friendly technology [...] is often more expensive than its rivals' (Mckay 2010, 15) so market forces would either force co-operatives to ignore eco-friendly alternatives, or have their survival threatened. He continues:

> In terms of environmental impact, a self-managed firm must still ensure sales exceed costs in order to survive and so the economy must grow and expand into the environment. As well as placing pressure on the planet's ecology, this need to grow impacts on human activity as it also means that market forces ensure that work continually has to expand (ibid., 16).

Furthermore, such projects 'could even degenerate back into capitalism as any inequalities that exist between co-operatives would be increased by competition, forcing weaker co-operatives to fail' (ibid.). Although anarchists must take these concerns with the seriousness they deserve, as out-right objections they are empirically contestable, and over-look two very important points that go to the very heart of the prefigurative project. On a concrete level, McKay's claim that co-operatives will be forced to abandon their principles to compete on the open market is simply untrue (assuming, as it appears McKay is willing to do, that we accept that the very act of setting up a co-op is not in itself such a compromise). In fact, many co-ops exist that stick firmly to their principles, even though they may well suffer economically as a result (a point I return to below), and McKay does their often-thankless work a great disservice by ignoring their efforts. Clearly, some give into the pressures (or promises) of the market, and slowly but surely their principles fade; and others, unwilling to compromise, do sadly fail. But what political strategy does not suffer from elements of failure? As Chris Carlsson argues

> all the foibles, contradictions, vices and confusions that beset anyone living in this mad world affect [such projects...]. Nevertheless, the experience that accumulates in them over time can be a fertile ground for new initiatives that might break out of this pernicious circle (Carlsson 2008, 236-8).

Holtzman et al. make a similar point, when they note that although such projects 'still take place in a monetary economy [...] commodities produced in a DIY fashion have expanded their use-values in relation to their exchange-value' (Holtzman et. al. 2007, 45). As such, these projects become 'part of the process of undermining capitalism by forming relationships not intended by capitalism' (ibid.). Whilst the problems of performing prefigurative politics within a capitalist economy must be constantly borne in mind, they do not ultimately diminish the importance of such projects. And, as noted, McKay's arguments also miss two core features of social prefiguration. McKay argued that market pressures would force co-ops to run in environmentally unfriendly ways, because the market would force them to pursue economic, rather than ecological, goals. However, once again, this is countered by real examples, and by a wider theoretical argument; many co-operatives exist with a strong emphasis on *creating*, or relearning, viable alternatives to unjust or unsustainable practices (see Carlsson 2008 for a lengthy analysis of this point). *Growing with Grace*, the local workers' co-op where I get my vegetables from, is dedicated to growing food in as sustainable way as possible. As such, its members are playing a vital role in the much needed process of recreating a viable food production system in this country; something which we have all but lost in the last fifty years or so. They also offer much needed pockets of bio-diversity, as well as helping maintain traditional seed lines, without which we would lose many varieties of fruit and vegetables which, unlike most of the food we currently eat, is suited to the local environment and therefore essential to any sustainable, localised community. Although referring to intentional communities rather than workers' co-ops (which often perform similar functions), Geoph Kozeny highlights succinctly the value to be gained from prefigurative projects:

In the twenty-first century, the experimentation extends to technological innovations and environmental practices, with members of intentional communities at the forefront of implementing and testing such technologies as straw bale construction; solar, hydro, biodiesel, and wind-powered energy systems; composting toilets and managed wetland water treatment; and organic agriculture and permaculture (quoted in Coates 2007, 13).

Without such projects, any potentially sustainable world that may come once McKay's preferred revolutionary tactics became effective would suffer from a very real lack of essential knowledge, skills, and environmental potential. Here and now, anarchists must begin the process by which they might eventually achieve, not only metaphorically, but also quite literally, 'the conquest of bread' (Kropotkin 1985, 66-88).

The second point is that a critique of *'market* pressures' can often obscure the fact that all manner of *pressures* exist, and will continue to exist, whatever the economic or political system we adopt. The critique of the previous chapters suggests that the freedoms demanded by individuals may conflict with one another, and that there will be unavoidable power relations between them; this point, I argued, is frequently missed by anarchists, and this is perhaps no more evident than in many radicals critique of the market. I am no fan of capitalism, but it has not created every problem in life, and a non-capitalist world would still be one where difficult choices have to be made between the producers or providers of certain services and goods. Such decisions are not simply a result of the way the world is currently organised; *market* pressures also relate to very real limitations in resources, of time, of people, of the environment, and such limitations will always exist. The market may currently bully companies into cutting corners to save money, but libertarian communities will also face pressures to make environmentally unsound decisions when doing so will result in greater luxuries or easier working conditions. To believe that it is only the market which creates such conflicts is to believe in a possible world where there are no constraints on resources; a *post-scarcity* anarchism, as Bookchin called it (1974). Bookchin's astute environmental observations, however, were clouded by a naïve optimism in the potential of technology to solve problems of production and consumption, a position which is no longer deemed tenable by many anarchists, and rightly so (see Gordon 2008, Ch. 5, for a useful overview of this). Communities will always have to make decisions about how they want their lives to be organised; and such decisions will often involve workers, for example, and tensions may grow between producers and other members of the community, or between two groups of producers. Such conflicts and tensions are not, in other words, simply the result of a market economy, but are an inevitable consequence of a plurality of values existing on a finite planet (see Fairlie 2010 for an interesting discussion about the many ethical and cultural choices about food production that communities will need to make in a post-oil world). Such problems will not simply disappear if and when state-capitalism does, but we can always make better choices with the limitations we will inevitably still face. Developing procedures for making this easier is a process of individual learning, not the creation of rigid protocol. Once again, the benefits of beginning such a process now cannot be overstated.

Furthermore, such projects should not only be viewed in isolation. Radical Routes,[50] a network of radical co-ops based in the UK, is active in supporting housing and workers' co-ops. As I write, some of its members are busy trying to get the best possible results out of the government's decision to disband the Financial Services Authority. This engagement with government (which created considerable discussion about reformist politics within the network) could be seen as akin to the sort of politics that unions often undertake. Indeed, there is increasingly excited discussion within the network about the potential for a radical co-operative movement to expand in a more organised, and explicitly political, direction; one which could potentially engage with politics, as unions do, but which was also prefigurative. Not only is each co-op within Radical Routes based on anarchist principles, but so is the network as a whole. Such an approach could help unite many of those involved in such projects (who tend to also be engaged with the movement I have been discussing) with other, more traditional anarchist trajectories, such as Solfed, or the IWW, for example.[51] Malatesta, again, saw the role of co-operatives as similar to that of trade unions, as both offered the possibility of experimenting with new forms of relationship, and so preparing people for an anarchist future (if and when unions were run alongside more libertarian grounds) whilst both offered more immediate reforms which could help bring working-class people, unwilling to wait for a revolution, on-board (Malatesta 1965, 115-6; see also Sparrow 1997).

So, social prefiguration offers a multitude of direct and indirect avenues for anarchists to pursue their political goals; it provides a concrete way to engage with anarchist politics, is often personally rewarding and inspiring, and it creates much needed space to experiment with and reflect upon the process of reducing hierarchies and living with fewer and fewer levels of authority and control. One slightly critical note I would add is this: as I have argued so often in this work, anarchists display a strong tendency to be too uncritical about their own politics. Not surprisingly, discussions about these prefigurative projects tend to over-emphasise the positives, and under-emphasise the negatives. Radical Routes is one more example used by activists to point to the viability of anarchism, and in particular, of the consensus process; yet there are already signs that, as the network grows, Radical Routes is struggling to achieve consensus on certain issues, occasionally reverting to voting (Nicholson 2007). Although this uncritical support is under-standable, it is ultimately damaging. If the process of social prefiguration continues to grow, critical voices will no doubt appear, but the sooner they do, and the more they come from *within* the movement itself, as supportive, rather than dismissive criticism, the better. *Social* prefiguration is also made much stronger, and is often entirely dependent on, a more personal approach to political change. I turn now to the question of personal prefiguration, or lifestyle politics.

Personal Prefiguration: No Gods, No Masters … No Excuses.

Although the subject generates frequent and heated debates on anarchist email lists, at gatherings, and so on, the issue of lifestyle politics has rarely been written about in depth. Not only academic, but also activist literature, tends to ignore the issue. One very well-known text which people may refer to with reference to the lifestyle debate is Murray Bookchin's essay, *Social Anarchism or Lifestyle Anarchism* (1995). It is worth explaining briefly then why Bookchin's essay, and his use of the term itself, has no real relevance to my own discussion. For Bookchin, 'what passes for [such lifestyle] anarchism [...] is little more than an introspective personalism that denigrates responsible social commitment', that 'arrogantly derides structure' and therefore presents no more than 'a playground for juvenile antics' (Bookchin 1995, 10). He continues: 'Lifestyle, like individualist, anarchism bears a disdain for theory, with mystical, and primitivistic filiations that are generally too vague, intuitional, and even antirational to analyse directly' (ibid., 11). However, it is, apparently, not quite so vague as to escape Bookchin's wrath, and he goes on to deride the fact that

> lifestyle anarchism today is finding its principle expression in spray-can graffiti, postmodernist nihilism, antirationalism, neoprimitivism, anti-technologism, neo-Situationist "cultural terrorism", mysticism, and a "practice" of staging Foucauldian "personal insurrections" (ibid., 19).

This text has rightly been critiqued for its own lack of consistency and clarity (Black 1997). Bookchin's claim that lifestyle is too vague to analyse, for example, arises principally from that fact that he 'cobbled together all his self-selected enemies' (ibid., 51) under the term lifestyle anarchists; certainly, Bookchin's caricature of lifestyle anarchism does not relate to any self-identifying group of theorists or activists, or indeed to any recognisable trend within anarchism. As Bob Black correctly suggests, lifestyle anarchism for Bookchin simply denotes those elements of anarchist theory of which he disapproves, regardless of whether such elements have in fact any relationship with one another, which, more often than not, they do not. Most regrettably, rather than inventing a new term to disabuse those he disagreed with, Bookchin (for no obvious reason) chose to label them as lifestyle anarchists, a term which had a very real, and very different, meaning for those who *did* identify with the label.

The lifestyle anarchism (henceforth, simply lifestyle, or

personal prefiguration) I wish to discuss is more commonly understood as referring to the prefigurative notion where one must put into practice here and now those principles one would hope to see in an anarchist society. However, rather than simply seeing this as a question of what I have called social prefiguration, lifestyle understands prefiguration on the personal level as well. Not only is the anarchist to create *collective* spaces to work, to live, to grow food and be educated, she is also to live, day to day, according to her principles, acting, where possible, in ways consistent with her own values. Although this may seem perfectly reasonable, and a logical extension of the sort of prefigurative politics I discussed above (and, indeed, I would suggest it is both those things) lifestyle is often greeted with considerable criticism. There are, I believe, two reasons for this; one, to do with its perceived reformist nature, and the other, to do with a more complex ethical problem relating to issues of responsibility and blame; I discuss these in turn, and, in tackling them, present the case for an increased support of lifestyle politics.

Lifestyle Politics: Revolutionary, or Reformist?

Lifestyle, then, is often dismissed as, at best, ineffective reformism; individual actions make little difference to the larger picture, and, in suggesting that the individual has real power to do good without radically changing the world, it supports a liberal view of the individual, freely choosing one act over another. In a discussion of ethical consumerism (which is one, but only one, element of lifestyle) the *Anarchist FAQ* presents a fairly standard position, not condemning lifestyle per se, but questioning its ultimate worth:

> This is not to suggest that we become unconcerned about how we spend our money. Far from it. Buying greener products rather than the standard one does have an impact. It just means being aware of the limitations of green consumerism,

particularly as a means of changing the world. Rather, we must look to changing how goods are produced. [...] Because green consumerism is based wholly on market solutions to the ecological crisis, it is incapable of even recognising a key root cause of that crisis, namely the atomising nature of capitalism and the social relationships it creates (2007, 470, my emphasis)

This statement makes explicit an assumption that underpins most critiques against lifestyle, and which is entirely misguided. The argument here is that shopping ethically is all well and good, but it will not help address the way goods are produced. I would suggest that lifestyle does in fact do that, that it has the potential to do it with considerable effect, and that it does much else besides. On what basis is the claim that 'green consumerism is based *wholly* on market solutions' made? Clearly, some green consumerism is little more than the support of green-wash by companies that have no real interest in working towards a just or sustainable world; but I would argue that rather than being a critique *of* ethical consumerism, this ought not be seen as ethical consumption at all. In other words, for consumption to be ethical, it must, for an anarchist, go beyond this superficial greening, and incorporate genuinely radical values. Lifestyle is by its very nature *not* a simplistic approach to shopping where some companies are boycotted and organic vegetables are bought from supermarkets; it must integrate a far more holistic approach. One obvious factor in this, almost always over-looked by critics, is that ethical consumerism is, first and foremost, about consuming *less*, and a broader lifestyle approach is about finding ways to satisfy needs without shopping, by growing one's own food, by learning to live with less, and so on. Another way to reflect upon this is to consider the distinction to be made between ethical *consumerism* and ethical *consumption*, with the former understood as a surface greening of an essentially unsustainable economic structure that demands perpetual growth, and the latter designating an attempt to make sustainable and just the production and provision of things that are seen as being of genuine worth[52] (Seyfang 2005).

Although it must rank amongst the most frequently quoted anarchist texts, it is worth here making mention of Gustav Landauer's view that 'the state is a social relationship; a certain way of people relating to one another. It can be destroyed by creating new social relationships; i.e., by people relating to one another differently' (Landauer 2010, 3). Applying this analysis to our everyday lives, we can see that our every act is played out within certain cultural, and practical, parameters. Shopping at a local workers' co-op, rather than a supermarket, even when doing so relies on standard economic transactions, helps create and define new social relationships: it helps people operate such ventures (because, as I suggested above, without people actively choosing to support them, they would not exist); it helps people learn to think and act in more localised, community oriented ways, with *people* replacing *workers* and *customers*; it helps create broader social relationships, the local shop buying food from the local farm, and so on; and, once again, it helps make clear the issues raised in the previous chapter, as people's needs and desires are not simply theoretical, ideological hopes, but day-to-day, practical realities, with tangible consequences. In short, it helps people experiment with and move towards the sort of social and economic arrangements anarchists might hope to some day see realised. Again, Geoph Kozeny puts the point well:

Many topics about which people in the mainstream culture may be reluctant to talk (relationship dynamics, for example, or differences in values and priorities) tend to get discussed more openly in intentional communities because their members are attempting to design their lives intentionally. They are trying deliberately to address and change culturally ingrained habits; generally they are trying to move from individualistic behaviour towards actions based on co-operation, sharing and collaborative decision-making (Kozeny, quoted in Coates 2007, 13).

Trust, values, friendship and a shared sense of responsibility and interdependence replaces the soul-less transaction of a super-market check-out. Abstract principles become the matter of concrete and daily decisions, and this includes responding to the difficult dilemmas that any such activity necessarily creates, and which would, if my analyses in previous chapters are correct, continue to exist in some form in an anarchist society. David Graeber recognises the difficulties created by engaging with a society at odds with anarchist principles:

> A revolutionary strategy based on direct action can only succeed if the principles of direct action become institution-alised. Temporary bubbles of autonomy must gradually turn into permanent, free communities. However [...] these communities cannot exist in isolation; neither can they have a purely confrontational relation with everyone around them. They have to have some way to engage with larger economic, social, or political systems that surround them. This is the trickiest question because it has proved extremely difficult for those organised on radically democratic lines to so integrate themselves in any meaningful way in larger structures without having to make endless compromises in their founding principles (Graeber 2009, 210-11).

I would suggest that personal prefiguration offers an excellent site of struggle, where responses to the problems raised by Graeber can be constructively considered, by creating much needed spaces in which emotional, cultural, tactical and practical issues can be addressed, experimented with, and improved.

As noted, lifestyle is much more than ethical consumption,

and, furthermore, ethical consumption is much more than ethical *shopping*. Learning to live with less, learning to grow at least some of our own food, to brew our own beer, to repair instead of discard, to share and hold in common, to structure our lives in ways that help, rather than hinder, our attempts to reduce our impact on the planet and all that lives on it. And, as I shall explain in the next section, it is about reclaiming *responsibility* for our own actions.

Responsibility in an Unjust World.

The notion that anarchists, or indeed any individual, should take responsibility for their actions within a world which is mostly at odds with their own values is obvious to some, but extremely contentious to others; as I suggested earlier, the argument that people have responsibility would appear to rest on the prior claim that even within state-capitalism people are genuinely empowered to act in whichever way they chose; something which any radical analysis of capitalism and the state would appear to deny. Whilst I would accept that people's actions are seriously limited by their context (and this is true of some individuals much more so than others) I would also argue that there is in fact considerable space in which we *can* move towards more consistent lives. Once again, Landauer makes the point powerfully, in a letter to Max Nettlau, in which he states that he

refuse[s] to divide people into those who are the masters of the state and those who are the state's servants. Human relationships depend on human behaviour. The possibility of anarchy depends on the belief that people can *always* change their behaviour. In order to change ourselves and our social conditions, we must use the limited freedom that we have. It is up to no one but ourselves to do so and to create as much freedom and unity as possible. Who can deny that we have made very little use of the possibilities we have? (Landauer 2010, 309).

In other words, the argument that people are disempowered and disenfranchised by the state, and capitalism, need not result in the conclusion that people are therefore completely incapable of making small but important changes in their everyday lives. Ironically, doing so results in still further disempowerment, and anarchists must be cautious of the disabling potential of their own radical critique. The issue of responsibility also touches upon the wider points made by this work; the more the notions of freedom, power and ethics are problematised, the more we see how important, and difficult, the making of daily decisions is. Such an argument, however, forces anarchists to accept an uncomfortable problem; namely, that *they* would, in an anarchist society, be put in a position where such decisions needed to be made. At present, lifestyle is often dismissed as being divisive, because it assumes moral judgements are being made *within* the anarchist community. Here I believe we see tangible evidence that the basic issues raised by this work have yet to be properly addressed. Somehow, the differences between anarchists, between meat-eaters and vegans, to cite one common example, is seen as being an unnecessary distraction; the real battle is between anarchists and the state. We are back to a simplistic analysis of the world; a world of 'one no, many yeses'. Whereas the postanarchists argue that such a position rests on underlying metaphysical assumptions, I believe that there are also more personal reasons, relating to questions of guilt and personal responsibility; such issues are much easier to deal with when the moral universe is neatly divided into the good guys and the bad guys. Certainly, the question of lifestyle, whilst remaining an apparent irrelevance for academics, as noted by the lack of discussion on the matter, is one which never fails to illicit a strong emotional response from the wider anarchist community. A quick glance through any anarchist email list will quickly reveal similarly passionate, defensive and often even highly confrontational discussions whenever the subject of personal prefiguration is raised. Such moral concerns, it would appear, are supposed to remain personal, once again echoing the liberal division between individual morality and public politics.[53]

However, the arguments I have presented in the preceding chapters suggest that this division is an illusion; anarchists need to accept that questions of ethics will remain pertinent, and at times conflictual, within libertarian societies; at present, the way questions of personal moral choices (or lifestyles) are dealt with suggests a movement that has failed to acknowledge the potential for moral divisions, *without the state*. Personal prefiguration, then, is important not only because it helps sustain *social* prefiguration, but because it helps foster both a sense of responsibility and forces anarchists to begin working through ways of responding to ethical conflicts. Rather than a distraction, disagreements about lifestyle should be seen as an integral part of the challenge anarchists face in the long battle to create new cultural and political tools to replace those of the authoritarian state with which we have all been raised. Indeed, one of the strongest arguments against the state is that it infantilises those it controls, by taking away the individual's moral responsibility. Kropotkin, for example, in his essay *Law and Authority* argued that people

> are so perverted by an education which from infancy seeks to kill in us the spirit of revolt, and to develop that of submission to authority; we are so perverted by this existence under the ferrule of a law, which regulates every event in life [...] that, if this state of things continues, we shall lose all initiative, all habit of thinking for ourselves (Kropotkin 1970, 197).

Following Kropotkin, Randall Amster makes much the same argument. Any 'reference to external, written laws represents an abdication of the subject's capacity for moral self-direction, an essential element of a social order without institutionalised coercion' (n.d). Such a critique, however, implies that people must relearn (or, more accurately, create afresh) these things; they will not, in other words, simply awaken once the state is destroyed. Making ethical choices in one's daily life now plays a crucial role in this respect.

Now, anarchists opposed to, or indifferent towards, personal prefiguration may take umbrage with my apparent suggestion that they are, by rejecting lifestyle, *not* making ethical decisions; clearly, they are. Their anarchism is the result of a moral choice, the result of which is an ethical condemnation of capitalism and the state, and there will no doubt be countless other examples; their outrage about a war, a particularly offensive policy, a corporation's especially ruthless approach to business, and so on. But whereas such ethical choices will lead to people holding certain (often long-term) political views about how the world could or should be organised, personal prefiguration encourages the individual to act, as much as is possible, according to those ethical decisions. As such, the practical and philosophical complexity that arises in making certain decisions that affect *one's daily life*, decisions which are often much more personal, and much less black and white, than questions of, for example, foreign policy, means that such decisions provide much more profound and informative, and often challenging experiences for the individual (see Trujillo 2010 for an informative discussion on the difficulties, and political relevance, of trying to live according to environmental values). Social and personal prefiguration works on many levels, then. Although neither will bring about radical change on their own, I believe they are both necessary elements of any attempts to create a more libertarian society. They offer small but important forms of daily resistance (which could become much bigger, the more they are adopted) as well as offering spaces for much needed experimentation and learning.

Furthermore, these acts of prefiguration also suggest ways in which anarchists might more comfortably deal with the question of defining how an anarchist society might function. The rejection of blue-prints is based on a number of legitimate concerns; the fear of a vanguardist approach to politics, the recreation of hierarchies, and the illegitimate universalising of political responses to complex and contextualised problems. However, attempts to prefigure an anarchist politics will necessarily provide clues as to how many of life's problems may be solved if and when the state and capitalism disappear. Such experiments must be understood with reference to their necessary limitations, performed as they are within the confines of the state, but as long as this is acknowledged, and claims are not made that they provide a genuine example of entirely anarchistic forms of organisation, then what they *can* offer is of considerable value to anarchists, because rather than abstract principles, acts of prefiguration provide daily examples that anarchists can begin to learn from, and which can, with necessary caution, begin to shed light on how such processes may grow and flourish as the state withers and dies.

Once again, there remains an undeniably large step between such projects and life in a fully-fledged libertarian society. So although prefiguration can respond to some of the fears about blue-prints, it by no means does away with them entirely. However, I believe that such fears, however valid, must be balanced with the need to ask questions about how anarchist societies might work, and the need to respond to people's legitimate concerns about challenging what most people see as essential features of modern life. Now, then, I want to explore this matter, and suggest that the unequivocal rejection of blue-prints is one more anarchist principle in need of moderation.

Rethinking Blue-prints: Positive Visions or Authoritarian Models?

We saw in Chapter 1 how Michael Albert argued that 'citizens of developed countries are not going to risk what they have [...] to pursue a goal about which they have no clarity' (Albert 2001, 326-7). Like Bookchin, Albert stresses the need to respond to the questions which anarchists have so often refused to answer (see also Shukatis, 2009; Purchase 1994). He also argues that as well as providing a more long-term vision, such discussions can help inform anarchist responses to contemporary political questions. Unfortunately, also like Bookchin, Albert appears unable to resist taking an overly personal tone against those with whom he disagrees. In the article from which the above quote is taken, he refers to those trends which reject the creation of blue-prints as 'distasteful anarchism' (ibid., 322). Not only is this counter-productive, in terms of winning support for his argument, which *is* legitimate; it is also misguided. The anarchist rejection of blue-prints is not some whimsical position, dreamt up by 'distasteful' people; it is a thoughtful response to the problems of, amongst other things, knowledge, hierarchy, authority and control. What I would urge is a meeting of these two concerns, where one does not cancel out or dismiss the other, but where each *informs* the other. There is a crucial distinction to be made between arguing that an anarchist community *would*, or *should* organise according to blue-print A, and arguing that an anarchist community *could* organise in such a way. Put simply, offering people a vision of how anarchists *might* deal with anti-social behaviour, for example, is not the same as arguing that such a society *must*, or *necessarily would*, follow such a vision. Of course, it is true that there is always the danger that ideas presented initially as *possibilities*, over time became ossified dogmas, which is precisely why the critique of blue-prints must not be entirely forgotten. But an out-right rejection of blue-prints is equally dangerous, because whilst it offers a less risky strategy *in theory*, it is, as Albert rightly suggests, unlikely to ever win widespread support. In other words, *it* runs the risk of giving far more openly authoritarian ideologies a free hand at convincing people that anarchism is a hopelessly utopian dream, and a liberal state, at best, the only viable alternative.

It is also crucial here to disentangle two different but over-lapping reasons for rejecting blue-prints; the more common argument given, as we saw in Chapter 1, is that to predefine how a society might organise at some point in the future would in itself be an authoritarian act, potentially limiting the capacity for those who would actually live in such a community to decide for themselves how their lives should be organised. However, there is, especially in recent years, an increasing resistance to the idea that the sort of institutions Albert and Bookchin discuss should exist *at all*, and with this view comes a rejection of blue-prints as being not only dangerous but ultimately unnecessary. As Albert suggests, many contemporary anarchists dismiss 'political forms, per se, or institutions, per se' (Albert 2001, 322). What I hope to have shown in this work is that the dream of a perfectly libertarian world is just that, a dream. However they might be imagined or realised, societies will create systems by which some form of social cohesion is created, and order maintained. Some communities may adopt formalised methods that approach what we currently understand as institutions, and *certain* institutions, such as the police force, at that. In doing so, they will run the risk of slipping back into more authoritarian forms of politics. Others may rely more heavily on cultural tools, such as the creation of moral taboos, for example, to create some degree of conformity and order. In doing so, they too will run the risk of slipping back into more authoritarian forms of politics. In other words, anarchists cannot simply deny the legitimacy of institutions and therefore hope to have solved the problems of authority per se, because other social tools have proved just as effective in creating authoritarian spaces. It seems, then, that the refusal to at least contemplate questions about how an anarchist society might run is considerably weakened. Its premises should not be dismissed, however, but incorporated as legitimate concerns that may rightly limit, guide, and inform such endeavours. So how might anarchists respond to these arguments, and incorporate them with lessons learnt from prefigurative experiments, to begin to sketch out the necessary outlines of a future world without the state?

I argued above that conflicts between different producers of goods and services, and between such producers and those they provide for, ought not be seen as simply the result of a market economy; such conflicts are, ultimately, inevitable, though we might hope they would be greatly reduced without the additional aggravating factors of a profit-centred economic system. As such, workers' co-ops and their customers must, to some extent, already begin to experiment with ways to respond to such conflicts.[54] For example, by breaking down the division between workers and customers, collective processes of decision-making can be established, and refined. Operating outside the relative simplicity of a temporary autonomous zone, such processes offer a far greater wealth of experience and insight into how difficult decisions might be made, and how conflicts may be resolved when full agreement is not possible. The needs of the workers, the consumers, and the local environment, therefore, will be taken into account, not as a theoretical experiment, but as a concrete procedure, with very real consequences affecting everyone concerned. I also mentioned earlier that Radical Routes is, at the time of writing, engaged in a complicated process of responding to the government's plans to abolish the Financial Services Authority (FSA), the body which until now had overseen the running of co-operatives. A particular concern for members of Radical Routes is an issue known as *carpet-bagging*, where members of a co-op effectively de-mutualise it, and turn it into a standard business, or house. Although strictly illegal, incidents of carpet-bagging have long been ignored by the FSA, which has created problems for the co-operative movement. Some members of Radical Routes are therefore hoping to convince the government that the co-operative movement itself should have control over individual co-ops. The process is extremely interesting for anarchists,[55] because it presents the possibility of a movement which operates according to many radical principles being given quasi-governmental authority. How this organisation might perform would therefore be of considerable theoretical and practical interest; if (deemed) successful, it could provide concrete ideas as to how institutions holding some degree of authority, and the power to act on it, may operate in a more libertarian context. The processes and structures employed could well provide an outline for other, similar 'institutions', becoming more localised and independent over time. Of course, if it fails, it may suggest either that radicals made one compromise too many, or that the possibilities of anarchistic organisation ought to be considered as even less realistic. Another example worth briefly mentioning is that of attempts to deal with cases of sexual harassment and assault within the anarchist community. Cleary a serious and sensitive issue, responding to allegations about rape and other similar offences without recourse to the usual legal bodies has proved a challenging, stressful and often demoralising experience for many. Yet much has been learnt from these experiments, both on a practical and a more philosophical level. Concrete questions of how to ensure an individual does not act in a similar way in the future, or, to think of it another way, how to keep a community safe, merge with ethical considerations of justice and retribution. No perfect answer has been found (and it is unlikely there really is a perfect answer) but that is beside the point. Again, in terms of both theory and practice, anarchists are slowly learning ideas and procedures to deal with such issues on their own; ideas which might seep into not only the broader anarchist common sense, but, eventually, throughout the wider community.

The creation of tentative blue-prints, then, can inform, and be informed by, anarchist experiments with prefiguration. How much detail such outlines might provide is not itself a question that can be answered in any great detail; some anarchists may, for example, consider general proposals for a rotating system of individuals, empowered by their community, who would act as 'police officers', and no more; others may feel that such an open-ended suggestion is more problematic than one with greater clarity, preferring to address particular concerns directly. Either way, I believe anarchists must come to terms with the tensions involved in thinking about such matters, and begin to consider more detailed ideas about the functioning of libertarian communities. And, in doing so, they may come to see that, rather than closing off possibilities, discussions surrounding these ideas are likely to lead to engaged and useful debates, prompting still more ideas; indeed, this must very much be about presenting a *plurality of visions*, rather than one, as authoritarian politics tend to do, or none, as anarchists have all too frequently done.

Conclusions.

In this final chapter, I have outlined some broad and tentative proposals for making anarchism a more viable political force. As well as responding directly to critiques I made in the opening chapter, I have also argued that a stronger emphasis on prefigurative strategies, as well as a rethinking of the absolute rejection of blue-prints, are appropriate responses to the core arguments of the work, which suggest that anarchism must accept that social order without the state can only be considered possible by accepting some limits to basic libertarian demands. This does not mean that anarchism needs to accept the state as a necessary political tool, but that it must come to terms with the need for some forms of organised politics, and with the need to begin to outline what such organisations might look like. Doing so can help anarchism escape the criticism that it offers no real alternative to the liberal state, as well as providing stepping-stones by which genuinely radical change might occur. All of the strategies I have proposed are already part of the anarchist tool-kit, but they are too often over-looked, or even considered as little more than a well-meaning distraction to the real goal of revolutionary struggle. By providing them with more of a theoretical under-pinning, I hope to have shown that such strategies can play a crucial role in the sort of social change anarchists wish to see. My support of such tactics does not deny their inherent problems, but rather suggests that at times, these problems are themselves of value to people hoping to create forms of politics that *deal* with conflict, rather than stamp it out. If my proposals appear to step out onto the slippery slope, precariously waiting to slide into an authoritarian, vanguardist revolutionary movement, or into liberal reformism, my response would be that this is precisely the challenge which anarchism must face; ironically, the absolutist positions of so many anarchists are themselves simply attempts to control the political terrain, to prohibit certain actions because of their supposed potential to become authoritarian or reformist. Anarchism must resist becoming what it has so relentlessly critiqued, but it must be mindful of the potential that, in doing so, it runs the risk of simply recreating its own forms of absolutist and dogmatic politics. Anarchism, we might say, is the art of politics, not in the safety of the state, or the party, *or* the autonomous zone, but rather, it is precisely the politics of the slippery slope.

Conclusion: Rules without Rulers?

Anarchists have always argued that *another world is possible*. Indeed, perhaps one of anarchism's most persistent and admirable features is its refusal to accept the inevitability of the state, the market, of inequality, of hierarchy; its refusal, in other words, to accept the inevitability of *this* world. When Margaret Thatcher stated that 'there is no alternative' to capitalism, it is clear that this is not precisely what she meant; what she meant to say was that there is no *desirable* alternative. Indeed, the Iron Lady was well aware that alternatives existed, and she thoroughly despised them. Although it might seem mere pedantry to point this out, I think it is informative to consider the likelihood that no one really thinks there is no alternative, or that, conversely another world is *not* possible. What people question are the declarations by individuals, or political groups, that they can offer not only *another* world, but a *better* one.

The other world that anarchists insist is possible is, however, supposed to be a better one. Indeed, whilst anarchists deny they are utopians, if by utopia we understand a world of uninterrupted happiness and perfection, they do nonetheless suggest that theirs is a world where everyone is free to pursue their own dreams, where no one will coerce anyone else, where any inequality is the result of natural difference and not social division. It is, politically speaking, perfect. Stated so categorically, anarchists may deny that this is what they believe, but if it is not, they are seemingly unwilling to admit which flaws we might expect to encounter: if there is to be coercion, we are left none the wiser as to how this might arise; if there are to be social inequalities, we are left none the wiser as to why they may come about; if there are to be limits to freedom, we are left none the wiser as to which liberties may be denied. Anarchism appears to offer everything, and explain almost nothing.

In this work, I hope to have shown, though with regret, that anarchism *is* all too often presented as a simplistic and utopian fantasy, with little awareness or acceptance of its own limitations, and the limitations inherent within the complexity of human life. Absolute freedom cannot be guaranteed, and, consequently, no society can promise that no one within it will ever be coerced. Disagreements about what it means to be good, about what is useful for society, about what constitutes harm, are not solely the product of an unnatural power held within the state, however much social divisions may have been exacerbated by hierarchical and deliberately unequal ideological systems. There is no natural harmony to be found within human nature, and theoretical and practical conflict is, to some degree, inevitable; consensus will not always be reached. When anarchism is presented as a once-and-for-all resolution to the inequities of capitalism and the state, is it any wonder that people refuse to accept such a promise, however appealing it might be? Yet when pushed, and at times of their own volition, anarchists do recognise that such problems exist; why, then, is anarchism so consistently presented as little more than a collection of absolute moral demands? Even when theories of social organisation are being experimented with by groups and networks, the rhetoric is not only one of success, but of a success which proves that an anarchist society of liberty, equality and consensus is possible. But anarchism cannot offer such a world; a world without conflict is not possible, no matter what ideological path we pursue. An anti-authoritarian politics must be one which recognises, and learns to live with, the limits of freedom, and, in doing so, recognises that therefore anarchy is precisely an ever-changing interplay between its own libertarian values and the countless other values that exist within and shape our world. Anarchism should not be seen as a refusal to engage with this world, but a certain approach to it; a way of learning to live with the inevitable consequences of power. Anarchism *is* life on the slippery slope, and a refusal to shepherd everyone to the 'safety' of the top, or the bottom. As Saul Newman argues

> anti-politics makes sense only if it takes seriously the task of politics: building, constructing, organising, fighting, making collective decisions and so on. Such practices are in no sense irreconcilable with libertarianism, on the contrary, they are its very condition. Put simply, a politics of anti-politics points to the possibility of a libertarian politics outside, and ultimately transcendent of, the state and all hierarchical structures of power and authority. To counteract such structures requires, however, the development of alternative libertarian and egalitarian structures and practices, coupled with a constant awareness of the authoritarian potential that lies in any structure (2010, 139)

Such a view chimes, perhaps somewhat unexpectedly, with the work of Murray Bookchin, a point which Newman himself recognises, suggesting that in 'Bookchin's idea of municipalism as the basis for a new politics of citizenship and democratic decision making, we find many interesting and appealing ideas for libertarian institutions and practices, including forms of council democracy and decentralisation' (151). With another slightly ironic twist, I would suggest it is the contemporary anarchist movement, supposedly inspired by much poststructural thought, which has failed to recognise the persistent possibilities of coercive power, and the inevitable limits of freedom; hence the claims that consensus is a viable tool for organising society. If my arguments have been convincing, such criticisms might lead the reader to wonder if there is anything in anarchism worth saving. In fact, I believe that there is, but only if anarchists themselves are prepared to recognise the limits of their ideology. If they do so, then they may begin to ask more honestly and critically what anarchism has to offer, and they will come to see that there is much to be said in its favour. The basic idea of democracy, so powerful in the western world, is more and more being placed under scrutiny, not only by academics (Hirst 1994; Douglas Lummis 1996), but also by the population at large, increasingly fed up with the political system and its claims to be democratic, equal and just. This *political system*, however, is more than happy to offer a few politicians themselves as sacrificial lambs. These proverbial bad apples are habitually presented to the public as scape-goats, in order that the system itself is never placed under scrutiny. Anarchists have seen through this, and recognised that a change of the guard still ultimately leaves us guarded. But in refusing to discuss how life might work without the state, and in refusing to accept and explore the ways in which life might reasonably be expected to continue without disintegrating into violent chaos, anarchists have helped ensure their ideas are easily and thoroughly dismissed, even by those utterly uncon-vinced by and unhappy with the status quo.

Anarchists must begin to accept that whilst they themselves may be fanatical lovers of liberty, liberty itself is not so easily loved; freedom for the pike is death for the minnow, as R.H. Tawney once wisely said. A society without the state must therefore be a society with some form of order, if it is to become not only another world, but also a better one. The promise of absolute freedom is as simplistic as it is false. Getting rid of the guard, as anarchism rightly demands, does not, and indeed must not, entail getting rid of order, but rather suggests making that order more equal and more free. Anarchism is neither chaos nor utopia, it is a world of rules without rulers. The sooner anarchists accept this, the sooner we might come to know this entirely possible world.

Bibliography.

Albrecht, G. (1994) 'Ethics, Anarchy and Sustainable Development' in *Anarchist Studies* 2:2, 95-118.

Anonymous (n.d) *The Anarchist Manifesto*, available from http://www.anarchy.net

Anonymous. (2003) *Do or Die: Voices from the Ecological Resistance* Issue 10 2003 (Do or Die: Brighton).

Antliff, A. (2007) 'Anarchy, Power, and Poststructuralism' in *SubStance* 36:2, 56-66.

Adams, J. (2003) Postanarchism in a Nutshell The Anarchist Library, available from http://theanarchistlibrary.org/.Accessed 24/04/10.

Albert, M. (2001) 'Anarchists' in Bircham, E. & Charlton, J. (eds.) *Anti-Capitalism: A Guide to the Movement* (Bookmarks: London).

Albert, M. (2003) *Parecon: Life After Capitalism* (Verso: London).

Alexander, R. (2002) *The Anarchists in the Spanish Civil War: Volume One* (Janus Publishing Company, London).

Alexander, R. (2007) *The Anarchists in the Spanish Civil War: Volume Two* (Janus Publishing Company, London).

Amster, R (1998) 'Anarchism as Moral Theory: Praxis, Property, and the Postmodern' in *Anarchist Studies* 6:2

Amster, R. (et. al.) (2009) 'Introduction' in Amster, R.; DeLeon, A.; Fernandez, L.A.; Nocella II, A.J.; Shannon, D. (eds.) *Contemporary Anarchist Studies* (Routledge: Oxon).

Bakunin, M (1973) in Lehning, A. (ed) *Michael Bakunin: Selected Writings* (Jonathan Cape: London).

Bakunin, M (1984) *Marxism, Freedom and the State* (Freedom Press: London).

Bannister, R.C. (1979) *Social Darwinism: Science and Myth in Anglo-American Social Thought* (Temple University Press: Philadelphia).

Barclay, H. (1997) *Culture and Anarchism* (Freedom Press: London).

Barclay, H. (2005) 'Power: Some anthropological perspectives' in *Anarchist Studies* 13:2 104-117.

Bauman, Z. (2001) *Community: Seeking Safety in an Insecure World* (Polity Press: Cambridge).

Bauman, Z. (2003) *Postmodern Ethics* (Blackwell, Oxford).

Berkman, A. (1973/1929) *ABC of Anarchism* (Freedom Press: London)

Berlin, I. (2002) in Hardy, H. (ed) *Liberty* (Oxford University Press: Oxford).

Biehl, J. (1997) *The Politics of Social Ecology: Libertarian Municipalism* (Black Rose Books: Montreal).

Black, B. (1997) *Anarchy After Leftism* (Columbia Alternative Library: Columbia).

Blackwell, T. & Seabrook, J. (1993) *The Revolt Against Change: Towards a Conserving Radicalism* (Vintage: London).

Bobbio, N. (2005) *Liberalism and Democracy* (Verso: London)

Bookchin, M. (1974) *Post-Scarcity Anarchism* (Wildwood House, London).

Bookchin, M. (1991) *Libertarian Municipalism: An Overview*, http://dwardmac.pitzer.edu/Anarchist_Archives/bookchin/gp/pe rspectives24.html Accessed 14/03/09.

Bookchin, M. (1995) *Social Anarchism or Lifestyle Anarchism: An Unbridgeable Chasm* (AK Press: London).

Bookchin, M. (2007) *Social Ecology and Communalism* (AK Press: Edinburgh).

Brown, L. S. (1994) *The Politics of Individualism: Liberalism, Liberal Feminism, and Anarchism* (Black Rose Books: Montreal).

Bufe, C. (1994) 'Introduction' in Purchase, G. *Anarchism and Environmental Survival* (See Sharp Press: Tucson)

Bufe, C. (1998) *Listen Anarchist!* http://theanarchistlibrary.org/HTML/Chaz_Bufe__Listen__Anar chist_.html

Carens, J. H. (2004) 'A Contextual Approach to Political Theory' *Ethical Theory and Moral Practice* 7:2, 117-132.

Carlsson, C. (2008) *Nowtopia: How Pirate Programmers, Outlaw Bicyclists, and Vacant-Lot Gardeners are Inventing the Future Today* (AK Press: Edinburgh)

Carter, A. (1993) 'Some Notes on 'Anarchism' in *Anarchist Studies* 1:2 141-45.

Chambers, P. (2006) 'Anarchism, Anti-clericalism and Religions' in *Anarchist Studies* 14:1, 36-47.

Clark, S. (2007) *Living Without Domination* (Ashgate, Hampshire).

Clastres, P. (1987) *Society Against the State* (Zone Books, New York).

Class War (1986) 'What Do We Do When The Cops Fuck Off?' in *The Heavy Stuff*, 2.

Cooper, D. (2004) *Challenging Diversity: Rethinking Equality and the Value of Difference* (Cambridge University Press: Cambridge).

CrimethInc (2000) *Days of War, Night of Love* (Demon Box Collective: Sundybyberg).

Cullen, S. (1993) 'Anarchy and the Mad Axe Man' in *The Raven* 6:2. 136-142

Curran, G. (2006) *21st Century Dissent: Anarchism, Anti-Globalisation and Environmentalism* (Palgrave: Basingstoke).

Davis, L. (2010) 'Social Anarchism or Lifestyle Anarchism: An Unhelpful Dichotomy' in *Anarchist Studies* 18:1, 62-82.

Davis, R. (1991) *Death on the Streets: Cars and the Mythology of Road Safety* (Leading Edge Press: Hawes).

de Angelis, M. (2001) 'From Movement to Society' in (anonymous editorial) *On Fire: The Battle of Genoa and the Anti-Capitalist Movement* (One Off Press: no publishing address given).

Douglas Lummis, C. (1996) *Radical Democracy* (Cornell University Press: London).

Ehrlich, H.J; Ehrlich, C.; De Leon, D. & Morris, G. (eds.) (1979) *Reinventing Anarchy. What are Anarchists Thinking these Days?* (Routledge & Kegan Paul Ltd.: London).

Ehrlich, H.J. (1996) *Re-Inventing Anarchy, Again* (AK Press: Edinburgh).

Epstein, B. (2001) 'Anarchism and the Anti-Globalization Movement' in *Monthly Review* 53:4. http://www.monthlyreview.org/0901epstein.htm (Accessed 22/03/2008)

Evren, S. (2008) *Notes on Postanarchism* The Anarchist Library, available at http://theanarchistlibrary.org. Accessed 13/11/2010.

Fernandez, L. A. (2009) 'Being there: thoughts on anarchism and participatory observation' in Amster, R.; DeLeon, A.; Fernandez, L.A.; Nocella II, A.J.; Shannon, D. (eds.) *Contemporary Anarchist Studies* (Routledge: Oxon).

Foucault, M. [Gordon, C. ed.] (1980) *Power/knowledge: selected interviews and other writings 1972-77* (Pantheon: New York).

Foucault, M. (1990) *The History of Sexuality, Vol. 1* (Vintage Books, New York).

Foucault, M., [Faubion, J. ed.] (1994) Power: The Essential Works of Foucault 1954 – 1884, Vol. 3 (Penguin, London).

Franklin, J. (1997) (ed.) *Equality* (London: IPPR).

Franks, B. (2006) *Rebel Alliances: The Means and Ends of Contemporary British Anarchisms* (AK Press: Edinburgh).

Franks, B. (2010) 'Introduction' in Franks, B. & Wilson, M. (eds.) *Anarchism and Moral Philosophy* (Palgrave: Basingstoke).

Fraser, R. (1981) *Blood of Spain: The Experience of Civil War, 1936-1939* (Penguin: Harmondsworth).

Freeden, M. (1996) *Ideologies and Political Theory* (Clarendon Press: Oxford).

Freeman, J. (originally published in 1970) *The Tyranny of Structurelessness* (Struggle, available at http://struggle.ws). Accessed 06/01/10.

Gellner, E. (1994) *Conditions of Liberty: Civil Society and its Rivals* (Penguin, London).

Gibbs, B. (1976) *Freedom and Liberation* (Sussex University Press: London).

Goaman, K. (2004) 'The Anarchist Travelling Circus: Reflections on Contemporary Anarchism, Anti-Capitalism and the International Scene' in Purkis, J. & Bowen, J. (eds.) *Changing Anarchism* (Manchester University Press: Manchester).

Goldman, E. (1972) *Red Emma Speaks: Selected Writings and Speeches* [compiled and edited by Shulman, A.K.] (Random House: New York).

Goodwin, B. (2007) *Using Political Ideas* (John Wiley & Sons: Chichester).

Gordon, U. (2007) 'Practising Anarchist Theory: Towards a Participatory Political Philosophy' in Shukaitis, S.; Graber, D. & Biddle, E. (eds) *Constituent Imagination: Militant Investigations, Collective Theorisation* (AK Press: Edinburgh).

Gordon, U. (2008) *Anarchy Alive!* (Pluto: London).

Gordon, U. (2009) 'Utopia in contemporary anarchism' in Davis, L. and Kinna, R. (eds) *Anarchism and Utopianism* (`Manchester University Press: Manchester).

Gordon, U. (n.d.) *Consensus Games:* Towards a Democratic Theory of Consensus Decision-making Conference paper.

Graeber, D. (2002) *The New Anarchists* (The Anarchist Library, available from http://theanarchistlibrary.org/.). (Accessed 04/03/10)

Graeber, D. (2004) *Fragments of an Anarchist Anthropology* (Prickly Paradigm Press: Chicago).

Graeber, D. (2007) *Possibilities: Essays on Hierarchy, Rebellion, and Desire* (AK Press: Edinburgh).

Graeber, D. (2009) *Direct Action: An Ethnography* (AK Press: Edinburgh).

Graeber, D. & Grubacic, A. (2004) *Anarchism, or The Revolutionary Movement of The Twenty-First Century.* (The Anarchist Library, available at http://theanarchistlibrary.org) Accessed 20/01/09.

Graham, R. (2004) 'Reinventing Hierarchy: The Political Theory of Social Ecology' in *Anarchist Studies* 12, 1: 16-35.

Graham, R. (2009) (ed) *Anarchism: A Documentary History of*

Libertarian Ideas Vol. II (Black Rose Books: London).

Gray, T. (1991) *Freedom* (Macmillan: London).

Gray, J. (2000) *Two Faces of Liberalism* (The New Press: New York).

Gumbs et al, n.d. *The Revolution Starts at Home: Confronting Partner Abuse in Activist Communities* (samizdat zine)

Trocchi et al, (2005) in D. Harvie, K. Milburn, B.Trott, & Watts, D. (eds) 2005. *Shut Them Down: The G8, Gleneagles 2005 and the Movement of Movements* (Leeds: Dissent and Autonomedia).

Hahnel, R. (2005) *Economic Justice and Democracy: From Competition to Cooperation* (Routledge: London).

Hartley, D. 'Communitarian Anarchism and Human Nature' in Anarchist Studies 3:2, 145-164.

Hayek, F.A. (2003) *The Road to Serfdom* (Routledge: London).

Hawkins, M. (1997) *Social Darwinism in European and American Thought, 1860-1945* (Cambridge University Press: Cambridge).

Heckert, J. (2004) 'Sexuality/identity/politics' in Purkis, J. & Bowen, J. (eds.) *Changing Anarchism* (Manchester University Press: Manchester).

Heckert, J. (2010) 'Listening, Caring, Becoming: Anarchism as an Ethics of Direct Relationships' in Franks, B. & Wilson, M. (eds.) *Anarchism and Moral Philosophy* (Palgrave: Basingstoke).

Hirst, P. (1994) *Associate Democracy: New Forms of Economic and Social Governance* (Polity Press: Cambridge)

Horton, D. (2006) 'Demonstrating Environmental Citizenship? A Study of Everyday Life among Green Activists' in Dobson, A. and Bell, D. (eds.) *Environmental Citizenship* (M.I.T Press: Massachusetts).

Holtzman, B., Hughes, C., Van Meter, K. 'Do It Yourself...and the Movement Beyond Capitalism' in Shukaitis, S.; Graber, D. & Biddle, E. (eds) *Constituent Imagination: Militant Investigations, Collective Theorisation* (AK Press: Edinburgh).

Hurl, C. (2005) 'Anti-Globalization and 'Diversity of Tactics'' in *Upping the Anti, Vol.1* http://uppingtheanti.org/node/1334.

Accessed 29/08/08

Illich, I. (1979) *Energy and Equity* (London: Marion Boyars)

Jun, N. (2010) 'Anarchist Philosophy: Past, Problems and Prospects' in Franks, B. & Wilson, M. (eds.) *Anarchism and Moral Philosophy* (Palgrave: Basingstoke).

Kempton, R. (2007) *Provo: Amsterdam's Anarchist Revolt* (Autonomedia: Brooklyn).

Kuhn, G. (2009) 'Anarchism, Postmodernity and Poststructuralism' in Amster, R.; DeLeon, A.; Fernandez, L. A.; Nocella II, A. J. & Shannon, D. (eds.) *Contemporary Anarchist Studies: An Introductory Anthology of Anarchism in the Academy* (Routledge: Abingdon).

Jensen, D. (2006) *Endgame: Vol 1: The Problem of Civilisation* (Seven Stories Press, New York).

Kingsnorth, P. (2004) *One No, Many Yeses* (The Free Press: London).

Kinna, R. (2007) *Anarchism: A Beginner's Guide* (Oneworld: Oxford).

Kinna, R. (2009) 'Anarchism and the politics of utopia' in Davis, L. and Kinna, R. (eds) *Anarchism and Utopianism* (`Manchester University Press: Manchester).

Klosko, G. (2000) *Democratic Procedures and Liberal Consensus* (Oxford University Press: Oxford).

Kropotkin, P. (1985) *The Conquest of Bread* (Elephant Editions: London).

Kropotkin, P. (2008) *Mutual Aid* (Forgotten Books: Marston Gate).

Kymlicka, W. (1995) *Multicultural Citizenship: a Liberal Theory of Minority Rights* (Clarendon Press: Oxford).

Kymlicka, W. (2001) *Politics in the Vernacular: Nationalism, Multiculturalism, and Citizenship* (Oxford University Press: Oxford).

Kymlicka, W. and Norman, W. (2000) *Citizenship in Diverse Societies* (Oxford: Oxford University Press).

Kymlicka W. (2002) 'Liberal Individualism and Liberal

Neutrality' in Smith, G. W. (ed.) *Liberalism: Critical Concepts in Political Theory* (Routledge: London).

Landauer, G. (2010) *Revolution and Other Writings: A Political Reader* (Edited and translated by Gabriel Kuhn) (Merlin Press Ltd.: Pontypool).

Leach, R. (1996) *British Political Ideologies* (Prentice Hall: Hemel Hempstead).

Levine, C. (2010) *The Tyranny of Tyranny* (The Anarchist Library, available from http://theanarchistlibrary.org/). Accessed 16/04/10.

Lutz, C. & Lutz Fernandez, A. (2010) *Carjacked: The Culture of the Automobile and its Effects on Our Lives* (Palgrave Macmillan: New York).

MacCullum, G.C. (1967) 'Negative and Positive Freedom' in *Philosophical Review* 76:3, 312-334.

Mackie, J.L (1977) *Ethics: Inventing Right and Wrong* (Penguin: Harmondsworth)

Maddock, K. (1987) 'Primitive Societies and Social Myths' in Ward, C. (ed) *A Decade of Anarchy: 1961-1970* (Freedom Press: London)

Maeckelbergh, M. (2009) *The Will of the Many: How the Alterglobaisation Movement is Changing the Face of Democracy* (Pluto Press: London).

Malatesta, E. (1965) *Life & Ideas* (Compiled and edited by Vernon Richards) (Freedom Press: London).

Margolis, J. (2004) *Moral Philosophy After 9/11* (Pennsylvania State University Press: University Park, PA).

Marshall, P. (1993) *Demanding the Impossible: A History of Anarchism* (Fontana Press: London).

Martin, T.S. (1998) 'Bookchin, Biehl, Brown: An Unbridgeable Chasm?' in *Anarchist Studies* 6:1, 39-44.

May, T. (1994) *The Political Philosophy of Poststructuralist Anarchism* (University Press, University Park: Pennsylvania State).

May, T. (1995) *The Moral Theory of Postructuralism* (University Press, University Park: Pennsylvania State).

May, T (2007) 'Jacques Ranciére and the Ethics of Equality' in *SubStance* 36:2, 20-36.

McClaughlin (2007) *Anarchism and Authority: A Philosophical Introduction to Classical Anarchism* (Ashgate: Aldershot)

McKay, I. (2007) *An Anarchist FAQ Vol.I* (AK Press: Edinburgh).

McKay, I. (2010) 'Mutualism, Yes and No' *Shift Magazine* Issue 8.

Midgley, M. (1991) *Can't We Make Moral Judgements?* (The Bristol Press: Bristol)

Morland, D. (1997) *Demanding the Impossible? Human Nature and Politics in Nineteenth-Century Social Anarchism* (Cassell: London).

Moseley, A. (2007) *An Introduction to Political Philosophy* (Continuum: London).

Mouffe, C (1993) *The Return of the Political* (Verso: London).

Munson, C. (2010) *Debunking Nonsense in the Anarchist Movement* (The Anarchist Library, available from http://theanarchistlibrary.org/). Accessed 24/04/10.

Neal, D. (1997) *Anarchism: Ideology or Methodology* Available from http://www.spunk.org/library/intro/practice/sp001689.html. Accessed 16/03/08.

Newman, S. (2001) *From Bakunin to Lacan: Anti-authoritarianism and the Dislocation of Power* (Lexington Books: Oxford).

Newman, S. (2008) 'Editorial: Postanarchism' in *Anarchist Studies* 16, 2: 101-106.

Newman, S. (2010) *The Politics of Postanarchism* (Edinburgh University Press: Edinburgh).

Notes From Nowhere (eds.) (2003) *We Are Everywhere* (Verso: London).

Nozick, R. (1996) *Anarchy, State and Utopia* (Blackwell: Oxford).

Nursey-Bray, P. (1996) 'Autonomy and Community: William Godwin and the Anarchist Project' in *Anarchist Studies* 4:2, 97-113.

Parekh, B. (2000) *Rethinking Multiculturalism: Cultural Diversity and Political Theory* (Macmillan Press, London).

Paterson, M. (2007) *Automobile Politics: Ecology and Cultural Political Economy* (Cambridge University Press: Cambridge).

Pilgrim, J. (1993) 'Crime, Delinquency and the State' in *The Raven* 6:2, 114-120.

Plumwood, V. 'Feminism, Privacy and Radical Democracy' in *Anarchist Studies* 3:2, 97-120.

Prichard, A. (2010) 'The Ethical Foundations of Proudhon's Republican Anarchism' in Franks, B. & Wilson, M. (eds.) *Anarchism and Moral Philosophy* (Palgrave: Basingstoke).

Purchase, G. (1994) *Anarchism and Environmental Survival* (See Sharp Press: Tuscon).

Purkis, J. & Bowen, J. (eds.) (1997) *Twenty-First Century Anarchism* (Cassell: London).

Purkis, J. & Bowen, J. (eds.) (2004) *Changing Anarchism: Anarchist Theory and Practice in a Global Age* (Manchester University Press: Manchester).

Rawls, J. (2005) *A Theory of Justice* (Belknap Press: Cambridge).

Rawls, J. (2000) 'Political Liberalism and the Idea of an Over-Lapping Consensus' in Gowans, C.W. (ed.) *Moral Disagreements* (Routledge: London).

Rawls, J. (2001) in Kelly, E. (ed) *Justice as Fairness: A Restatement* (Harvard University Press: Cambridge, Mass.).

Read, H. (1974) *Anarchy and Order* (Souvenir Press: London).

Read, H. (1974) *Anarchy &Order* (Souvenir Press: Norwich).

Richardson, B. (1987) 'Freedom and environment' in Ward, C. (ed) *A Decade of Anarchy: 1961-1970* (Freedom Press: London).

Richards, V (ed) (1993) *Violence and Anarchism: A Polemic* (Freedom Press: London).

Ritter, A. (1980) *Anarchism* (Cambridge University Press: Cambridge).

Rose, K. (2004) *Powers of Freedom* (Cambridge University Press: Cambridge).

Sahlins, M (1974) *Stone Age Economics* (Tavistock Publishing, London).

Scott, J. (2009) *The Art of Not Being Governed: An Anarchist History of Upland Southeast Asia* (Yale University Press: New Haven)

Schmidt, M. & van der Walt, L. (2009) *Black Flame: The Revolutionary Class Politics of Anarchism and Syndicalism* (AK Press: Edinburgh).

Seeds for Change (2007a) 'Doing it Without Leaders' in Trapese Collective (eds.) *Do It Yourself* (Pluto: London).

Seeds for Change (2007b) *Doing it Without Leaders*, full length version, available at: http://www.seedsforchange.org.uk/free/resources#grp, last accessed: 8/07/09.

Seeds for Change (2009) *Facilitating Meetings*, self-published pamphlet.

Soper, K. (1993) 'Postmodernism, Subjectivity and the Question of Value' in Squires, J. (ed.) *Principled Positions: Postmodernism and the Rediscovery of Values* (Lawrence & Wishart: London).

Squires, J. (1993) (ed.) *Principled Positions: Postmodernism and the Rediscovery of Values* (Lawrence & Wishart: London).

Stamm, E. (1995) *Consent or Coercion* available at: http://www.spunk.org/library/intro/sp000985.txt Last Accessed 20/12/07)

Taylor, M. (1982) *Community, Anarchy and Liberty* (Cambridge University Press: Cambridge).

Tester, K. (2007) *Moral Culture* (Sage: London).

Tormey, S. (2005) 'From Utopian Worlds to Utopian Spaces: Reflections on the Contemporary Radical Imaginary and the Social Forum Process' in *Ephemera* 5:2, 394-408

Torres, B. (2007) *Making a Killing: The Political Economy of Animal Rights* (AK Press: Edinburgh).

Trujillo, A. (2010) *Being Green in a non-Green World: Theories of Difference, Ecological Values and Everyday Life* (Unpublished doctoral thesis, Reading University).

Walter, N. (1979) 'About Anarchism' in Ehrlich, H.J; Ehrlich, C.; De Leon, D. & Morris, G. (eds.) *Reinventing Anarchy*

(Routledge & Kegan Paul: London).

Walzer, M. (1995) 'The Communitarian Critique of Liberalism' in Etzioni, A. (ed.) *New Communitarian Thinking: Persons, Virtues, Institutions and Communities* (University Press of Virginia: Charlottesville).

Ward, C. (2008) *Anarchy in Action* (Freedom Press: London).

White, S. (2007) 'Making Anarchism Respectable? The Social Philosophy of Colin Ward' in *Journal of Political Ideologies* 12:1, 11-28.

Wieck, D.T. (2009) 'The Realisation of Freedom' in Graham, R. (ed) *Anarchism: A Documentary History of Libertarian Ideas Vol. II* (Black Rose Books: London).

Williams, B. (2000) 'From Freedom to Liberty: The Construction of a Political Value' in *Philosophy and Public Affairs* 30:1, 3-26.

William, B. (1993) Ethics and the Limits of Philosophy (Fontana: London)

Williams, L. (2007) 'Anarchism Revised' *New Political Science* 29:3, 297-312.

Wolff, J. (1996) *An Introduction to Political Philosophy* (Oxford University Press: Oxford).

Young, I. M. (1990) *Justice and the Politics of difference* (Princeton University Press: Princeton).

Young, I.M. (2000) *Inclusion and Democracy* (Oxford University Press: New York).

Young, I. M. (2001) 'Equality of Whom? Social groups and Judgements of Injustice' *The Journal of Political Philosophy* 9:1, 1-18.

Zerzan, J. (2002) *Running on Emptiness: The Pathology of Civilisation* (Feral House: Los Angeles).

Endnotes.

1. Of course, this is supposed to be true of all anarchists; the following work suggests otherwise.

2. Climate Camps are organised along anarchist principles, but not everyone involved is necessarily an anarchist. See http://climatecamp.org.uk/ for more info. I also discuss the Camps organisational methods in Chapter 6.

3. See http://dysophia.wordpress.com/2010/01/ for one such discussion (last accessed 31/12/2010).

4. The extent to which people's interests will inevitably *clash* is a question I explore in depth in Chapter 3.

5. I recognise significant problems in using the term *primitive*, but given the consistent use of the term by anarchists, both to describe stateless societies, and as a particular form of anarchism, i.e. anarcho-primitivism (Zerzan 2002), it seems appropriate to continue to use it in the way they intend; without, that is to say, any normative connotations of inferiority, etc.

6. The Anarchist Teapot is an anarchist collective that cooks food for large activist events and gatherings.

7. It is perhaps worth reflecting briefly on the fact that neither Gellner nor Moseley are anarchists, a point which perhaps allows them to see more clearly the problems of stateless societies – an insight that is crucial in reference to the libertarian demands of anarchists.

8. As I suggested earlier, questions of anarchism's viability in relation to other existent, non-anarchist, societies are beyond the scope of this work.

9. I discuss the idea of a common good, whether such a thing is possible, or indeed desirable, in Chapter Three.

10. The argument presented in the article this quote is taken from suggests that by 'curious', Chambers is implying that such a suggestion is in fact wrong.

11. As I noted in the Introduction, the following work does not discuss the work of anarcho-capitalists, who may in fact be sympathetic to Hayek's arguments.

12. Although I disagree with much of Bookchin's work, and the manner in which he presents it, I cannot help but sympathise with his increasing frustration with a philosophy whose adherents so systematically fail or refuse (with a few honourable exceptions) to engage in self-critical analysis and to ask some fundamental questions such as those I pose below. I should add, however, that whereas Bookchin lays the blame for this on an ad-hoc collection of groups and discourses of which he disapproves, such as postmodernism, spiritualism, and, seemingly, youthfulness, I have already offered in Chapter 1 what I believe are more convincing reasons for this state of affairs. It is, in my view, deeply regrettable that Bookchin wrapped the seeds of some important insights in such heavy, muddled and embittered rhetoric.

13. I noted in the Introduction the commonplace claim that contemporary anarchists have expanded their focus to look well beyond these more traditional foci of authority and power, to explore issues around race, gender, and so on. However, I would suggest that whilst this is reflected in the way anarchists think about the world, the targets of anarchist activism remain much the same as they always have: corporations, institutions, and governments.

14. Berlin's work itself goes into much greater detail; for example, within the notion of positive freedom he discusses the question of self-determination. However, for the purposes of the following discussion, this level of enquiry is not necessary, and indeed may well confuse matters.

15. This is not to say I agree with Nozick's analysis, but that the basic problems he discusses are worthy of our attention.

16. Anarchists often make the point that, whatever the arguments regarding the conduct of individuals, the crimes of the state are

always far worse.

17. See Hawkins 1997 for an interesting discussion about Kropotkin and the wider context within which he, and man others, on the right and the left, used Darwin's theory to promote their own ideological positions; Robert C. Bannister, 1979, also provides another interesting account.

18. Though Bookchin clearly owes much to earlier thinkers, most notably Kropotkin, and potentially many others, such as Henry David Thoreau, for example.

19. There is considerable disagreement about what, if anything, distinguishes ethics from morality; as there is no clear agreement, and as, in any case, I see the distinction as ultimately false, I use these terms interchangeably. See, for example, http://www. philosophyblog.com.au/ethics-vs-morality-the-distinction-between-ethics-and-morals/ and Bauman 1993.

20. Benjamin Franks and I edited a book, *Anarchism and Moral Philosophy* (2010) which was an attempt to tackle what we both felt to be a problematic lack of explicitly ethical reflection within the anarchist canon.

21. Of course, it could be argued that such deaths were in fact an inevitable consequence of Stalin's utilitarian approach, whereby people were consciously sacrificed for the (supposedly) greater good. What I mean by suggesting a lack of intent is that, communism, per se, does not have as one of its goals the destruction of a certain group of people, as fascism does.

22. Indeed, this is precisely why anarchists place such a strong emphasis on prefiguration; sadly, however, this is not a panacea for any and all unintended problems arising from a particular ethical position.

23. In recent years, a number of theorists have challenged the idea that poststructural theory is incapable of engaging with ethical discussions, except to dismiss them (Squires 1993; Bauman 1995). As Todd May puts it, poststructuralism has often been accused of 'a reticence toward and an inability to justify ethical principles'

(May 1994, 121). Interestingly, however, it is perhaps the postanarchists May and Saul Newman who have most explicitly placed ethics at the heart of their discussions on anarchism in recent years.

24. Alan Carter (2003) makes the point that, because of their commitment to social equality, anarchists may at times prefer a large socialist state, which has the capacity to redistribute wealth, to a liberal minimal state, which, however 'weak', may nonetheless act to preserve such inequalities. Whilst this is a perfectly valid point, it does not detract from my arguments here.

25. This is not of course to say we must not criticise liberalism, and I will offer many reasons for doing so below, but rather to say we must engage with liberal arguments and challenge them accordingly, and not simply dismiss what liberals say as some sort of ideological mask for domination.

26. Of course, conflicts are not necessarily always between only two groups – indeed, they can often be far more complex, but the point remains the same.

27. Bookchin also considered diversity to be a fundamental part of nature, and thus of morality; as I argued previously, however, I do not consider his ideas on these matters to have been especially influential, so I will not discuss them here.

28. See Kuhn, 2009, for a useful discussion on the short but already complicated history of postanarchist thought.

29. Both writers discuss much more than power, of course, but I am mostly concerned here with what they have to say on this matter.

30. Again, I would note that I disagree that what is commonly referred to as a poststructural, or Foucauldian understanding of power should in fact be understood entirely in this way; many anarchists understood the pertinent points that were later made by Foucault and others long before poststructuralism appeared. I simply use this terminology at times to draw a recognised

distinction between different understandings of power.

31. We might also note that such a view of power relies on an equally diverse understanding of freedom; just as power is not simple exploitation by the state, or market, so freedom is not simply freedom from the state, or a degree of economic liberty.

32. Freeman has been referred to as both as Leninist (Munson 2010) and as an anarchist (Franks 2003), but for my argument it is not relevant whether either of these claims are true.

33. Mundane it may be, but as I discuss briefly in the following chapter, 'sound pollution' is not only a very real problem in our daily lives, a problem which, like power, goes largely unnoticed, despite its significant impact; it is also a constant problem in temporary autonomous zones.

34. I say 'appear' because often there will be *underlying* ethical or political reasons; but these may well not be explicit, and indeed may elude the knowledge of those favouring certain decisions. The example of transport is a case in point; whilst there are clearly strong economic and political dimensions to transport policy, people in their daily lives are often unaware of this. Either way, the key point is that not all disagreements will be of an obviously political nature.

35. I ignore here the critique of all technologies offered by anarcho-primitivists such as John Zerzan and Derick Jensen, because, whilst interesting, they are in my opinion of little practical value.

36. At least it is *perceived* to be all of these, though very often it falls far short of its promises; it is certainly not safe compared to other forms of transport, for example.

37. Again, the postanarchist critique maintains that we are indebted primarily to Foucault for this understanding of power, a claim I and many other anarchists disagree with. However, I believe the important factor for all anarchists is how to respond to the complexities of power, whoever we might turn to in order to better understand it.

38. Consensus has been advocated by earlier anarchists (see, for example, Ehrlich et. al. 1979, 15) but, given its centrality and popularity within contemporary anarchist movements, I have chosen to focus on these recent articulations. However, the theoretical elements of the following discussion are applicable to consensus as a philosophical concept, independent of its support and application by particular groups.

39. It is of course no coincidence that this model resembles in some important ways that of the federalist principles of earlier anarchist discourses such as anarcho-syndicalism, as well as drawing on the structures of the anarchist tradition of 'affinity groups' (Dupuis-Déri 2010).

40. Seeds for Change is a workers' co-operative that has been involved in the movement for many years now, helping activists learn the necessary skills to use consensus decision making; the texts I reference in this chapter are written for activists, as educational tools, and are not intended to be academically rigorous. Consequently, I feel a certain discomfort in subjecting them to what amounts to a highly critical analysis. However, the claims made by Seeds for Change are exemplary of a wider discourse, and these claims are ones which, as I hope to show in this chapter, are in need of serious critical engagement. My hope, then, is that my criticisms are taken as a genuine attempt to encourage a constructive dialogue, and not as the arrogant and disinterested dismissals of an arm-chair theorist.

41. Of course, in theory, a majority can also block a decision. However, the way consensus works, it is extremely unlikely that a proposal will ever reach the stage where people are asked to support or oppose it, if a majority appears likely to block the decision. This is seen as being one of the many positive elements of consensus, but it is worth considering briefly the cultural and political impact that blocking might have on minority groups, and, conversely, the fact that majorities may never *appear* to be blocking decisions; the potential for a majority to exploit their

apparent libertarian credentials, by demonstrating that they have never opposed a decision, or for a minority to appear to be overly confrontational or divisive, because they are forced to block decision, should be of real concern. When we think back to the arguments of Iris Marion Young, who argued that the views of the privileged were often presented as normal, helping defend them against the supposedly selfish claims of minority groups, we can see how even consensus may lead to establishing imbalances of power over time.

42. Graeber does not indicate precisely what he means by *violence*, but it must be assumed that he is referring to what might also be termed *coercion*; if people cannot come to consensus, then some people will be forced to do, or prevented from doing, certain things. Because Graeber sees coercion as potentially avoidable, he therefore sees any incidents of it as being illegitimate, and therefore equates them with violence. However, I see some coercion as inevitable, so I prefer to avoid using the term violence, which suggests a degree of illegitimacy that, given coercion's inevitability, seems ill-placed.

43. Some people do suggest moving to some form of voting, but with a much higher standard than a simple majority. A figure of eighty or ninety per cent agreement has at times been mentioned, which simply leads to the questions: what if *that* can't be reached? And how are these decisions to be enforced?

44. This raises another question which should be of interest to anarchists, about paternalistic care, and the extent to which communities may want or need to coerce certain individuals in certain ways, due to mental health issues for example.

45. By this I do not mean that the distinction discussed above, between anarchism as a certain approach to life and anarchism as a way of organising an entire society is broken down, at least not in a significant way. In experimenting with prefiguration, anarchists claim to be *experiencing* another world, a claim I have already dismissed in Chapter One. Rather, I believe that they are

slowly *creating* another world, but one which continues to exist within the old world. I believe the philosophical and practical consequences of this must be more openly and clearly acknowledged, and to do so we must accept the distinction, although not always perfectly black and white, between prefigurative experiments performed within state-capitalism, and a society entirely organised along anarchist principles.

46. As I explain in this chapter, there are numerous ways in which we might consider anarchist ideas are able to contaminate liberal democracy, by expanding libertarian practices (and thus reducing the need for statist institutions) and by a discursive exchange, whereby, for example, some of the more realistic ideas behind consensus are encouraged within more hierarchical institutions (local councils, for example). This vision clearly runs the risk of being, or being perceived to be, an unhelpful compromise, and there is no hard and fast rule as to how, when and where this notion of contamination might succeed: the context is crucial. What matters here is that anarchists begin to emerge from their purist tendencies and experiment with the basic idea that, through exposure to dialogue and example, individuals, institutions and discourses that are currently inclined towards hierarchical, statist forms of politics might slowly become more open to other, more anarchistic ways of organising.

47. As I am discussing principally western anarchist discourses, my arguments are similarly focused on the liberal world in which they operate; I am unqualified to discuss how my ideas might translate into non-liberal contexts. Presumably, in other social and political environments, there would be important differences but also important points of convergence.

48. The Haringey Solidarity Group (HSG) is involved in numerous activities, including residents' associations which include many non-anarchist members of the community; rather than creating temporary autonomous zones, HSG 'aims to practice, encourage and support self-organised struggles by

ordinary people within Haringey'. See http://en.wikipedia.org/ wiki/Haringey_Solidarity_Group for more info (last accessed 23/01/2011).

49. An Earth First! Pamphlet entitled Direct Action, for example, focuses solely on such actions, and makes no mention of other forms of direct action, such as the creation of workers' co-ops.

50. See www.radicalroutes.org.uk

51. See www.solfed.org.uk and www.iww.org.uk

52. Of course, the question of which things we need to live becomes a very complicated one, the moment we step beyond the realm of those things, such as food and shelter, that are absolutely necessary; and even here, there are questions about which food, and what sort of shelter, we might demand. What is clear to anarchists, however, is that, at present, we live in a world that has gone too far in its obsession with material wealth, and that, consequently, a reduction in consumption is necessary (in the West, at least). Conversely, an anarchist society would, in theory, make discussions about necessity more equitable and just; as C. Douglas Lummis puts it: 'The sorting out of our true needs from those that are the maimed consequences of the fear and envy of class society would happen slowly and naturally in a society that was genuinely just, equalitarian and safe' (Douglas Lummis 1996, 78). Rather than suggesting this is not a difficult question, personal prefiguration turns such theoretical questions – what do we need to be happy? – into a matter of concrete, daily life.

53. Of course, there are also reasonable disagreements about which values ought to be pursued – a fact which may muddy discussion of lifestyle somewhat, because there are no clear acts which a lifestyle anarchist would necessarily perform, or abstain from. This diversity of values makes it hard to assess the extent to which anarchists embrace lifestyle, and adds an additional dimension to debates about prefiguration, which often makes such debates not only confusing but also even more emotionally

charged. Although this fact makes it more difficult to analyse with any certainty how lifestyle is viewed by anarchists exactly, I believe this makes my argument for a more explicit approach to lifestyle stronger, rather than weaker.

54. And, indeed, much wider networks may slowly be established; a local farm, for example, may also engage in discussions with producers of farming equipment operating in other parts of the country, or even the world. As such, we can already see the development of a federated system of decision-making, where the needs of two communities, separated by geography, are united by shared, though possibly conflicting, interests.

55. It is also interesting to note how readily people approved the proposal that the network should engage in this process, seemingly unconcerned by the extent to which this simply replaced a governmental authority with a co-operative one. On a personal level I was heartened to see so many anarchists willing to make what I believe to be a worthwhile and certainly educational compromise, but also deeply concerned that this was happening because of an ideological blindness which was focusing people's attention on the problems of the state, and not on the broader question of authority per se. Indeed, as I hope my work has shown, the concern that anarchists could well, given the chance, and with the best of intentions, simply replace state authority with an equally problematic 'libertarian' authority remains very real, but woefully under-acknowledged.

Contemporary culture has eliminated both the concept of the public and the figure of the intellectual. Former public spaces – both physical and cultural – are now either derelict or colonized by advertising. A cretinous anti-intellectualism presides, cheerled by expensively educated hacks in the pay of multinational corporations who reassure their bored readers that there is no need to rouse themselves from their interpassive stupor. The informal censorship internalized and propagated by the cultural workers of late capitalism generates a banal conformity that the propaganda chiefs of Stalinism could only ever have dreamt of imposing. Zer0 Books knows that another kind of discourse – intellectual without being academic, popular without being populist – is not only possible: it is already flourishing, in the regions beyond the striplit malls of so-called mass media and the neurotically bureaucratic halls of the academy. Zer0 is committed to the idea of publishing as a making public of the intellectual. It is convinced that in the unthinking, blandly consensual culture in which we live, critical and engaged theoretical reflection is more important than ever before.